Delhi
Mostly Harmless

Delhi
Mostly Harmless
one woman's vision of the city

Elizabeth Chatterjee

RANDOM HOUSE INDIA

Published by Random House India in 2013
1

Random House Publishers India Private Limited
Windsor IT Park, 7th Floor
Tower-B, A-1, Sector-125
Noida 201301, UP

Random House Group Limited
20 Vauxhall Bridge Road
London SW1V 2SA
United Kingdom

978 81 8400 356 7

Typeset in Sabon by R. Ajith Kumar

Printed and bound in India by Replika Press Private Limited

Well, he was mooning about Delli, that highly pestilential place, possibly in search of some undiscovered facts...

—Joseph Conrad, *Victory*

CONTENTS

1

THE BEST-LAID PLANS

Wherever she went, including here, it was against her better judgment.
—Dorothy Parker's proposed tombstone

*N*othing, in all my heaps of books and strategies, had prepared me for the cold wetness spreading beneath my buttocks.

The interview was not quite going to plan.

Outside, Delhi had begun to boil. Back when this was all an idle library fantasy, I'd pictured a white-hot city, wholesome white like milkmaids' pails and American teeth. But this felt yellowish-hot—the colour of nicotine fingers, tabloid splashes, warning lights. Delhi's rulers have always fled the heat whenever possible, the Mughals to Kashmir, the British to Shimla, today's lot to the more glamorous American and European cities. With impeccable timing I'd travelled the wrong way around.

But inside everything was frozen. Ice stacked in giant cubes: thirty tonnes of them, I read later, 'Crystal Clear' and imported from Canada. Against one wall stood a sculpted ice animal. It appeared to be a wolverine, though that seemed a puzzling choice of whittled ice mammal, and had melted slightly under the rumps of posing customers.

A perfectly sensible place for an interview, I tried to tell myself.

But whatever else you might say about the place, Delhi is always generous when doling out life lessons. Not least of these is that it is unwise to interview a powerful man in fluffy mittens. Something had gone wrong somewhere. Several things, actually.

Half an hour earlier, pants still mercifully unsodden, I'd arrived downstairs to case the joint. The mall lay spreadeagled under the sky's murky eyeball. It hadn't been my suggestion. That was the first error of the afternoon, deceptively tame but spinning inexorably towards calamity. The interviewee had bowled me a right old googly.

A guard pawed me through a security scanner. The interrogation would take place in one of Delhi's many glossy coffee shops, I decided. I would order a tea, with a poignant comment about the shared tastes of Britain and India. The interviewee would open up like a broiled oyster.

Be prepared, a voice said somewhere among my little grey cells. It was satnav-cool and, like all the best prophets, managed to sound both vague and ominous.

The interviewee arrived exactly on time. He looked like Luigi, the better-looking Mario Brother: same moustache, bulbous nose, coquettish eyes. *Establish control*, the satnav voice said, *but be reassuring. Create rapport.* We shook hands at the mall's entrance. I squeezed firmly, exuding rapport from every pore, just as I'd practised in the autorickshaw on my own left hand.

So far, so good. *Control the agenda. Lay out your goals.* The planned questions ticker-taped through my head. I was the David Frost of PhD research, cool, charming, incisive, I was the fusion of Letterman and Oprah and Karan Johar. I rehearsed the introduction in my head, formed the first line—

'Do you want a drink?' Luigi said. The *t* in *want* thudded against the roof of his mouth.

'Um,' I said professionally, and consulted the satnav-cool voice.

Retain control, but, it said, *but, er, create rapport.* Unfortunately the good cop—bad cop dilemma appeared to be the satnav's Achilles heel. *The interviewee is more likely to talk if you seem perfectly harmless. Authoritative but, like, harmless.*

There was a pause, then quietly at the very edge of my grey cells: *Bugger.* The satnav lapsed into guilty silence. Touché, Luigi, touché.

'Come.' Luigi left no room for an answer. I looked longingly at the coffee shop as we swept past.

And so I found myself in a bar made entirely of ice, draped in a waxy borrowed poncho and praying to all the gods of India that this would bring a cartful of rapport. Our smoggy breath mingled awkwardly. The place itself was peculiarly distracting. It was small, our footprints invisible on the clinical tiles. Besides the ice wolverine, the walls glowed the hot pink neon of a suburban lapdancing club. In one corner, a barman was discreetly turning blue. The door had an unreassuring industrial heaviness. I thought of airlocks and quarantines and zombie apocalypses.

The whole place was like a psychotic Narnia and must have taken the energy of a small town to keep frozen 50°C below the outside world. It was vigorously tasteless. At least for the first time in months I wasn't sweating from my eyebrows.

'What will you take?' said Luigi.

RETAIN CONTROL, said the satnav voice.

'Um,' I said. 'A tea, I think, please'—though it would probably freeze over and taste like a Yorkshire millpond—'just a cup of tea, please. Isn't it funny how Britain and India both—'

'No.' His moustache had taken on a decidedly dictatorial aspect. 'You will take something interesting.'

Two drinks in ice glasses appeared on the ice table. They were bright red and sticky and altogether un-tea-like. The barman emitted a censorious tooth-chatter in my direction. Any remaining poise, gravitas and grasp of Interview Techniques 101 quietly perished. I was prepared for jargon, mistrust, slipperiness—even silence. I was not prepared for cocktails.

Each drink cost around ten times the controversial figure selected a couple of months earlier as the official daily poverty line for urban India. The government was in the process of a characteristically slow and quarrelsome retreat, while we sucked and slurped icy handfuls of rupees, tossed monthly incomes down our frost-huffing throats.

The bar was quiet, at least. Most of the clientele was male

and grinning and suspiciously young. The boys shivered in small homoerotic clumps, heads steaming like horses, and whipped out their smartphones. They took turns in posing for photos with an ice mannequin, loaned mitts groping her cold curves. Her face was blank.

I shifted in my ice chair, which had begun to melt disconcertingly into my trousers. (Tight black jeans: the informal uniform of an international generation, a half-solution to that elusive Goldilocks midpoint between Indian conservatism and elite Delhi-mall-rat cool, and sensible for neither yellowish-hot nor frozen conditions.) This sort of thing didn't happen to Oprah.

Luigi watched me intently, stroking his moustache, as I picked up the glass. I looked away and gave a discreet cough, which formed a small guilty cumulonimbus at my shoulder. The satnav voice shrilled: *Make U-turn when possible!* I knew in India only bad girls drink. Worse, he knew that I knew.

'Cheers,' I said.

Opposite me Luigi's moustache shuffled with pleasure, and he began to talk. He was wearing a poncho over his office shirt; its furry collar was the exact texture of his moustache. He was waxing lyrical about coal-fired power plants he had known and loved: the sensual curve of a special cooling tower, the thrust of a favourite turbine. His waxing sent little plumes of steam into the air.

As Luigi's glasses misted over with enthusiasm, I pondered some crucial life questions. How had this happened? What was I doing there in Delhi, the City Formerly Known as My

Second-Least-Favourite Place on Earth? And was that a hand I felt upon my thigh?

It is a truth universally acknowledged that nobody who lives there, nobody at all, has much good to say about Delhi. Along with Milton Keynes, Detroit and Purgatory, it is one of the world's great unloved destinations. Its inhabitants, Dilliwallas, take a perverse pride in complaining about it. At best they tolerate it. At worse, some despise it with the fire of a thousand June suns. In his novel *Delhi* (1990), the irascible Khushwant Singh describes how the city appears to a stranger:

> a gangrenous accretion of noisy bazaars and mean-looking hovels growing round a few tumble-down forts and mosques along a dead river… [T]he stench of raw sewage may bring vomit to his throat.

—and he's a fan.

Sure, there have been writers who praise the city's magnificent imperial past as the heart of Mughal civilization. But they lament its subsequent decline into Punjabi aggression and consumerist bling. Others damn it with faint praise, as though reluctantly reviewing a friend's very bad restaurant. They call it *contradictory* or *interesting*—the décor's OK and the waitresses are pretty, but for God's sake don't put anything in your mouth.

Delhi's inhabitants are scarcely more popular. According to stereotype, there seems to be some terrible syndrome that afflicts big-city folk. New Yorkers are foulmouthed, over-caffeinated snobs. Parisians are viciously rude and dipsomaniacal sexual deviants (if exquisitely dressed). Londoners are famously grumpy, as territorial and hostile to eye contact as feral dogs. Narcissistic, consumerist, restless, aggressive, neurotic, media-obsessed, social-climbing, credit-card-wielding, lonely—the clichés locate Western megacitizens somewhere between *Sex and the City* and *American Psycho*.

Other Indians are just as brutal in stereotyping Dilliwallas. In this bitchy vision, Delhi's citizens look like the cast of Dante's Hell. Abandon all hope, ye who enter here: it is a city of touts, thugs, gluttons, brats, voyeurs, hustlers, crooked politicians, suits, pencil-pushers, pimps, perverts—every kind of sinner. Khushwant Singh again:

> They spit…; they urinate and defecate whenever and wherever the urge overtakes them; they are loud-mouthed, express familiarity with incestuous abuse and scratch their privates while they talk.

For all their bad reputations, New York, Paris and London can at least claim grudging recognition of their dominance from the rest of their countrymen. Delhi can't even manage that at home, let alone in the world. Independent India's founding fathers, especially Gandhi, had a famously ambivalent attitude to cities. India's soul was in its villages, the Mahatma argued, not in the dark satanic mills of the crowded cities, cheap imitations of the imperial West.

Delhi's rivals today are on the doorstep—rival cities hate

each other like warring ex-wives. Its worst critics are Mumbai's great fans, who contrast their hometown's Bollywood curves and sea views with the capital's bureaucratic grumpiness. Bombay (as the crème still call it) is the younger, taller, better-read sibling. It even does sinning better, with more glitz and glamour: its gangsters, religious rage and dancing girls have attracted the best of India's urban chroniclers. Just look at its nicknames: Maximum City, city of gold, gateway to India.

Delhi is starting with a handicap. It might be heralded as one of the twenty-first century's rising world cities—but no wonder it has an inferiority complex.

I too arrived with a host of preconceptions, some concealing a grain of truth. One hoary old myth, though, would be proved emphatically wrong as soon as I set foot in the city.

It's often said that India is blessed (cursed) with a strange timelessness, as constant and otherwordly as the sun's arc. Delhi scorns this notion. It isn't changeless: today you can practically hear the hourglass frothing—even if IST, 'India Stretchable Time', does run a little less predictably than GMT.

At least until 2012, Indians were among the most optimistic people in the world today, confident that India is not just another Third World country, but a civilization which will eventually inherit the century. India is going places—and Delhi is too, at least its richest segments. On my evening jaunts, people often remarked on the change with a sort of smug astonishment. 'Five years ago there was nothing in Delhi. Nothing at all. But now, *but now*…'

Soon middle-class Delhi won't be content to be compared to other Indian, or even Asian, cities. It wants *recognition*. It wants to be a real, undeniable world city, in your face and by every metric—trade, tourists, summits, dollars, nukes, haute cuisine.

Such rapid change inevitably brings a crisis of identity. The city is in either its seventh or tenth or twelfth incarnation, depending who you listen to, with a history stretching back at least three thousand years. At the same time it is an adolescent city, wrestling with the wake of Partition, waves of migration, and hypertrophic growth, and reborn yet again with the economic opening of 1991. It is both a city of past glory and get-rich-quick newcomers, big-spending populists and big-spending corporates, incredible wealth and even more incredible corruption. It is the skittering heart of a democracy claiming to represent over a billion people, yet just as often governed by elite privilege and authoritarian fiat.

Yet Delhi's swagger is fragile. It is at once expansively confident and deeply insecure, as the recent turmoil in India's financial markets has shown. Middle-class urban Indians are beginning to doubt, railing at the corruption and ineptitude of their New Delhi rulers, even as the fundamental strengths—and weaknesses—of the Indian economy remain. India's growth will slow and its politicians will falter; the city's roads will become ever more choked and its throat parched. But Delhi's murky star will continue its uneven rise, yellowish-hot.

I only ended up there half by accident, half out of duty, deep in the heart of wealthy, middle-class Delhi. Somehow as I came into contact with its various evolving faces I almost came to love it, in an embittered and judgmental fashion—or at least to respect the scale of its ambition.

But as I sat wet-buttocked in the ice bar and peered at Luigi's misty spectacles, the warm fuzzy feelings were a long way off.

2

HOME AND AWAY

An adventure is only an inconvenience rightly considered.
An inconvenience is only an adventure wrongly considered.
—G.K. Chesterton, 'On Running After One's Hat'

August, 2009 or maybe September: I first set eyes on Delhi. It wasn't exactly love at first sight.

It was a flying visit. Delhi—c. 2,500 years of history and power and spilt blood—was just a slightly inconvenient airport on the way to the hills. I felt obliged to experience it firsthand, if only to complain convincingly, so I decided to stick around for a handful of days. Plus I had a World To Do List ('bucket list' sounds too morbid, 'world agenda' too Hitler) including several railways, carnivores, irritable ex-colonies, and a couple of hundred cities. These I planned to work through over the next three-score years before death, collecting snap judgments to wear at dinner parties.

It wasn't my first Indian adventure. The previous year

I'd briefly swanned about in South India, green and wet and toothsome. I hoovered up vast amounts of coconut-based produce and watched clumps of invasive water hyacinth float by, mindless and smothering as jellyfish.

But everyone assured me Delhi was different and much more hostile terrain. I made the mistake of reading about it first, as bookish kids tend to do even when things are best left under-researched, like young love or hiphop lyrics.

More horror stories surrounded the place than Halloween. A week earlier, a friend's pre-university Gap Yah adventure had lasted precisely six hours before he fled in terror all the way back home to the cider apples and clotted cream of Devon. Well-meaning acquaintances kept consoling me that at least I'd come back thin. The Mothership, a woman whose sunny optimism I've inherited, dropped dark hints about writing a will. In between motorbike accidents and outbreaks of dysentery, I should expect to be blown up at least three times by terrorists and/or bootleg machinery. And then my corpse would be mugged.

She shook her head with finality. 'And the insurance company probably won't even pay to send your body back.'

By the time I landed I was hyperventilating so hard I could barely carry my suitcase of toilet paper. Reeking of antiseptic hand gel and fear, I walked around expecting the worst and Delhi helpfully delivered.

I took a taxi from the airport. It was black and yellow and pungent and listed to one side like an old tugboat. There was no seatbelt. I clung to the sticky seat and, snail-eyed, peered warily out of the window. Big roads, barricades, clumps of policemen. Then honking and signboards and endless blocky buildings. The air was hot and dry on my face. When we arrived I panicked and tipped twenty times too much with my fat airport bills.

New Delhi Railway Station was carpeted with bags and bodies. Indian Railways is one of the world's largest employers, with over 1.4 million workers; a guesstimated eight billion journeys are made on it each year, and it shows. At any one time half the continent seems to be lurking around with sacks and suitcases on heads and fistfuls of snacks. Shysters pursued tourists through the dank corridors and to the counters and queues outside, offering fictional tickets from fictional offices. Mile-long blue locomotives crawled in and slumped, hissing gently. In the distance their lost number let out mournful Chewbacca hoots, like whales in the deep. Overhead the loudspeakers blared out a tinny *TA-DAH!* every fifteen seconds in celebration of arrivals and six-hour delays alike.

Like a lot of first-timers I wound up in Paharganj, the grimy huddle of narrow streets just west of the station. It's one of the crummiest parts of town, as though Delhi is intent on making tourists battle uphill to like it. The alleys were fringed with stalls selling fake designer bags and those Aladdin pants that make owners look like they're wearing a soiled nappy. Blurry faces inside: 'Hello-o, madam, which country?' Dreadlocked Germans stomped by, haggling over badly printed postcards of the Taj Mahal and jaggedly stitched North Fake gear. Puffs of incense and weed drifted over the potholes.

(Two years later looking at the main strip would be like wearing X-ray specs. The government would solve the problem of illegal encroachment onto the road by simply smashing the fronts off the buildings. Passers-by gazed into storerooms and bedrooms. The odd toilet hovered in plain sight. At night the flames of blowtorches licked the concrete shells.)

The hotel, once I finally found it, was a multi-storey concrete block which threw in loud drilling and hammering noises for free. At intervals sleazy waiters knocked on the door and my heart drilled too. I spent my first evening aligning my toilet rolls and looking meaningfully out over the city. I tried for the eighteenth time to make it through *Midnight's Children*, Salman Rushdie's bearded visage smirking over me like an evil genie. I even saw a cockroach, though admittedly a rather small torpid one.

All this was par for the course, traditional even, to welcome me and prove my grit. The bed retained the imprints of previous tourists, just my shape and size and sweatiness. Even the cockroach looked bored, like an extra who'd appeared in the background of one too many coming-of-age stories. The predictability was reassuring. I felt in control, just. Then the rains began.

At the burnt end of summer, the sky heaves its bosom and spews forth a sultry green new city. Spit and a bush leaps up: the Victorian colonizers must have been scandalized. The rain soothes Delhi's nerves a little, greening it even as the roads overflow. Unfortunately Paharganj had yet to smear the ground with uneven concrete. Instead it seemed to be a gigantic plughole, a drain down which all the city's grubby fluids gurgle.

On the third evening, the cockroach having given up any attempt at self-concealment, I headed out. A debonair and swashbucklingly bearded former classmate was escorting me to a snazzy 'pink rupee' fundraiser (Delhi's gay rights activists being both active and corporate-savvy). Encased in squirtings of hand sanitizer, I stepped gingerly out of the hotel, balancing on a pair of bricks in the stream. The street appeared to be drenched in greasy French onion soup. A dead rat floated past my foot, emitting villainous smells.

My phone rang, and I hovered precariously on one soggy foot to answer it. From the briny depths of their shops the locals regarded me with interest.

It was my classmate. 'I'm only forty yards away in the car,' he said, with the irritating composure of the rat-free man. 'Can you make it?'

Forty yards of glutinous, scum-encrusted, corpse-reeking liquid. A veritable shit creek. The skies were just reopening overhead to sluice further waves of sewage down the lane. My shoes were adventure shoes, sold with promising phrases like Neoprene and Gore-Tex and TC5+ Rubber—but they were also too new and pretty for anything like this. The villainous smells would follow me into the car and the evening and the city, thwarting my dreams of an urbane new life. And when I returned the road might be up to my nostrils in the soupy remains of expired rats.

'No. No, I can't do it.'

Defeated. I retraced my steps over the dead rat, its eyes gloating, and slunk back into the hammering. Back into my chrysalis of hand sanitizer. The other damp youngsters on the roof top ignored me, too busy chain-smoking over their own *Midnight's Children*s.

Aside from this sewage-induced house arrest, my overriding memory of that first visit is of a small boy grabbing my left breast in the street with a disinterested look on his face. I looked at several monuments, red and white like candy canes, and bought some curly-toed slippers I would never wear. My train out went from Old Delhi, and for several blocks on the journey to the station two boys on a motorbike followed with detailed commentary on my imagined underwear.

As the train pulled away, at the sort of weakling speed that enables an entire Bollywood scene to take place during departure, I caught a final *TA-DAH!* from the station speakers. I settled back to write my verdict on some badly printed postcards of the Taj Mahal: Delhi deserved a minor natural disaster. Nothing too destructive, but something that might wipe the smirk off a few sleazeballs' faces and prompt some minor remodelling. A plague of locusts, perhaps, or a B-movie tornado full of sharks.

But in February 2012 I found myself going back, *harder better faster stronger*, and on a mission—

'—Chatterjee?'

The passenger next to me was studying my business card. (I had two hundred, all stowed in my hand luggage just in case. These are the handshake and *namaste* of twenty-first-century Delhi, palmed around by even the most remotely businessy people by way of introduction. Young ambitious types collect those of the powerful like they're trading Pokémon cards.) He was a businessman, he said, on the way back home to Delhi after some 'bijniss' in London.

The man was a Talker alright, blight of the skies. We were still on the tarmac and he was firing up conversation ready for the next nine hours, preempting my antisocial headphones manoeuvre. This was dangerous. Aeroplanes make me weirdly overemotional. I think it's the detachment from ordinary time, the hospice food and the way the stewardesses meet your eyes. I didn't want the Talker to catch me sobbing like a mad cat-wielding spinster over the in-flight romcoms—or worse, over the adorably tiny cans of Coke. Already I was getting damp-eyed with Delhi reminiscences. Again I cursed the airport gods. The middle seat is like most Facebook updates: awkwardly intimate, all too public, but with no real views on anything.

'Elizabeth *Chatterjee?*' he said again. 'This is the name you use in India only, *na?*'

I blinked. Did people really do that, invent entirely new names for their overseas jaunts? I eyed the implausibly vast list of qualifications on his business card with renewed mistrust.

'Or,' he brightened, 'probably you are married to an Indian. Yes, I think you like Indian men…' He reclined his chair with a suggestive lurch.

It was going to be a long flight.

I took a deep breath. 'No, it's my real name. I know I don't look at all Indian but—'

Chatterjee. Aka Chattopadhyay, to use the older version rejected by the British as too complicated. It seems to be unspellable to British ears, and got me teased at school as *Chatterbox* or *Chimpanzee* or (once, impressively) *Lady Chatterley*. The name is Bengali, and I've always liked it because it almost rhymes with lots of things: *strategy, flatter me, what-can-the-matter-be?*

But the Talker was not the first sceptic. I don't look Indian, or sound Indian, or feel Indian.

In fact, my usual haunt is exceedingly British, as British as boiled ham and stiff upper lips and Hogwarts. It is perched in a pale spined building at the heart of Oxford, high above a row of crumbly black gowns. Even the bed I'd abandoned that morning, and in which I'm writing now, is exceedingly British: it's an awkward size called a Gentleman's Occasional—for occasional gentlemen, I like to believe. The room is wood-panelled and the window porthole-round, like a tiny ship's cabin. The porthole overlooks a small manicured garden in which a blue sculpture of a Greek boy winks his buttocks. My nearest neighbours are gargoyles, some of them rather eminent in their fields. Tourists take pictures of us when we go downstairs for afternoon tea.

The room is lined with books: bought, begged, borrowed, and then ordered by colour just to throw off undergraduates. (This is an autistically pretty but useless system: I spend hours most afternoons ransacking the room for a particular volume.) In one corner is a fireplace, boarded up now but still full of geriatric creaks and moans in high winds. On it stand a bottle of Scotch and a series of kitschy souvenirs—Putin-Yeltsin-Lenin-Stalin Russian dolls, a goggle-eyed Sri Lankan mask, a little red Chairman Mao alarm clock with Mao's arm as the minute hand (now broken). I dust them when I remember.

The air smells sepia, like old teabags. On one wall maps are beginning to yellow in the genteel Oxford sun. India is reduced to three feet of crisp paper. A brown heavy-hipped body is hedged in green, and pirouettes on a fat sandy tail. It is topped with a quiff streaked in rocky orange and pale mauve: Kashmir. Travels—real and aspirational—are marked across the map with a scattering of dots.

The whole scene is static and sombre, like a photo of dead relatives in the days before the photographic smile was invented. (This is an invention that has not really reached India, so that in most of my photos I look like I am holding the locals hostage.) Downstairs a duck's head sits in a tiny case stapled to the wall. He has been there for two centuries, fading and musty. I often find myself in front of the case, staring into his glassy eyes with a strange sense of communion.

Leather armchairs, portraits, tweed. In the good old days explorers and prospectors set down their snuffboxes and set off from similar surroundings. Some travelled to exotic empty places that only the elite could afford to suffer: the Sahara, Antarctica, the deep wet heart of the Amazon. They spent the time naming and claiming things, and writing flowery tracts about cannibals and frostbite.

Others headed off to India, to trade and privateer, later to hunt and survey and rule. (From these same armchairs sprang three viceroys, one India Secretary, and later the second president of independent India. In Delhi I planned only to mention the latter.) India was already famed for many things—its elephants and snakes, palaces and hovels, sages and collaborators, its many gods and tongues. You might, like Mark Twain, kill thirteen tigers on your first hunt. You might classify verbs or skull sizes. You might go out to find yourself a husband from among the eligible young lieutenants and polo players. Of course, you might find the life out there all 'stupid dull and uninteresting', like a 21-year-old Winston Churchill. All this lay at the end of a tedious months-long journey over the waves.

At the other end of that voyage was my family, and other animals.

My grandpa, my father's father, grew up in Calcutta. A sociable younger son, he trained first as a classical Indian singer and later as a lawyer. (This law degree was obtained in a fit of pique: after his father called him a flibbertigibbet, he studied at night just so he could slam the certificate down on the table in the next argument.) In photos he has sleek hair and a Hitler moustache: Nazi Germany was a big hit with the young idealistic Bengalis of the 1930s and 1940s (and their champion, Subhas Chandra Bose, looks oddly like the melting Gestapo agent in *Raiders of the Lost Ark*). In fact, the Nazis are still popular in India. The state of Maharashtra is full of Hitler brands, *Mein Kampf* is still a big seller, and I saw a DJ in one upmarket Delhi bar proudly wearing a T-shirt emblazoned with the red, black and white swastika (he was reclaiming it, he said). There was even a recent TV serial about a very stern female breadwinner, set in Delhi: it was called *Hitler Didi*.

But six decades ago, my grandpa abandoned newly independent India for the bright lights and loose postwar immigration policies of the imperial motherland.

From Trinidad to the Netherlands, South Africa to Canada, the world is full of Persons of Indian Origin. The diaspora outside India includes between 9 and 30 million of them, depending on how propagandistic your definition of Indianness is. They have poured from the subcontinent in overlapping waves. Merchants to the four corners of the earth: from Russia to Kenya, Indonesia to Persia. Sailors and indentured labourers and imperial policemen across the British Empire, from Hong Kong and Singapore to the Caribbean. More recently, academics, doctors, entrepreneurs and the IT lot to the rich West. Now another surge of poor workers clean the Gulf states' toilets. Everywhere they have been unpopular: thrown out of Idi Amin's Uganda and coup-ridden Fiji, 'curry-bashed' in Australia, second-class citizens in Malaysia, Guyana, Sri Lanka, and the Gulf.

Many migrants fight hard to preserve their homelands' cultures overseas. They force their children to take traditional dance classes, learn the mother tongue, marry within the community. Over time, as the motherland changes but the diaspora group does not, this can have quite weird effects (just look at V. S. Naipaul). They can become more Indian than the Indians, militantly committed to a very particular idea of India. And ordinarily, no community is more militant about this cultural preservation than the Bengalis.

In India, the 'Bongs' are stereotyped as brainy dweebs. My former professor, himself owlish and clever, told me regretfully that they used to be considered great marriage catches, until the rise of the musclebound cash-wielding Punjabi in films and firms. Bengalis are bespectacled, soft-handed and sweet-toothed intellectuals, most often to be found spouting leftwing political philosophy late into the night. The only thing they love more than fish is arguing, and the only thing they don't argue about is Bengali culture: they are utterly convinced that their language, literature and brains are the greatest in all world history.

But in London my grandfather's plucky Bengali spermatozoa encountered my grandmother. In this formidable Finnish ice-hockey player with a taste for bespectacled brown men half her height, he met his match. The two nationalities could not be more different. Bengal is muggy, filled with mangrove swamps at one end and the hilly tea plantations of Darjeeling at the other; Finland is flat and icy. The population of the Kolkata metropolitan area alone is almost three times the entire population of Finland; its population density is a thousand times greater. The Bengalis chatter and eat sweets and dodge sport; the Finns ski in grumpy silence. The two share only a depressing handful of things: the aforementioned love of fish, the ability to survive sauna conditions, and a disproportionate propensity to commit suicide.

The compromise between the two extremes was English, football, and the suburbs. Their three children—my father a jolly and perpetually nude baby in the middle—grew up speaking neither Bengali nor Finnish, understanding neither Hinduism nor Lutheranism. They might have reclaimed this heritage in one of the attacks of genealogical panic that seems everywhere to seize the middle-aged. But into this mongrel mix was thrown the Mothership's side of the family too: a Scottish-Irish muddle of customs officials, conscientious objectors, and even one shipwreck-prone whaler who apparently confessed on his deathbed to cannibalizing a cabin boy. In this melting pot, Bengal was boiled up with all the other ingredients and transmogrified into little more than bad eyesight and a surname.

My home turf in northern England was full of South Asians, and all that entailed: great curry houses, sketchy corner shops, headscarfed mothers, rightwing politics, a race riot in 2001. If we were lucky, on the way home from swimming lessons we'd stop for *gulab jamun*, sticky-sweet fried dumplings, alongside our fish & chips. I remember giggling over the chorus to Cornershop's smash hit 'Brimful of Asha': 'everybody needs a bosom for a pillow, everybody needs a bosom'. I never knew that 'Asha' was in fact one of Bollywood's greatest singers. I remember casting my first vote, glad to see that the idiotic racist vote would be split three ways by three idiotic racist parties. I remember filling in a tickbox form and choosing my ethnicity as 'White Asian'; it sounded exotic and faintly incredible, like a white tiger.

There were hints of Indianness in our house. The Mothership gamely discovered cumin before all the other mothers, and once spent an entire day boiling pints upon pints of milk to make a microscopic amount of kulfi icecream, an attempt never to be repeated. In my bedtime stories Ganesh got his elephant head, Krishna sucked his demon nurse dry (terrifyingly illustrated), and Rama battled for pages and pages to free Sita from the demon king Ravana, only to chuck her out again in a moment of alpha male paranoia. Every few years relatives arrived with gold rings for my brothers and complaints about the cold. One sari-clad woman insisted we call her 'Grandma', which we knew to be an alarming lie. She was probably my grandpa's cousin; we were never entirely sure because all Bengalis all have two names: a perfectly respectable one plus an arbitrary two-syllable family nickname, so that your stern elderly relatives might introduce themselves as, say, Pinky, Hippo and Tushy.

But really, India left barely a mark on my childhood. In terms of impact on my youthful consciousness it was somewhere above Thatcherism but below the Spice Girls. In the late 1990s, I remember watching the sitcom *Goodness Gracious Me* together on the sofa. (The rasp of my father's crisp packet, the exasperated sigh of the iron. The Mothership perhaps cradling a glass of wine, back when Chardonnay was still the apex of British middle-class leisure, a small brother slumped over each sofa arm.) One of the sketches that evening involved the provenance of the British royal family:

> They all live in the same family house together: Indian. All work in the family business: Indian. All have arranged marriages: Indian. They all have sons; daughters no good: Indian!

It seemed plausible. I think I assumed *everyone* had a few Indian relatives, scattered here and there across the family tree like brightly coloured birds.

We spent many summers in Scotland and its soggy family sites with their soft names: Paisley, Pumpherston, Campbeltown, Craigellachie. We visited Finland and the more clipped places of my grandmother's past: Helsinki, Lahti, Tampere, Ruka. We met family from New York, Toronto, Sydney, Melbourne.

But we never visited India. My father had been, and assured us it wasn't worth it. He told tales of despotic relatives, diarrhoea and magpie-sized cockroaches, in various combinations. The only Indianness I carried from my childhood was a sort of dark shapeless curiosity that rusted in the corner like an old heirloom, turned in my fingers every now and then. On the map India remained a flat unfamiliar diamond, surprisingly small as it dangled into the blue.

By this time the Talker, thoroughly out-talked, was slumbering on my shoulder. Each breath made small confidential rustlings, like a badger in the undergrowth, and a tender tear pricked my eye. He was in many ways the ideal listener. I ordered another whiskey and miniature coke, and decided I might as well keep talking.

Now, as I say, I was heading to Delhi on a mission. Three times I'd visited India: as a tourist, then a rather useless language student, and finally a researcher of toilets. (This might sound like Michael Jackson preaching the virtues of a teensy pharmaceutical pick-me-up now and then, but India *is* addictive.) Quite clearly, the logical next step was to do a PhD—specifically, a PhD on the glamorous topic of Pressing Questions in the Indian Electricity Policymaking Process. And as everyone knows, from Margaret Mead to the Mormons, fieldwork is an essential component of any decent mission.

The process of doing a PhD, especially a PhD involving fieldwork, is much like the quest yarns of yore. There is a feckless young hero, probably spotty and pubescent at first. (Never mind that at the crusty old age of 26, I am older than half of all Indians. In fact at independence in 1947, Indian life expectancy was only 32—it's now 66. But in the West, I am part of the so-called 'Peter Pan generation'.) Unfortunately, our hero lives in a callous and gerontocratic society. He is exploited by his seniors, who have grown long malicious beards and forgotten their own feckless youths. He chafes at the homeland's pointless superstitions and at his subordinate role in its rigid hierarchy, and is prone to staring into middle distance as the sun sets. But then there comes to him a rumour on the wind. There exists a miraculous beast or holy grail or golden fleece, recovery of which will guarantee him fame and fortune or at least a tenure-track position. At first our hero is reluctant, but his wise ageing mentor cryptically spurs him towards his destiny. He departs, carrying only a small knapsack and the *Lonely Planet*.

Our hero ventures to a faraway land on his quest for the miraculous unicorn or magic ring. The faraway land contains vicious mountains, poisonous beasts, and many foreigners with amusing accents. Amongst them, our hero overcomes adversity and passes a series of tests, to grow into a man with manly skills and a sword and designer stubble. He makes peace with the spirits of his ancestors—Marx, Foucault, Max Weber—or at least learns to ignore their voices in his ear. Through trial by fire, he has arrived at the Truth, or at least some moderately convincing approximation of the Truth that fits into 80,000 words.

Finally, with the trusty sword and his newfound skills, he defeats his nemesis and seizes the scroll of knowledge. He returns triumphantly home to claim his kingdom/bride/ tragically overrated educational qualification from the bearded old men. He then discovers the quest was only symbolic all along and, chuckling wryly, writes his memoirs and retreats into happy obscurity to grow his own beard.

So we have the key ingredient of a decent rite of passage: separation from the world you knew before, ready for the dramatic transition from naïve caterpillar to worldly butterfly. The problem is that rites of passage can be quite painful. A substantial chunk of the internet is devoted to lists of such masochistic practices. The least imaginative involve isolation, the equivalent of the dweeby history PhD student locked away in a dusty Soviet archive for a year. The most dramatic incorporate poison, hallucinogens, and self-cannibalism. Wannabe men in one Amazonian tribe, for example, traditionally must dance wearing mittens full of poisonous ants (after the ice bar I feel their mittened pain). In many Indian universities entry is marked by 'ragging', a euphemism which covers everything from forced public nudity to fatal beatings.

Fieldwork comes somewhere in the middle of these extremes. It involves a journey into the unknown, with exciting possibilities for collecting scars, public humiliations, and native amulets. In fact, it is basically a more sophisticated version of the Gap Year. Like the PhD, the Gap Yah was once the preserve of drifters too dishevelled and socially awkward to flourish in society. Now it is *de rigueur* for the British middle-class adolescent seeking some padding for a CV: six months of menial labour, followed by sunburn, cheap Asian liquor, and sexual embarrassment.

I belong to a Department of International Development, bursting at the seams with intrepid souls. All the other kids seem much hardier and more heroic, and grow up to be real academics like Indiana Jones. Their fields seem authentically distant and full of threatening vegetation. They battle typhus and dodge bullets and are periodically falsely imprisoned in Côte d'Ivoire. Back home they show off their ringworm, and tell tales of the sex workers, child soldiers, and drug lords they interviewed. Their quests and obstacles overcome would make for good old-fashioned rollicking adventure yarns.

Alas, this is not one of those tales. Delhi today is no blank space on a map marked Here There Be Dragons, but a global city. Indians are not an isolated tribe stuck up a river and waiting for literacy, but inhabit all four corners of the earth and even some corners of my family. English is widely understood, and it is easy to buy everything from Kentucky Fried Chicken to haute couture.

But debutante balls, *quinceañera* and bat mitzvahs are rites of passage, for all that they feature prom dresses and bitchy aunts rather than wrestling lions. The princess with the pea under the mattress was proving something, even if it was that girls with soft hands are far too thin-skinned for their own good. I hoped that my time in Delhi, too, would lead me out of intellectual puberty. A quiet adventure, with internet and inflight entertainment.

With little fanfare, an anonymous warehouse in Middlesex dispatched my visa. I was going.

Oh God, I was going.

Into the belly of the whale, the gates of Mordor, the tiger's lair. Time, my dear Talker, for my first dance.

3

RENT

...and once arrived in the City, he dispersed utterly and
gratefully in it like a raindrop fallen into the sea.

—John Crowley, *Little, Big*

*B*efore any glamorous electricity research could
begin, I had to go on a terrible journey to the
bowels of Delhi and the very depths of the human soul: I had
to find a place to live.

Leaving the exhausted Talker far behind, I bounded off the
plane filled with foolish confidence. Delhi is a city of almost 23
million, if we include the towns it's chomping up daily. Some
experts predict by 2030 it will have 46 million inhabitants, twice
the population of Australia. (Mind you, these are the same
people who in the 1970s predicted Kolkata's population would
reach 50 million by the year 2000, versus the 13.2 million of
reality. In fact, Delhi isn't growing all that quickly compared
with some of the global South's other rising cities. But India

has always provided a steady source of income for prophets of the Apocalypse.)

So how hard could finding a place be for little old me? Surely I was a catch, what with my student salary, adorably frail grasp of nineteenth-century Hindi, and reluctance to commit to a deposit. What's more, I'd chanced on an expat mailing list. Alongside adverts for Chihuahuas, pre-loved rocking chairs, and one memorable plea for an elephant and a marching band, it advertised a variety of rooms for the commitment-phobic newcomer. I'd be fighting off the offers!

Oh, foolish youth.

Cities are humanity's great steaming engines of economic, social, and culinary progress. In general they seem to muddle along fairly well. Yet for all that from afar they appear like single organisms, harmonious wholes like hives or coral reefs, the reality is something more complicated.

Like London, the so-called city of villages, Delhi is a more or less badly stitched patchwork quilt. Its clumps of settlements seem thrown together half by accident, held together by a wispy thread of loyalty—and not all clumps are equal. It is a Victorian attic of a city, all odds and ends, old and new and grim and fair heaped upon each other.

Actually, though it claims to be three or four thousand years old, the city might not even be Victorian. Though often described as a great Mughal city, it was already in decline even before the vicious British retaliation for the 1857 'Mutiny'.

It might be more accurate to date the birth of today's Delhi to 1911, when it abruptly became the British Indian capital and began to grow rapidly. Or to 1947 and the great waves of migration that followed Partition and independence, changing the city's temperament forever. Or even to 1991, the year of India's 'big bang' economic opening, when Delhi scored its own legislative assembly and began a conscious reorientation 'from walled city to world city' (the *Times of India*'s neat marketing slogan) with its eye eventually on the 2010 Commonwealth Games.

Delhi is the incarnation of an old philosophical chestnut. Can you ever step into the same city twice? (You might manage to step in the same Yamuna River twice: on its bad days it seems neither liquid nor solid, but a murky fume-belching chemical state between the two. Delhi's once-great tributary of the Ganges, choked with much of the city's sewage, has been declared officially dead. Which makes doubly troubling the novelist Javier Marías' comparison of his heroine's eyes with the Yamuna's 'blue water'.)

Imagine a great decaying ship. Its components are repaired and replaced one at a time—a jigger here, a mizzen there—until from crow's nest to poop deck not a single inch of timber is original. Now imagine this full-scale rebuilding has occurred not only once, but seven or twelve times. When does it stop being the same ship? Humans have inhabited the city's rough area continuously for thousands of years. Monuments from many of these eras visibly survive. But the city has been changed and chipped and retrofitted by each war, exodus, regime change, and geographical shift. 'There are only about

200 original Dilliwallas in the whole city,' said one Delhi University scholar.

The great ship's mystique has survived: Delhi the city of power, the eternal emperor's court, and nerve centre of India. Delhi today, the city of 1911 and/or 1947/1991/2010, makes much of this timeless prestige. Yet, for large chunks of history it languished in moderate obscurity, often barely more than a provincial town with pretensions. A series of small capitals wandered gradually north in present-day Delhi, culminating in the great seventeenth century 'Old Delhi' (then, of course, New) of Shah Jahan, builder of the Taj Mahal in Agra and, in Delhi, the great Red Fort, Chandni Chowk and Jama Masjid. But as the British expanded from their Bengali foothold and the Mughals slumped, so did Delhi, revived only with the government's return in 1911.

Such a chaos of mixed time, in which history is marked and markedly ignored, is perfect for a Generation Y-er like me. Not to put too fine a point on it (Generation Y is famous for its narcissism), we are both the soulless children of global homogenization and the people most likely to Wikipedia 'Shah Jahan'. We know that ruins are inevitable and everywhere and symbols of the futility of our aspirations: the seminal event of our generation was 9/11. We know too that they make an excellent soulful background on Instagram. In this jumble of eras and settlements as temperamentally different as herons and haberdashers, and with almost zero prior knowledge, I knew with utter certainty that my life would be over if I didn't choose the right neighbourhood.

The first viewing slightly dented my confidence. I had

narrowed my focus to South Delhi. The British created a dual city, and built to the north a civilian-military combination of civil lines and cantonment for themselves quite distinct from the native city of Old Delhi. Today, apart from the slogan-spattered hubbub of Delhi University's 130,000+ students, who never seem to study but all hang around in cafes outside, North Delhi has faded. Civil Lines' leafy avenues and once-lavish Maidens Hotel are mired in somnolence. Since independence, Delhi's centre of gravity has gradually oozed southwards. South Delhi is now a sprawling series of wealthy, introverted quarters, each with their own parks and markets.

Safdarjung Enclave seemed an appropriately ambivalent historical area. The neighbourhood is named after an opportunistic nobleman. Just down the street sits his bulbous-headed tomb and gardens, 'the last dying flicker of Mughal architecture', largely constructed of cheaper materials and scrappy marble nicked from a general's older tomb. It is an affluent area of modern residences and gossiping neighbours.

This particular flat, though—only the rich own full houses—was on a dingy back street and up eight flights of stairs. The door was heavy with locks. Electricity wires of dubious legality hung in thick parasitic clumps and mistletoe sprigs. Traffic jangled below.

The ageing, blue-jawed owner had a dramatic pair of seagull eyebrows, a son in America, and an enormous rattling chain of keys. His eyes were seamed with veins, but sharp and sidelong. Once he had recovered from the climb, he eyed my whiteness.

'I think you saw a wrong number. What can I do? It is like this only.' The price mysteriously leapt by a third.

I felt a twinge in the region of my pocket. As the novice —isolated, marginal, betwixt and between—goes through the rite of passage like 'water being heated to boiling point, or a pupa changing from grub to moth', in the words of the anthropologist Victor Turner, described her condition—as one of 'sacred poverty'. The formidably dangerous fieldwork sites of all my International Development chums are, crucially, often pretty cheap. I had haughtily surveyed Delhi on Google Maps (lightly fictionalized for the city, I would discover during a physics-defying car journey through a market) and assumed I would be living in a princely mansion in the location of my choice.

The scales were falling from my Oxford-coddled eyes. Delhi is certainly not the place for sacred poverty. In fact, it is jolly bloody expensive—perhaps especially in terms of accommodation.

Forget the stereotype of impoverished old India, with its begging bowl in one hand and leprous stump the other. Or at least set it aside for a moment: of course India still boasts poverty, malnutrition, and over half of the world's remaining lepers. But there is a lot of money in Delhi—and I mean a *lot*. You can almost smell it in the air: the warm and faintly sweaty vegetable smell of old paper money.

Money washes over the city in waves. It congeals in malls and mansions and the fatty gleam of SUVs. It seeps into surprising cracks. My favourite tale of excess is that of a competition running in the robotically shiny atrium of a shopping complex. The prize: several thousand rupees for the person carrying most pictures of M.K. Gandhi. Of course, the Mahatma's toothless smile appears on all Indian banknotes. The winning family rushed to an ATM and took out a sum of cash that far dwarfed the prize itself. That whooshing sound isn't Gandhi's noble spinning wheel: it's his ashy phantom cycloning on his slick black Raj Ghat memorial.

It's horrifying in retrospect to see how quickly I internalized the importance of this kind of conspicuous consumption. I'd managed to claim one crucial pillar of Dilliwallihood, a SIM card, thanks to a thoughtful young shopkeeper who generously took it upon himself to Photoshop my passport photos until the government had no chance of recognizing me. It was obvious I ought to be flaunting a snazzy phone; everyone else did. There was just one problem: my smartphone didn't actually work.

Nonetheless, I devotedly flashed it around, an expensive idiot. For the niche matter of actually making calls I concealed about my person a cheap plastic phone that seemed to horrify all who saw it: 'a farmer phone, shudder.' Occasionally it buzzed incriminatingly in my bag. 'What? No, I didn't hear anything.'

A lot of the money swilling around is black, or at least dark grey: money from scams, corruption, crime, tax avoidance, under-the-table industry, cheaply privatized state assets and natural resources, and other slightly dubious and unsavoury sources. It flows into land and property (along with India's addiction of choice, gold), partly because keeping aspects of property deals quiet and largely untaxed is far cheaper for all parties. Indians are also not a very urban lot, perhaps surprisingly: two-thirds of the population still live in rural areas. Perhaps as an agricultural hangover, land is perceived as safe and bestowing status. It is prestige given concrete and inheritable form—'a real estate Rolex', in the words of the *New York Times*.

Until 1990, India was famous as the land of the Licence Raj, a morass of red tape and the dismally low 'Hindu rate' of economic growth. In the 1980s, under Indira Gandhi and later her son Rajiv (neither related to the Mahatma, though their far less popular memorials are close to his at Raj Ghat), the country began in fits and starts to become more pro-business. In 1991, facing the realities of a post-Cold War world and a short-term external payments crisis, the government opened to the world economy with a bang. In selected sectors it reduced tariffs, permitted some foreign investment, and allowed private competitors in alongside government corporations. Many tariffs remain comparatively high, state corporations are still powerful, and the bureaucracy still produces Five-Year Plans. Nevertheless, slowly but surely over the two decades since 1991, India has reoriented itself towards the market.

Consequently, Delhi doesn't have a single ruling elite. On one hand is its peaceably globalized Anglophone upper crust, with their Western educations and accents and, more rarely, nostalgic attachment to the leftwing ideology of the pre-liberalization era. On the other is a rather more rambunctious—and increasingly wealthy—crowd. Set foot in the westerly neighbourhood of Karol Bagh, for example, and you'll see a swirl of garishly sequined clothing, imported electronics, and hard-drinking Punjabi men.

On one side is the power of snobbery and 'high culture'; on the other, that of popular politics and cold hard (or perhaps warm soft) cash. From this latter group Delhi rather unfairly gets its frontier town reputation: that beneath the veneer of universities and galleries lurks a semi-wilderness of casual violence, opportunism, machismo, and enormous self-made fortunes. The old elites watch the challengers' rise with a kind of dull refined horror, lamenting their avarice, knowing the money and the power is beginning to flow elsewhere. But some of the old trappings of power—English, overseas education, corporate employment—are still attractive to the upwardly mobile. Their sons and daughters may appropriate these trappings to secure their own position. The result is an uneasily shared city.

Occasionally these loose groups clash head-on. One evening in an upmarket bar I witnessed the launch of a book of queer erotica, followed by a glossy Audi event. A trio of burly turbaned sardars must have arrived early for the red-blooded German sports cars. They awkwardly threw back whiskey, beards bristling, while a lipsticked man simulated a startling range of same-sex practices with wooden puppets.

The upshot of this moneyed ferment is that house prices, and increasingly rents, are becoming more and more expensively bubbly, hitting Manhattan or even Moscow levels. A lawyer chum acting on behalf of a group of farmers selling land just outside Delhi expected the deal to be in the tens of millions.

'Of rupees?' I asked naively.

'No, dollars.'

Central Delhi prices are even more grotesquely inflated,

especially in the wide avenues of imperial New Delhi. In March 2012, a run-down, water-stained bungalow near Lodi Gardens sold for US$29 million; the Mexican ambassador's residence was valued at $110 million. Much of this area, often called 'Lutyens' Delhi' after the architect of its most famous buildings, is still devoted to government housing, giving the Government of India control over one of the world's more valuable real estate portfolios. The death of ministers and former presidents leads to vicious squabbling over the villas. Green and spacious, stalked by peacocks, the pressure to seize and develop the space is immense.

There is so much money swilling around the city that high house prices alone can't make people spend it fast enough. Home improvement is one option for the big spender, especially for those who want to show they have good taste. There are even consultants who thoughtfully help you spend your cash. *Vaastu* is an Indian version of feng shui which promises peace and prosperity. It's now big business: earlier confined almost exclusively to temple architecture, it has found favour for the new houses of metropolitan elites. Pricey consultants use this 'ancient science' to produce prescriptions on everything from the position of air-conditioning units to the direction your feet should point when sleeping, lest the house be attacked by Negative Forces.

'We had a terrible time with our new place,' my friend sighed over breakfast one day. She is a true elite Dilliwalli, always immaculately dressed and attached to her Blackberry; she even has a tiny adorable dog. 'We'd already finished building it when we called in the *vaastu* guy. It turns out we did it all wrong. The entrance is bad because it faces south. My room should be next to the door because I'm an unmarried daughter and will be the first to leave the home, or presumably the first to be murdered by any passing maniac. And it turns out the house is unlucky because it's on a T-junction—we've had to put up a convex mirror to compensate. He wanted us to rip up the entire place. It's *jinxed*.'

Back in Safdarjung Enclave, I pointed out that there was no kitchen. 'Oh, we'll build that this weekend,' the blue-jawed man said cheerfully. I could almost see his seamy eyes calculating my weight in gold, a seedy Archimedes.

I must have looked unconvinced, so the man upped his sales pitch: 'We'll treat you like our own daughter.' It became clear over the next few minutes that this meant he would generously treat me to the finest despotism the Evil Patriarchy had to offer. I would be banned from leaving the house after dusk, and my calls, callers and diet monitored. He looked affronted when I asked whether the bedroom door locked. 'Why would you lock out your own father?'

When he went next door, the walls were so thin that I could hear him breathing.

As I went back downstairs he called after me, 'By the way, you're not a Muslim, are you?'

Thankfully, I had found somewhere to rest my head during the search. In the most appalling breach of British etiquette of my life thus far, I threw myself on the kindness of virtual strangers.

A good Englishperson would sleep in a septic tank rather than actually take up an acquaintance's offer of hospitality. I spend much of my time apologizing to Indians for this fanatical hostility to overnight guests—in the subcontinent, by contrast, 'the guest is God'—along with the ghastly dishes the British serve up in the name of korma. But hey, I was throwing out the English rulebook; besides, I'd have my own place in no time. And so I ended up staying with the great Family Roy.

(Here I must assuage the social horror of my British readers. In one of the bizarre twists that characterizes India, three months later I found out I was actually related to the Roys, via a clump of undiscovered relatives living only two doors down.

'Well, yes,' said Mrs Roy reasonably, 'I did wonder if you were related to those Mukherjees. I knew they had a Chatterjee relative who moved to England, married an extremely tall Finnish woman, and had a Yorkshire-born granddaughter who went to Oxford... But I thought there must be a lot of those about.')

For decades the Roys had lived in the southeastern neighbourhood of Kailash Colony, named after the residence of the gods on Mount Kailash (more meditative and unbitchy than Mount Olympus). When they arrived the colony was separated from the city proper by dusty farmland filled with oxen, but now it is appealingly central.

Prices rocketed with the arrival of the metro in the run-up to the 2010 Commonwealth Games—an event we shall tactfully call a slight goof, more on which later—and the main road is now lined with coffee shops and gyms sporting the tangerine likeness of David Hasselhoff. Within a warren of quietly bustling streets, sleek, energy-hungry new houses are replacing the faded older terraces and their traditional heat-defying architecture. In a vain attempt to stop middle-class bickering over the vast number of cars that cram the roads, garages are to be compulsory. The Roys were being gently evicted a month later by developers eager to thrust a sleek substitute upon them. I helpfully showed up in the middle of their packing four generations of old clocks and model planes.

Throughout the agony of my homelessness the Roys were probably the only thing standing between me and a murderous rampage through the streets, and they also provided a wonderful and bemusing early education in the ways of Delhi. I learnt, for example, that it is impossible to sit around compromisingly clad in only your pants, because at least twenty people—salesmen, builders, acquaintances, lost citizens, indeterminate others— will ring the doorbell before lunch.

One special feature of daily life particularly struck me. A cultural quirk of the British is the tendency to eat our evening meal very early, before we all crowd around the wireless and sing God Save the Queen. Indians typically dine a lot later, as do all the other grown-up nations of the world—but the Roys took this to a whole new level. Immediately they warned that dinner would be around 11 pm. In fact, sometimes they would call their British-based son, my wise friend and newfound cousin Indrajit, and all eat together across the airwaves on Skype despite the five-and-a-half-hour time difference.

'Why?' I asked.

So came the shamefaced revelation. The family was nursing a serious addiction—to serials. At first, I heard 'cereals', and thought this was some late-night jonesing for the Honey Monster, a little muesli-snorting. We've all been there. In the United Kingdom, the lurid American cereal Lucky Charms and its creepy leprechaun mascot are considered so dangerous that they are banned, lest all the nation's schoolchildren lapse into a diabetic coma.

But no, the Roys were addicted to good ole-fashioned soap operas. I was fascinated, and sat down with them to watch.

There are hours of these serials each day, drip-fed in tiny ten-minute crack-morsels in between adverts for biscuits and whitening cream. They are quite clearly directed at the advertisers' beloved demographic of podgy but well-meaning females who don't get out of the house all that much. Every ten minutes an extended break aimed to entice me into buying chocolate, shampoo, or electronics.

Luckily, there's so much English in the dialogue that I could get the gist of the least ludicrously implausible episodes. (This was a lot more successful than my first foray into Bollywood, when I watched ninety whole minutes of *Kaminey* before realizing that the plotline revolved around that hoary old chestnut, identical twins. I had assumed the hero just had a very bored costume designer.)

Generation Y also knows that you should never, ever underestimate the power of TV. It can make and break communities, creating identities and stereotypes in equal measure. Through TV you belong differently to the world. Your spheres of empathy expand and shift even while you are shut up alone, watching. India is no exception. The TV version of the epic *Ramayana*, serialized between 1987 and 1989, broke viewing records. Crowds gathered around the sets and cities came to a standstill. It's almost a cliché to credit (or blame) the TV show for helping to create Hindu nationalism as a key political force in the 1990s.

Until 1991 there was only one broadcaster, the state-owned Doordarshan. Satellite TV arrived alongside the opening of the rest of the economy, and viewing exploded. First global channels and then Indian entrepreneurs quickly got in on the act. Twenty-four-hour television news has particularly boomed, in a variety of languages. Doordarshan and the state All India Radio still have a vast budget ($2 billion in the five years to 2012), but the government's bland and propagandistic voice is generally outshouted in the cacophonous market.

A myriad of commercial channels chase down the news in its goriest, sexiest, and most populist varieties. They are credited with deepening Indian democracy, but it is an amoral phenomenon: they also spread fear, stoke nationalism, hound their objects, and prize the superficial. Their pretty anchors and epileptic graphics, says one commentator, 'whirr like fans on a hot day—fast and furious'. Another claimed that today's Indian politics is like 'a mutated version of *The Truman Show*', except that the politicians know it's there and have adapted strategies to cope. For the first time I heard a country's senior journalists pleading for state media regulation, lamenting the decline of quality and ethical standards in their own industry.

Mrs Roy's serials themselves turned out to be a strange mixture of the progressive and the regressive. The protagonists are all in their mid-twenties and implausibly good-looking with vast hair. The men are either rugged child-schlepping love interests, or—once they've been pinned down by a large-haired woman—lazy, incompetent buffoons. Many of the women are bolshy and assertive, not simply decorative, but simultaneously their role as chaste and selfless wives, mothers and daughters-in-law is stressed. The villains are easy to spot, because they cackle a lot and have luxuriantly evil moustaches.

Alongside the traditional soap opera fallbacks (adultery, bereavement, poorly explained return from the dead), the plotlines lurch through all sorts of worthy subjects: corruption, child marriage, dowry payments, pervy bosses, wife abandonment, and the relationship between the dreaded mother-in-law and her daughter. At the same time, the focus is generally on the individual and family, not the nation. They seem to suggest that the only real option for social change in contemporary India is vigilante action, complete with firearms.

All this drama occurs to a thundering operatic soundtrack punctuated by inexplicable lightning strikes at moments of particular high tension, such as doors opening and tea being served. In one ten-minute segment, nine minutes were in slow motion; eight people were kidnapped; fourteen people got married; a grandmother menaced her family with a shotgun; two brothers unconvincingly pretended to punch each other with cartoon *thwocks*; a drug-addled middle-aged woman attacked people with a trident; and a lot of mobile phones rang whilst the camera swooped to and fro into each overacting *O.M.G. WHO IS CALLING ME* face. I went to bed with high hopes for Delhi life, and indigestion.

Delhi, with its architecture of draughts and gloomy coolness, is a city built to survive the bleeding hot summers. It whines in winter. By February there is still a slight chill now and then in the air. At night the odd fire still flares for warmth, although the air was clear, unlike January's choking smogs. Dilliwallas still wore a disproportionately forlorn refugee air, with the odd clothing and demoralized aspect of British tourists in the Heathrow homecoming lines. Guards wear woolly hats, auto drivers sport padded jackets and earmuffs, older women wear thick socks under their sandals ('We are defrosting,' Mrs Roy explained). I even saw one driver with beetle brows and what looked to be a fully ear-flapped Russian fur cap, a three-wheeled Brezhnev.

My Britishness stopped me from asking for hot water. This came from a geyser—not, as I thought, an Icelandic spring that periodically dispatched jets of boiling water across the kitchen, but a small water heater in the other room with an eerily flickering red light. Turning it on in time requires military-style planning skills that I lack.

So on the second optimistic morning of flat-hunting I hummed as I took a traditional bucket bath. I had finally worked out what '2BHK' meant ('two bedrooms, hall and kitchen'), set up several more flatmate dates, and expected to be installed in a new home just in time for my latest serials fix.

Undaunted by the Safdarjung strikeout, I headed further south to Saket. It was a little further out than I'd hoped, but Hauz Khas had offered nothing more than a mattress on the floor for US$400 a month. It was a shame: the location was great and full of unassumingly futile ruins. I spotted a squat tower filled with holes, allegedly for displaying the severed heads of thieves, but still the perfect flat remained elusive. A Green Park flat had been let five minutes before I arrived; the landlord in a boutique-heavy block of Greater Kailash-II suddenly stopped returning my calls. With a heavy heart I let Kalkaji go too, although it would have brought me close to my Bengali roots.

The Saket neighbourhood is famous for its vast glossy malls, so I decided to plunge through the ubiquitous security searches and sample one. After being thoroughly groped a few times by the security guards, I was inside. It was utterly forgettable, full of the same familiar brands and wearily smirking assistants of any other big city. Glossy-haired wives trailed their chubby polo-shirted husbands around a shrill-voiced woman trying to flog a sports car. Later, I would have the best haircut of my life here, although it took three men to blow-dry and made me look like a First Lady for the first 24 hours.

Moving into the belly of the mall, I was inspired to see the place full of gaudy red hearts. Richard Branson's grinning visage peered down from one side like a disconcertingly bearded Cupid. A Valentine's Day celebration! Sponsored by Virgin! Rarely has naked consumerism made me so cheery. The Indian festival calendar is already bursting with lights and incense, but this could actually be a progressive woman-friendly addition to a set that otherwise revolves heavily around fasting for husbands, brothers, and sons. And it was surely a good omen for my next flat-date.

Further away from the malls, the traffic lapsed a little further into chaos. The flat turned out to lie alongside a gigantic open sewer. Nonetheless, I forged ahead—and suddenly found myself in the middle of a beauty contest. The Machiavellian flatmate-in-chief worked in social media in one of the events-based jobs that Delhi has invented over the last couple of years, and consequently had an acute sense of how accurately popularity contests can illuminate human value. He had invited several prospective tenants altogether for a sort of *Hunger Games*-style battle royale. Like displaying stags, we four challengers all vied to deliver the knockout blow and be the last man standing.

Sounding simultaneously visionary and ineffably fun is, however, difficult when asking questions about fridges and fan speeds. I've never quite trusted my laugh at the best of times—it sounds either too enthusiastic or slightly sarcastic. Now with horror I found myself emitting an obvious fake that sounded quite like a sea mammal's mating call. As if from a long way away, I could hear my own treacherous voice saying, 'Sure, I love early-morning vuvuzela concerts. You're right, this is a good space for a crack den. Yes, go right ahead and sublet the corner of my bed to the Forestry Commission—I'm, like, *so* chilled about personal space.'

Machiavelli watched, expressionlessly stroking his goatee. Occasionally he threw out impossible questions: 'Do you smoke?' The four of us spasmed. 'Um. Yes? No? Yes, but for you—for you, lovely handsome Machiavelli—I'd quit. No, but I simply love people blowing it in my face, and I buy cigarettes for all my smoker friends—no, packs of cigarettes! cartons! of rare Cuban cigars!' I hated myself. At one point I may even have called him 'dude'.

After some hours, Machiavelli seemed to be content with the volume of social awkwardness he'd extracted from our desperate-to-please veins, and dismissed us with a flick of his wrist. He was, of course, off to play golf.

We four challengers looked at each other with the peculiar embarrassed grin of people who both know you'd gladly stab each other in the back and sell the still-warm corpse. As I walked back down towards the giant open sewer, I fought the urge to grovel under the window.

Machiavelli never called.

By Day 3 I'm ashamed to say my morality—never my most robust attribute at the best of times—slunk off for some sightseeing and *chaat*. Promiscuity seemed the only answer. I honed an ingratiating smile and a patina of white lies like some nymphomaniacal estate agent, and flirted with every single flat out there. I admired sofas and sinks with the kind of coos reserved for newborns. 'What a charming cosy place! What a simply divine concrete view! Of *course* I didn't think "furnished" meant "contains a bed", or expect running water.' I feigned extreme religiosity, lied about my soufflé skills, and promised to shower only between 8.05 and 8.07 am.

They were either unconvinced or wanted vast unsanitary deposits of cash.

Those were the longest ten days of my life. I started to look further and further away from the fashionable neighbourhoods. By the end, I'd seen more flats and more slow-motion serial episodes than any mortal should ever have to, and felt dirty right down to my soul. The Roys started to suggest I should go through a broker, a shady-sounding figure who would carve off at least a month's rent in fees.

It was chastening. I'd imagined the city would bow down to me like some visiting dignitary. Instead I was more like the Hindustan Ambassador. This is not some top-hatted diplomat but an automobile, plump, white and ponderous like a beluga whale. It is iconic: 'virtually indestructible', with great goggling herbivorous eyes; the design was actually poached from an old Oxford-built model, the Morris Oxford III. For years the Ambassador was the pinnacle of aspiration, with a seven-year waiting list; its swollen bonnets are still frequently gilded with the telltale flags of official government power; and it was recently crowned the world's best taxi by *Top Gear*. The only problem is that nobody wants to drive one anymore. In 2012–13, 1,895,471 passenger cars were sold; only 3,390 were Ambassadors. The days of its unchallenged dominance are gone.

Just when I was abandoning hope and about to move into a hostel—where the landlord's first sentence was 'Don't worry, I'll tell your parents if you die'—I found the flat. Granted, it was in the distant, soulless southwestern suburb of Vasant Kunj. Approached across an area of dusty forest (which led occasional city-mouse auto drivers to plead, 'Madam, you take me in jungle. Very far, very dangerous, you give more'), it is a sprawling low-density area just south of Jawaharlal Nehru University's safari park of a campus. The Kunj—as nobody calls it, despite my Australian housemate's best efforts—bustles like a genteel ant hive in the morning and is pitch black and paranoid at night, the only sounds the clatter of the nightwatchman's stick and the roar of drunk drivers on the road to Gurgaon. It was a long way from my lofty central dreams. But the flat was light and airy, and the Roys were about to be evicted.

'I'll take it.'

Joyously, I threw my useless smart-phone onto my new bed. It hit with a sharp crack and fell apart. On closer inspection, the mattress appeared to be a solid block of stone, benevolently engineered by Gandhians to strip sleep of all pleasure. It also turned out to lie under a gigantic flight path. If we can infer international status from the reasonableness of the times planes pass overhead, Delhi is the grovelling Igor-like minion of America.

But it was Home. Stage 1 on the journey to becoming a Dilliwalli was complete. I fell asleep dreaming of Aeroflot crash landings and urban myths of frozen poo plummeting from the sky.

4

HANDS

Any woman who understands the problems of running
a home will be nearer to understanding the problems of
running a country.

—Margaret Thatcher

*T*he next morning, I was woken by an eruption right
by my head. A crash, followed by a long insolent
goat-like bleat. This was the discreet entrance of Kamala,
the most formidable and uncooperative maid in the whole
subcontinent.

She started shovelling dust onto my belongings. Groaning,
I inched off the stone mattress in a joy of semi-paralysis, and
tried to work out how to reinvent myself as an independent
young researcher. Kamala eyed me with cheerful malice, and
began blasting out tinny Bollywood tunes from her phone.

This was the morning ritual for the next few months—apart
from the times when Kamala mysteriously didn't turn up for

several days in a row, and then reappeared without explanation. Despite working in an Anglophone flat for two years already, she had resolutely refused to learn any English word except 'Morning', a greeting which she imbued with such withering diphthongic sarcasm that it sounded like a genealogical insult. With equal resolution she refused to recognize any of the sounds I emitted as anything resembling Hindi. Instead, she simply spoke more quickly and more loudly in her eccentric accent, until eventually giving up with a facepalm of disgust.

Less than five foot tall in bare feet (horny toenails painted) and curly black hair, Kamala cut a formidable figure. She was built like a wrestler, slapping dough and clothing in thick hands. She periodically let loose a throaty chuckle apropos of nothing, shaking her head so hard her earrings clicked. Several times a morning, her phone would ring and she would make it absolutely, eye-rollingly clear that she was gossiping about our idiocy. I once caught her red-handed in the bathroom, chain-smoking cheap hand-rolled *bidis*. She regarded me silently, took another drag, and tapped the ash into the laundry bucket.

As a result, Kamala's employment was characterized by a profound and humiliating asymmetry—on my part. My final realization that I was the beta female in the relationship—and quite possibly in life as a whole—came about two months in. She offered me a lychee, and I was strangely touched.

'Thank you, *dhanyavad*, *shukriya*!' I waggled my head so hard I almost choked.

She looked at me strangely, and ate several herself. Then she turned, threw the orange-brown rinds on the floor of the flat, and swept haughtily out.

I crouched and swept up her rubbish, filled with a strange feeling that prefigured my ice bar bemusement.

At our lowest ebb I even consulted the great Victorian classic *Mrs Beeton's Book of Household Management*. Managing the help, Mrs Beeton proclaimed darkly, was 'the greatest plague in life'. It is, of course, an especially female role. I learnt that I must be like the commander of an army, and that I ought to wear silks of a grave hue. There wasn't much else.

Oxford colleges are old-fashioned in many ways, not least the continued existence of 'Scouts' who clean the rooms. In the UK I'm an anachronistic weirdo—and quite possibly immoral— because someone arrives each morning to deliver post and take out the bin: a wonderful woman called Sue, who always bears enormous earrings and chunks of gossip. In India, however, it's still common for middle-class families to have at least one servant, often several. Reliance on them is deeply ingrained. These are the people who keep the city running.

Kamala's part-time appearances were enough for us, but vast inequalities in income mean that it's feasible to hire a maid, a cook, a driver, and a nanny if you're so inclined. The monthly salary of a chauffeur for six days a week, for example, might be only around £100, plus a little extra for meals on evenings out. A maid will be considerably cheaper, especially if you avoid going through a middleman firm. For both, though, foreigners often end up paying salaries an order of magnitude greater, much to their chagrin and the irritation of locals who claim they distort the labour market. Of course, the cheapest of all is the unpaid labour of the daughter-in-law—but that's for another chapter.

Trained and experienced staff fetch higher prices. Expats trade them for their skills in speaking English or chefing up French hors d'oeuvres. Otherwise it's a slow process, like the army breaking down and resocializing new recruits. I witnessed a Delhi-born friend 'breaking in' a new driver with good-humoured curses as he stalled and overrevved and tried to put on his own music over hers.

As we stepped out of the hot car, she glanced worriedly back at him settling for a nap inside. 'I'm not sure he'll think to open a window. I hope we don't come back to find him baked alive.'

It's frighteningly easy to get used to. Within weeks I found myself speaking like a nineteenth-century aristocrat. Over cocktails with some jaded longer-term expats, I congratulated myself for my thoughtfulness and generosity. 'Of course it is such a *crowded* country. One does like to create employment where one can.'

I jangled the ice in my drink, and continued, 'You *must* come and visit the new flat. Kamala's *vegetables à la dérision* are simply delicious.'

It is so much easier to be hospitable, to tell visitors grandly, 'For us, the guest is God, as the natives say', when someone else is washing the dishes. And it is so easy to find yourself barking orders and bitching to other wealthy women about the effort of it. I caught a glimpse of my reflection in the mirror of the bar, hazy in the tasteful evening lamplight. All of a sudden I realized my silhouette looked just like a colonial memsahib, lacking only a parasol. If this was Stage 2 of Dilliwallahood, I wasn't sure I wanted it.

The next day Kamala didn't show up again. Her phone rang and rang, with no answer, despite the fact it was perpetually suckered onto her hand in our flat. I was torn between resentment of a work ethic that involves one day's work being skipped every fortnight, relief that I didn't have to cook or do the laundry, and sympathy for the low wages and dull work.

We weren't good people to work for, I don't think. We might have been less dictatorial, but we never understood things like when to give festival presents and what recipes to suggest and that occasional random days off will be taken. Along with the other *firangi* in the flat I was largely clueless, while Alpha Housemate, the flat's Bengali chieftain, ruled with an iron fist.

Don't get me wrong: Kamala had any number of redeeming features. She was wonderfully no-nonsense: when I was still in denial that I'd killed the second of my plants, foolishly thinking the green bits were the mark of a living organism, she hacked every root and shoot out, and then watered the pot. She was impressively unfazed by the motley collection of half-naked refugees—friends, siblings, indeterminate others— who sporadically graced our floors, and would sweep dust over their sleeping forms with the exact same level of enthusiasm with which she swept it over my laptop.

There wasn't a cowed or obsequious bone in her body. Fittingly, Kamala means 'lotus', a plant whose seeds are 'tungsten-tough' and can survive a thousand years; whose flower can regulate its own temperature and manipulate pollinators; and which possesses a hidden solution for everything from piles and insomnia to erectile dysfunction. Redolent of purity and divine beauty, it is a symbol of Vishnu and Lakshmi.

Lakshmi: the goddess of wealth. Workers like Kamala are the backbone of India's prosperity. Like most other domestic workers, she was part of the vast iceberg of India's informal economy. Over 90 percent of Indian jobs exist in this murky category, without rights, without pensions, without a written contract, often without holidays or even regular hours.

Let's put this in context. Ask anyone from my Yorkshire hometown what the contemporary Indian economy is like, and they'll tell you it's founded on the IT and business process outsourcing (BPO) sectors. (That is to say, they'll complain about call centre workers who inform you their name is Mike and unconvincingly discuss the weather in Basingstoke and last night's *Britain's Got Talent*.) In this story, half of all India's workforce is allegedly made up of software technicians stealing jobs from the hardworking chaps of Newcastle or Arkansas.

In reality, even the most generous estimates suggest that the sector directly employs only 3 million people in a workforce of half a billion. Even then, many of these are so-called 'cyber coolies' like my ex-housemate in Bangalore. Her name actually was Lakshmi, though it had brought little wealth. She was large and quiet and always dressed in grave shapeless kurtas.

She proudly called herself a 'BPO' worker, though she wasn't sure what BPO stood for. Despite her commerce degree and command of English, she was bussed in and out to work long, dreary, monotonous nights at a call centre. Constantly monitored, abused by customers, and made to operate in an American timezone half a world away: unlike most, Lakshmi had lasted more than a handful of months. But at weekends she slumped on the sofa like a zombie, staring dead-eyed at the TV even after the power was cut, too tired even to wonder why she hadn't found the promised BPO husband.

In fact, India's much vaunted economic growth has largely been jobless. Employment creation remained more or less stagnant between 2005 and 2010. The formal sector—comprising those lucky few with legally recognized labour rights—has actually been shrinking over the last decade. China has become the workshop of the world. Even lucky Bangladesh has become its sweatshop. India has so far lagged behind, and policymakers are becoming quietly panicky as growth rates slow. Even its international standing as an outsourcing hub is threatened by rising wages and foreign resentment.

Into this gap steps the informal economy. It is often discussed as though it is a historical relic, rather quaint and soon for extinction, like crochet or the giant panda. Many migrants do wind up within it: Kamala and her husband, a driver, were both from Nepal. (Both of them hated Delhi.) The old stereotype suggests that raw-skinned rednecks arrive from their bumpkin villages or the poorer corners of the earth, and the informal economy catches them like a great benevolent net to ease the transition into the sophisticated ways of the *true* urban economy. But the formal economy has not expanded to receive them. The informal economy *is* the true economy.

This shadowy world contains a hugely diverse range of livelihoods and enterprises, most quite legal. Once I started looking, I saw the informally employed everywhere. This is the India that surrounds you in the lanes and bazaars, on the scrappy farms glimpsed from roads and railways and the little neighbourhood markets. Most people are effectively self-employed. The luckiest get a consistent wage; those less fortunate are paid by the hour or day or piece delivered and work multiple jobs.

There are the construction workers, much in demand in Delhi with its ceaseless striving for the new. These are not only the wiry male labourers who I often saw teetering up rickety wooden scaffolding, but also several million near-invisible women who bake and carry bricks. Other very visible individuals run small stalls, selling food or everyday goods or trinkets for ridiculously small profits. They colonize areas of the pavement, keeping an eye out for police, or push carts up and down the streets. Still other workers are artisans, crafting furniture and jewellery with skill to sell it in little specialized markets. Some parts of the country are renowned for clusters of them—Agra for shoes, for example, not just for sale but for international export.

Then there is the rubbish I managed to generate, even as the heat diminished my appetite and the rent my budget. It winds itself into a whole sophisticated economy of recyclers. They pick through the waste produced by urban lifestyles for valuable materials—paper for reprocessing, precious metals from phones—an essential service in a place where garbage collection services are virtually nonexistent.

Other invisible hands produce goods the West might expect to be produced in factories: clothing, pharmaceuticals, low-end electronics. Farming these out to dispersed individual home-based workers is even cheaper than factory labour. The homeworker can work late into the night or draft in the extra hands of relatives and children, without legal risk to the employer. Power cuts and machinery breakages fall upon the individual's head, not that of the transnational corporation.

Though many are left fluctuating in and out of poverty, not everyone in the informal economy is poor. Some earn far more than the national average income by running entire enterprises off the books, too small or too sketchy to be regulated by the state. In India the informal economy is officially called the 'unorganized' sector, but it is far from chaotic. Many small and medium enterprises are protected by guilds and business associations, often drawn up on caste, religious or party-political lines. The boundaries between formal and informal, too, are blurred. Virtually all wealthy Indians are implicated indirectly, whether through employing maids off the books, dodging taxes on property transactions, or corruption. Larger industries, including some government corporations, operate with substantial informal workforces.

India's current economic slowdown looks somewhat different in this light. Urban middle-class India, corporate India, may be gloomy, but consumer demand in rural India continues to grow. The informal economy remains resilient; Credit Suisse suggests it contributes at least half of India's entire GDP. Commentators are rapidly recasting it as a bright spot, for all that it limits the state's tax base.

This shouldn't have taken me by surprise. The informal economy is a very modern phenomenon, and not one confined to the developing world. It approximates the economist's wet dream of a flexible labour market. Workers without the right to organize, strike, sue, age or get sick are a lot cheaper. India is simply cresting the wave of global fashion.

As if to confirm this fashionability, I started spotting business books that glorified the informal economy's creativity and adaptability. Its potential for low-cost innovation has got a lot of press as Western economic models appear to be ossifying. The French call it Système D, allegedly named after the resourceful and self-reliant *debrouillards* or hustlers of francophone Africa—or perhaps instead after those willing and able to *se démerder*, to remove themselves from the stultifying shit of bureaucracy. The celebrated Indian equivalent is *jugaad*, the art and science of muddling through. The subtitle of a recent book explains the promised benefits: *think frugal, be flexible, generate breakthrough growth*. Don't be fooled by the shiny malls. Look more closely at the little stores and service workers that dot moderately wealthy neighbourhoods. These little hairdressers, takeways, and cosmetics stores are the face of the new India too.

Check the pavements of Connaught Place, probably where you'd turn when, scratching your head, you tried to pinpoint some sort of geographic centre to the city. CP was designed as Delhi's central business district. The pricey office space still houses some big firms and iconic names, at the heart of three rings like a great skull-white bullseye. Its egotistical colonial architecture sits uneasily with the grubby signboards and perpetual digging. Between the columns hawkers hawk a fine selection of pirated non-fiction books on the very business practices they epitomize.

Jugaad can indeed be brilliant. Early in my stay, a friend had a printer toner cartridge to deal with. We belted it over the undulating Outer Ring Road to one of the capitals of informality and *jugaad*, southeast Delhi's Nehru Place. Not too far away from C.R. (Chittaranjan) Park, where Bengalis self-ghettoize to hang out buying fish, the Place proper is flanked by large dirty grey buildings, dark eyeless windows looking out onto a bustling plaza full of little stores and courtyard merchants.

We grabbed a hot almond *badam* milk, marzipan delicious with a little caramelized skin on top. I looked around.

The atmosphere was oddly festive, with a brand of all-male restless optimism. Nehru Place is famous as a technology bazaar. No computer is ever entirely broken or useless: someone here can fix it. The merchants sell quasi-legal and pirated computer accessories of all kinds. Software, cables, batteries, monitors, motherboards, hard drives, Chinese-made USB sticks with giant erratic memories—they're all here, if you haggle. More impressively, so are the formal stores, from a host of banks to Microsoft itself. Here the informal economy has all but vanquished its formal enemy. Forget Linux: *this* is real open source innovation.

The skinny cartridge man, smart in a crisp white shirt, squatted down. His hands were ink-stained and prematurely wrinkled but swift as he surveyed the cartridge, prying open shelves and hatches. He smoothed out a couple of sheets of newspaper and set to work. He upended the cartridge. With a swift set of taps, he sent the old ink tumbling out, weirdly powdery onto the runic lines of upside-down Hindi. A few swipes with a cloth to clean it out, and then he carefully refilled it from a nearby container and sealed it neatly. All for a fraction of the price of a new cartridge. Nehru Place murmured approvingly below.

This is the opposite of getting a PhD: it's gutsy, self-taught, spontaneous and cheap. The PhD student famously knows more and more about less and less until he knows everything about nothing. The *jugaad* ad-libber instead does more with less. The do-it-yourself nation will inherit the Earth, so the tale goes, and Indians are particularly good at improvisation. They are the jazz musicians of management strategy, cobbling together a (relatively) successful economy with spit and duct tape. Where the West is fat and complacently addicted to the advice of experts, Indians flourish in adversity. As the protagonist—self-proclaimed 'thinking man' and 'self-taught entrepreneur'—of Aravind Adiga's *The White Tiger* (2008) advises, China leads India on all metrics,

> except that you don't have entrepreneurs. And our nation, though it has no drinking water, electricity, sewage system, public transportation, sense of hygiene, discipline, courtesy, or punctuality, *does* have entrepreneurs.

The cartridge man was just such a businessperson, plugged into twenty-first-century technology but offering a service much more cheaply than the titanic American originals. Forget the Protestant work ethic. In the twenty-first century, to be an entrepreneur against all the odds is to be Indian.

It seemed my lack of *jugaad* get-up-and-go was obvious to more than just Kamala and me.

Being the only academic at a titanic corporate networking event is like being a leper at a children's party. The venue, a glossy luxury hotel, was certainly decked out as if for a celebration. The streets leading there were decked in banners, the auditorium swaddled in decorations beneath its chandeliers, the waiters immaculately servile behind tureens of food. Yes, it was that highlight of the jet set's social calendar: the 7th Asia Gas Partnership Summit. (Over breakfast, I casually eyeballed the programme one final time—and nearly coughed out my dubious masala toast. I had managed to miss the headline event: a speech by the prime minister. This boded slightly ill.)

The other speakers were even more glamorous than the prime minister, himself an impressively impassive man (one cartoon shows his turbaned visage seamlessly morphing into an onion). Brits sweating in loud ties, a US State Department official with the helium voice of Bill Gates, a Turkmen with a sinisterly Gothic PowerPoint, a Gazprom chief who held the audience with a featherlight killer's grip and dead fish eyes, a Pakistani minister promising peace and harmony in a sarcastic tone. And in the final session, the real power players: some of India's own most influential energy politicians and technocrats, their state-fuelled power indicated by their casually crumpled shirts.

There was one snag. Everyone wore affiliation tags, marks of social status dangling at navel level on unmissable scarlet lanyards, and scanned those of strangers with avid snobbery. My own scarlet letter, unfortunately, screamed that I was not a CEO, or even a humble consultant, but a researcher. This was the equivalent of ringing a bell to announce my hunchbacked presence (though at least the 99 percent male population stared a little lower than usual). People backed away in horror, crossing themselves. My only hope was to seize a business card from the runts of the herd before they recognised my affliction.

At one point I thought I might finally have made a friend, a sweet Gujarati man called Abhinav. Most of the other conference attendees instantly dropped to sleep, smartphones glued to their hands with the devotion of teenage girls. But Abhinav followed all the conference talks with open-mouthed awe and giant Bambi eyes. There was something pleasantly herbivorous about him. I could tell he was relatively junior: his suit was crisply tailored, and his moustache—that Samson-like indication of seniority—still limp and sparse.

We shook hands, his fist pumping enthusiastically. He smiled with genuine warmth, and barely flinched when he found out I was a note-taking subhuman. We made small talk—power grids, gas markets, the open access provisions of the Electricity Act 2003—and he introduced me to some bigger moustaches. We sat together for the following session. I felt positively jolly.

At the day's end, Abhinav said, 'We will talk, Lidge.' (Zs are borrowed from Persian and Arabic, so now and then you find a Hindu who says *bajaar* not *bazaar*, and who calls me Elijabeth.)

'Yes, yes!' This was a break, I could feel it. 'I have so much to ask you about ultra mega power plants!'

He pressed something into my hand, and I beamed at him.

'I can tell you are lacking direction, Lidge. Look at this,' he wiggled his eyebrows suggestively, 'and we will talk.'

What? He headed for the exit, then turned dramatically, wearing a messianic look. 'I will make you *student cum entrepreneur!*'

I looked down. He had handed me a CD in an aggressively orange case. Despite the obvious hints to the contrary, I clung to the belief that it contained vast insights into the world of natural gas, and played it that evening.

Uh-oh. The only gas was metaphorical. It appeared to be a business motivation CD. While the others had shunned the research leper, Abhinav had come over all Mother Teresa and decided to save me from my own sad fate.

I idly googled the company. After a couple of brief detours—Google at first helpfully translated the company name into 'BBW', the 'big beautiful women' who tickle a certain type of internet inhabitant—I found it. Crikey Moses. It turned out that, again like Mother Teresa (if Christopher Hitchens' excoriating *The Missionary Position* is to be believed), Abhinav sought to get a little something himself out of his charitable act.

The company looked to rely on a classic 'multilevel market' scheme (obviously I won't say 'pyramid' or 'Ponzi', not at all) in which the top tier accumulates vast wealth from the efforts and hopes of a constantly rotating lower membership. Like a warped version of Avon, the bottom stratum must try to sell overpriced health food and cosmetics to their friends and family—and are encouraged to buy a big chunk themselves. The only way the system makes profits is by continuing to expand, bringing ever more sellers into its orbit and sending ever-greater profits upstairs.

But the company's biggest product was exactly the CD I was listening to: it sold *motivation*. Pre-packaged, gold-plated, Jesus-infused motivation.

The CD continued playing. Its cover showed a grinning middle-aged Indian-American couple; the married couple is the ideal business unit, I learned, obviously with the woman as primary homemaker. The couple looked motivated. You could see it in their teeth.

They dispensed positive thinking and a dollop of evangelical Christian rhetoric as though stacking a dishwasher. The pair had started out at the bottom too, they informed me, but had prayed a lot and taken out loans and worked twenty-three hours a day. Their rise was God-given, because God loves cold hard cash, but humility was not a virtue they took seriously. The inevitable victory was described with relish and a healthy dose of greedy materialism. To paraphrase only somewhat, 'Look how rich we are! Don't be a loser. Don't you want to be rich like us?' The wife described their cars—five! six! seven!—their beautiful house, their five-star lifestyles. Work hard, think big, *believe*, and all this could be yours. Who wouldn't want to be like them?

Weirdly, that wasn't the only time my interviewees dispensed well-meaning motivational advice to me. Others tried to convert me to Zen Buddhism and an expensive three-day-long, thirteen-hours-a-day forum. Setting aside what these recruitment efforts said about my own networking style, there was clearly something interesting going on.

In CP's pavement bookshops, too, self-help was everywhere. Spread across the slabs were American classics and more recent populist pseudo-psychology. There were feel-good spiritual healing texts from wealthy Indian-Americans and meditation tracts from religious gurus. There were innumerable volumes by Osho, which I first thought was a corporate brand but turned out to be a twinkly-eyed guru with a huge Gandalf beard. The 'rich man's guru', he littered his texts with jokes and sexual innuendo. By his death in 1990 he had accumulated a giant Oregon ranch, five private jets and become allegedly the world's single largest collector of Rolls Royce cars. His American followers renamed a town after him, and under a rogue lieutenant carried out the United States' first-ever bioterrorist attack in 1984. I think it's fair to say you couldn't make it up.

Together the books promised 'Six Ways to Make You a Leader', to influence people, to make you popular in eight or ten or twelve steps. (They all seemed to involve a lot of lists.) More than anything, they promised ways to get rich quick. Tellingly, the Hindi version of *Who Wants to Be a Millionaire*, *Kaun Banega Crorepati*, is still running and has spawned multiple regional language versions as well as *Slumdog Millionaire*. There were other genres too, sandwiched between chick lit. They promised muscles and makeovers, ideal husbands, the joys of sex, the deciphering of women from venus. 'Entrepreneurship' seems to have a very real currency.

Could these teach me to be a decisive researcher (and to control Kamala)? I felt my mind pulping beneath the pugnacious clichés: seize the day, embrace the now, learn to love yourself, feel the fear and do it anyway. It was the same language my interviewees used, full of tipping points and black swans. In the twenty-first century you can be whoever you want to be if you try hard enough, so the myth runs. Money is more fungible than ever, and on the internet nobody knows you're a dog. We are all of us in a constant process of fashioning newer shinier selves.

It seemed Delhi, like me, was on a mission for self-improvement.

Around Hauz Khas Village, the grubby fashionista heart that overlooks an old royal lake and some serene ruins, the elite returnees all have big dreams too. Their keyword is 'start-up', like booting a crotchety old computer. Everyone has one or wants one; everyone's in the perpetual process of beginning things.

'I have a start-up,' one recent returnee told me, punctuating his American-accented sentences with lazy swirls of his beer bottle. He was casually dressed and bling-free, expansive and charming with the Cheshire cat smile of an American teen drama. He was fond of making a gesture that looked like overturned stool: two fingers and a thumb made a semi-circle in the air, as though twisting a very small plum from a branch. It was distracting, because I'm sure Tony Blair used to do something similar when he was about to start lying.

The Returnee kept waving to new entries—'that's my old classmate from [insert nonchalant Ivy League college reference here]'. Not for nothing does HKV sometimes try to call itself 'the Village'. Its icons are international—currently Williamsburg, Brooklyn. The new entrants were instantly recognizable as an Indian take on that international brand, hipsters. A plethora of articles have attempted to define the Indian hipster; just as many argue he is a white elephant. You might think Indian returnees have a leg-up on their white counterparts. Many of the men are already skinny, multilingual, and vaguely metrosexual. The rooftop bar even dispensed hummus and indie music to make them feel at home. The uniform is remarkably similar everywhere: plaid shirts, vintage T-shirts, skinny jeans or shorts, MacBooks in satchels, Palestinian scarves, heavy-framed glasses. (Confession: I was also wearing at least two of the above.) The *Hindustan Times* claims, though, that the Indian hipster would have waited in line for the opening of Delhi's first Starbucks in February 2013, something that would have the Williamsburg crew choking on their organic hibiscus soda.

It is now compulsory for the hipster aristocracy (obvs as *true* hipsters they shun the label) to put the boot into Hauz Khas Village, claiming it's gentrifying too fast to be really credible and expanding too fast to survive. Further down the narrow road cars queued with painful slowness to dispense them at a barrier. The place swarmed under the night sky. The alleys below were a crumbling mass of scuffed bricks and signboards, the narrow unpaved lanes barely able to support the weight of canvas-clad feet. The authorities have threatened several properties with demolition and fines. Admittedly it can be pricey and slow to access, and you see the same people every time. But the rooftop bar was all mood lighting and clean wood. Lower down you find great cakes, artsy memorabilia, and earnest leftwing books. For now it's still just about likeable.

The Returnee had worked for a prestigious international consultancy. 'My parents just didn't understand why I gave it up! But I spotted a niche—there is always a niche in India— and I was sick of being a drone. I wanted to work for myself.'

He paused to drag on a cigarette and wave to some more new entries. A live world music band had wandered on. One straddled a cello, another wielded an oud, the stumpy fat-bellied Arabic lute. The straggly-haired singer was warbling so loudly that the Returnee had to shout the final words.

'But really I'm here to *give something back*.'

Elite Indians of my generation are very different to the previous lot. Firstly, they've embraced the corporate sector to an extent unimaginable to the old Nehruvian elite. Secondly, they can actually imagine returning to India for good. Not for them the safe world of state employment or the permanent relocation to Texas. At long last, India's 'brain drain'—to NASA, Silicon

Valley, and beyond—may be transforming into an elite-educated 'brain gain'. Thirdly, they are secure enough to think outside the profit box, confident they're employable the world over. Along with the rat race, they're just as likely to be found studying postmodernism, running non-profit organizations or doing a stint for 'Teach for India', the subcontinent's new equivalent of the huge American scheme. In fact, they are indistinguishable in many ways from my British-born Oxford classmates. They're just more confident—and more optimistic.

For the less well off, success is similar but perhaps less radical. Defining the 'middle classes' is difficult in any country. This is all the more true in India, where data on income is often sketchy and only 2.5 percent of people pay income tax. Sometimes the middle class is defined not by its income but by its conspicuous consumption, especially of white goods: television, fridges, scooters, cars, computers—all common dowry components.

Alternatively, you might spot the middle classes according to their future plans. The aspiring middle classes nurse a cult of the 'three Es': education, English-speaking, and entrepreneurship. It's there in the English-laden signboards, the roadside ads for computer lessons, the surfeit of business cards.

The first step is to move to the city and send your kids to school. Twice a day our road played host to a parade of SUVs. Chubby kids clambered in and out, into a school decked with computer labs and Hogwarts-style inter-house competitions.

There is a range to suit all budgets. At least a third of Delhi children attend private schools or top-up state education with private tutoring; a 2011 Credit Suisse survey suggested Indians typically spend 7.5 percent of their income on education, ahead of the Chinese, Russians and Brazilians. Aspiring parents, even the very poor, save up to ensure that some of their children, especially sons, can escape the government system. The cheapest schools cost only a handful of dollars a month, and many lack official recognition. The teachers earn considerably less than their state-employed peers—though they're more likely to show up.

'English medium' schools are especially popular, promising future salaries a third higher. At university, you won't study a subject like mine. Bachelors degrees in he humanities and social sciences are generally for dolts. The real kids study science, computing, engineering, commerce, and idolize the MBA.

In reality, much of the Indian education system does not encourage the development of entrepreneurs. Quite the opposite. It is famous for encouraging rote learning, right up to memorizing out-of-date facts and errors in the textbooks. The system is wracked by accusations of grade inflation and bribery. Amartya Sen's *Argumentative Indian*, with his fondness for debate and democracy, also only works up to a point: the schools are incredibly hierarchical. In Bangalore, I worked under a boss who wouldn't have recognized a good research design if it had brained him with a clipboard. My two Indian teammates realized in the abstract that he was a blithering idiot. In practice, though, when he entered the room to blither they stood and saluted. Employers complain they face a serious dearth of skilled, articulate labour.

The entrepreneurship dream can't match the reality. It's all very well valorizing high-reward risk-taking, but stability is underrated. Still a majority of youngsters aspire to work for the government. Corporate 'trainings' in personality development and soft skills also raise and dash expectations. They promise to unlock employees' potential and turn them into budding entrepreneurs. Workers are meant to internalize the demands of the workplace by fashioning themselves into competitive, self-motivated, perpetually smiling individuals—even when they are working as a cyber coolie in a call centre or in a faceless clothes factory for very low wages. One social anthropologist calls it an attempt to create 'shrink wrapped souls'. Huge numbers burn out, frustrated by exhausting realities.

The real strategies needed for success may be much less romantic. Mohsin Hamid's recent novel is structured like a self-help book, telling 'you' *How to Get Filthy Rich in Rising Asia*. It has some slightly more unsettling lessons than the classics on sale on the CP pavements. Befriend a bureaucrat, be prepared to use violence, and embrace debt. There may not be an entirely happy ending.

It might not focus on technical improvisation, but this is *jugaad* too. *Jugaad* can be a dark art. It's ingenuity and 'fixing' in the broadest sense. So much of Indian entrepreneurship relies on the shadowy network of fixers, middlemen and associations who regulate the structure and flows of the system. The banking system is timid and state-dominated, the state is aloof or compromised whilst still controlling access to a vast number of resources and licenses. Navigating the system takes *political* savvy, not just technical skill. Personal contact is all, seizing the moment to shove your way to the front and shake a tactical hand. Why else was Abhinav and everyone else at that conference? My own ticket came via an acquaintance's wife, the connection forged one rainy Oxford evening. There is no substitute for doing a favour or clapping a firm hand on a shoulder.

IT entrepreneurs like Nandan Nilekani, his Mr Bean appearance belying his eloquence and success at Infosys, might be twenty-first-century icons. Yet in reality such glossy firms do not dominate India's economy. Its largest firms are almost exclusively family-run, state-dominated, based on privileged access to natural resources, or some combination of the three. They have handed down wealth through the generations, like the Birlas and (until recently) the Tatas, or secured access through personal networks. They have been uncomfortably close to government ministries, or are directly vulnerable to political interference, as in the case of the great unsung behemoths of the stockmarket like Coal India and the Oil and Natural Gas Corporation, still largely state-directed. The Indian economy is more concentrated and old-fashioned than its global image suggests, still dominated by powerful family leaders with retinues of lobbyists. The room for most entrepreneurs is correspondingly more limited.

Jugaad may have lessons for the researcher and her general adaptation to new circumstances, notably Kamala. But Margaret Thatcher was wrong. Running a country is not like running a household. The *jugaad* path at a country level may come at the cost of transparency and long-term planning.

Though remember: the elephant-headed god Ganesh is carried by rats.

5

VEINS

There was no possibility of taking a walk that day.
—Charlotte Brontë, *Jane Eyre*

With months of fieldwork yawning ahead of me, I had a vague sense that it was somehow very important to get to know Delhi, to earn my stripes. I wanted to explore its nooks and crannies. I wanted to understand the wiring holding the whole place together, from the arterial roads to the less visible nervous systems: shared air, water, piping, and, of course, that great underrated topic, electricity.

The desire to explore had a fortunate side effect. Living in Delhi is like watching a horror movie. You scream, flinch, thrill, cry, nurse an impending sense of doom—and leave feeling refreshingly purged. Reviewing her last three years there, a perennially acute American friend wrote, 'The streets of this city are better than therapy.'

Nothing is more cathartic than locking horns with auto

drivers, a constituency upon which God bestowed meekness and financial probity with the same lavish hand he reserved for mining conglomerates and Wall Street. The autorickshaw is an iconic species of yellow-and-green beetle that farts and skitters its way around India. Riding one through Delhi is like navigating an Autobahn encased in nothing more than a sweet-wrapper. Sod your rollercoasters and psychoanalysts. The auto is equally effective and far cheaper.

If you can haggle, which I can't. Nearly all autos have meters, apart from in the futuristic wilds of Gurgaon where laws are passé. Most drivers are only moderately obstreperous about using them, and under the hawkish gaze of, say, Alpha Housemate even the stubbornest cracks. Unfortunately the proximity of white skin seems to make meters malfunction.

There's an auto parked at the edge of the road. I could just fling myself inside, but all too often this provokes the driver into parping off without a word or a meter, a long gleeful $$$-filled thought-bubble visibly puffing out from his skull. So instead I querulously call out the destination, trying not to sound too desperate despite the fact I have just had a phone call: 'The honourable Mr X has agreed to see you. Come immediately.'

The driver is thin and creased, his eyes spinning wheels of veins. '*Nahin, nahin.*' He waves me off. It's too long or short or congested or uninspiring a trip for him to bother. I wander away muttering. Delhi is a lot less strike-prone than West Bengal, where practically every day of the year involves some sort of shutdown, but the auto drivers are one exception. Thanks to their lobbying the Delhi government periodically hikes fares, much to commuters' ire.

On the other hand, auto driving is not exactly lucrative. The 80 percent who rent their autos take home only half the fares; the rest goes on fuel costs and payments to the contractor. Those who own their autos are often heavily in debt after paying huge amounts for licences, which sell on the black market for thousands of dollars, twice the price of the vehicle itself. Then the driver requires clearances, a uniform, and a sheaf of paperwork to be carried at all times. It's a complicated system—though a *dalal* or tout might make it faster, for a price, in another example of *jugaad*—and leaves him vulnerable to being stopped by the police and regularly 'fined'. I am briefly seized with an attack of white liberal guilt.

A second auto is whining along the other side of the road. I flap it down and he U-turns. He is dapper, his grey uniform old but carefully pressed.

We size each other up like chess players. First I check to see he knows the destination. He's unlikely to say he doesn't, but his hesitation might be revealing. The rare old hand is astonishingly knowledgeable, and most drivers know their own tiny patches. Further afield it all breaks down. Direction-givers are often kindly but fantastically misleading.

But I have to be a bit cagey when asking. If he realizes I'm not sure of the destination, he might be a little *too* keen to go on the meter and pump up the fare by meandering all over town. Thanks to consumer lobbies, the government has begun a slow, patchy process of introducing GPS navigation systems to stop this happening, and to make travel safer. Until this is complete—and enforced—sometimes fixed fares are your friends.

I use some dodgy Hindi to specify the location, which I like to think wins me a tiny grudging point. He pretends to wipe his seat with a grubby cloth, and spits out a price. My move. I feign horror, throwing my hands up and beginning to walk away.

If there were several drivers around they could act as economic theory suggests, competing to give me the best price. Or they could behave like the cartel that formed just outside our colony, a clutch of men eavesdropping and interfering to ensure nobody took a customer for anything less than extortion. (They are almost always men. I have heard rumours of odd female drivers, usually with NGO and state support, but I have never seen one.) This second driver is alone now the first has settled inside his auto for a nap. The negotiation could go one of two very different ways: he could agree to a lower price—or even to use the meter, shock horror—without his peers around to humiliate him, or he could smell a market scarcity and demand a premium.

Round two. He calls out a marginally lower price.

'Ha! Ha!' I continue walking.

'Madam, OK,' he calls, and drops the price further. Without waiting for a response, he guns the auto toward me. I calculate the distance. It seems reasonable. I clamber in.

The auto is a capricious and jittery little creature. The drivers must kick and cajole even to get their vehicles to start. Eventually we putter off with the characteristic tuk-tuk sound. Autos run on compressed natural gas (CNG), the result of a clean-air initiative. It sits in red containers at their rear, the green doors often secured only by a rattling scrap of string, so that the canister flashes out as if from an adolescent's low-rise jeans. More than once the gas abruptly ran out mid-journey and we wasted precious minutes (are my minutes really that precious?) refuelling.

At first I high-five myself for my negotiating skills. Yet the longer I sit there, the more I feel a nagging sense that I haven't won after all, especially after he pauses to spit in a way that seems just a little too jubilant. I frequently have this feeling in Delhi, the sense that my small triumph was an illusion. Why is it so important to win, anyway? Why do I so keenly feel my sense of self bound up with these awkward transactions? On bad days it's an indictment of my ability to cope with India, life outside the wood-panelled Oxford womb, the universe, etc.— let alone the imminent encounter with the honourable Mr X.

I brood.

The autos' interiors always cheer me up, though. Like many others, this one's customized. Glittery stickers of goddesses adorn the space above the driver's head. In the shell-like rear, I am flanked by big magazine cut-outs of Bollywood muscles. Lean, fox-faced, two thumbs, it's Hrithik Roshan on the left, facing some pert pectorals I don't recognize. The more enterprising are painted with adverts for acupuncturists and insurance agents. Occasionally they are kitted out with vast speaker systems too, half the size of the auto. Once we acted as a public service vehicle, blasting the cricket scores out at passers-by; once the driver excitedly put on his 'English' music: David Guetta's 'Sexy Bitch', blasting out into the night with a throb that shook the whole tin can.

The logic of the road is Might is Right, as even the law realizes: it futilely tries to counteract this logic by holding larger vehicles guilty for pulping smaller ones, something less than popular with my SUV-wielding acquaintances. The auto is a tinfoil bubble, just waiting to be popped or crumpled like a crisp packet under a more powerful beast. It must swerve out of the way of bigger, richer vehicles, zigzagging, and braking. This alone guarantees an adrenaline-pumping experience. I particularly recommend stuffing an implausible number of people in the vehicle so the prospect of toppling out becomes thrillingly real.

Corresponding almost perfectly to this vehicular muscle is a hierarchy of horns. On the horn metric the auto is almost at the very bottom of the food chain, just above the whimsically useless bicycle bell. For a second I hold my breath and wait. The horn comes on as if automatically. An audible whine of a horn signifies a healthy auto with a driver at least remotely interested in his continued existence. A muted buzz suggests even the other autos are capable of smashing us to a pulp. These drivers are the worst of all, recklessly swerving to drive the wrong way up a main road to save a little gas, switching 'lanes'—there are no lanes—with impunity. I unerringly find them.

Though the drivers themselves make some journeys more memorable than others ('You are only a guest in my country', 'Do you want some meat? Very good meat'), conversation is typically a little unoriginal. The inevitable question comes: 'Which country, madam?'

The auto passes a cycle rickshaw. The motorized equivalent certainly beats the heartwrenching awkwardness of this flimsy older version, to be found lurking in clumps around busy shopping streets. The cycle rickshaw ride is nasty, brutish and short, no cheaper and far slower than its motorized equivalent, but you are mostly paying out of guilt. These are some of the most poorly paid workers of all. The driver is all straining sinews and muscles over a skeletal frame; you'll wish you hadn't eaten that last snack, the memory of the crisp outer shell and explosive tang of a *pani puri* (in Delhi a *golgappa*) guilty in your mouth. My auto unsentimentally cuts him off, and the rickshaw-wallah tumbles off to push by hand. As the smallest fry on the street, he must twirl and wait and jangle his futile bells. Thankfully the hand-pulled rickshaw—hill stations used to have them, pushed by six strong men up the slopes—has all but died out outside Kolkata.

Back in the auto, conversation is progressing as expected. '*Shaadi-shuda?* Married, madam? Boyfriend?'

Sometimes I display a ring. Sometimes I suggest I have a mysterious hunk somewhere in the world, working or travelling; I usually stress how tall and musclebound he is, and how honourable and permanent his intentions. One really creepy time I showed a picture of Feckless Brother, my younger sibling.

Maybe I give off some spinsterish vibe, maybe it's that the ring is made of plastic, but they never really seem to buy it. My favourite response came from a handsome young driver with proper Delhi swagger: 'No problem, madam. I like fun only. My girlfriend, she is married also.'

Ahead flows a scooter with an entire family stacked upon it. They are lower-middle-class and law-abiding: the husband is wearing a shirt and suit pants—and a helmet, of course. His wife sits with suicidal decorousness: side-saddle like a Victorian, baby clutched to her bosom. Her sari dangles terrifyingly close to the wheels as the scooter sways. She has no helmet. At the very front is perched another child, wedged between the handlebars of her papa's moustache and those of the bike. 'It doesn't look safe, but it must work,' I think, and then remember that India has only 1 percent of the world's cars, and 10 percent of the world's road deaths. Up to 190,000 people a year die on Indian roads, more than Oxford's entire population.

The sluggardly trucks are banned from the city centre until deep into the night when they reel onto the roads, juddering fatly. They scar and eventually crumble the tarmac under their illegally heavy loads. In an industrial area outside Bangalore's Electronic City, we saw a pothole so large that one of the lorries had upended in it. For days the autos pottered ant-like around the edge of the crater, the lorry's flabby body still aswoon at the bottom.

Alongside prices (plane tickets, student fees), the drivers enjoy holding forth on how grim Delhi is. Like many others, this driver is from Uttar Pradesh, the big dry impoverished state to the east. His family remains behind in Agra. Delhi is too expensive and too dangerous to bring them over, he says, although he only makes the short journey back home a handful of times a year. He leans far out of the side of the auto and spits another meditatively bloody gobbet of *gutka* onto the road. He's careful with money, though—he doesn't have the vampiric rotted red mouth of the addict.

Overhead swoops the metro. It is undeniably classier than the rattling grime of the London Underground. Since my first abortive Delhi visit, its expansion has reshaped the feel of the city, bringing together opposite corners and liberating wealthier women. Passengers seem to be on their best behaviour inside. It is clean and cool and spit-free. On the other hand, I am deeply sceptical about claims it has taught Dilliwallas to queue. Bear in mind that I come from a country where the queue *is* civilization, and any breach of its logic a sign of moral degeneracy. In the Delhi metro everyone waits patiently along the painted lines until the train arrives—and then the civilized pretence breaks down. Sociopathic elbows everywhere, those trying to get on headbutt those trying to get off. For a month I hung back, tutting in British horror, but gradually I too turned *Lord of the Flies*.

A violent horn and a roar from behind, getting ominously close: a bus. The city's rapid transit buses largely cleaned up their act for the Commonwealth Games. Their hunchbacked green forms stalk the roads like mantises. The plan was to let them stalk dedicated bus lanes, though this plan proved way too controversial and has all but collapsed, leaving only treacherous lumps of concrete in the middle of the road. Some of the most deadly private buses—the famously murderous Bluelines—have been phased out or pushed to the city edges. Other private buses continue to ply the routes, however, often packed and full of groping hands.

The auto driver skitters to the left, horn whining madly. A big beefy SUV is coming up fast, blaring. Its windows are tinted, though tinting has been banned in a vain effort to prevent sexual assaults. I wonder who is at the wheel. Probably someone like the honourable Mr X: clearly able to afford a driver, but too impatient to sit through someone else's geographical ineptitude.

The SUV is so close that I close my eyes and resign myself to a sticky end. At least then the honourable Mr X won't see my auto-induced Afro.

The auto driver hunches forward on the horn and lets out a string of imaginative obscenities ('You *padkora* fried in the oil of a dirty…!'). The SUV's blare gets louder and louder.

Suddenly we lurch sideways at high speed. I'll say this for Dilliwallas: they really can drive. They have reflexes and spatial awareness I've never seen outside *2 Fast 2 Furious*, skidding and weaving fearlessly an inch away from the next car. Apart from the drunk drivers, of course.

The SUV roars past. We tuck in behind with a deferential parp and gaze at the prominent Germanic logo on its rear. It belches a gassy tail like a gleaming black comet.

Blow your nose in Delhi and you are greeted with a claggy mass of black, perhaps punctuated with interesting orange and brown flecks. This is the air Dilliwallas resentfully share, one of the great public goods. It hangs around and coughs and mutters dirty little mantras: NO_x, CO, SO_2, CH_4, plus tiny evil particulate matter, $PM10$ and $PM2.5$, which I'd never even heard of before I arrived, let alone inhaled. The sun, a groggy aspirin white, at times seems to dissolve altogether.

Virtually all contemporary cities are cursed by air pollution, but Delhi has the dubious distinction of the second-worst air quality in the world, narrowly behind Beijing but rising fast. Just living in its smoggy streets is allegedly worse than smoking a packet of cigarettes a day; jogging is a form of self-harm.

I proudly nursed an increasingly lavish cough as a badge of Dilliwallihood. Two in five of the city's residents suffer from respiratory illness, killing an estimated 10,500 a year; across India, Greenpeace claims coal-fired power plants kill 120,000 annually. Delhi is low-lying. The hot air doesn't shift in summer. The winters feature thick, greasy smog which resembles the 'pea-soupers' of pre-1950s London, 'the yellow smoke that rubs its muzzle on the window-panes'. And what, or who, is to blame?

It is Mumbai, not Delhi, which has become famous as the city of *Slumdog Millionaire* and Asia's largest slum, Dharavi. But Delhi has its slums and beggars too. They are simply less visible, and the city handles them with discreet authoritarianism.

Still virtuously exploring, I set off to explore the roads around our colony. A hundred meters from the guard, a paunchy man with a Freddie Mercury moustache and dreams of becoming a chef in London, was a *jhuggi-jhopri* cluster. It comprised a series of scrawny shacks with corrugated iron and blue plastic roofs, stretched in a narrow band along the roadside. On the pavements its inhabitants patted cakes of dung to dry for fuel. The women wore cheap polyester saris, partially concealing their faces, and squatted over small grills of food for sale at regular intervals along the road. Their children played cricket with a broken tennis racquet, the ball occasionally thwocking into the path of passing autos. An enterprising advertiser or homeowner had hung a gleaming Vodafone sign on the side of one of the huts. Overhead messy coils of wire poached electricity for the odd lightbulb and black-and-white TV.

The sky overhead looked like a wheezing lung, one of those sad cases who lights up and takes a drag through their tracheotomy tube. After five minutes my eyes were streaming. The road opposite the JJ cluster was a turbulent sea of thick choking smoke. My stomach shivered: burning plastic smells like something going very wrong on a molecular level.

The source of the smoke was a series of fires on the roadside, gasping smoggy creatures short on orange and hot on grey. Behind, a couple of skinny figures watched with scarves over their mouths. They poked the fires every now and then, tossed on more rubbish, and coughed as I did. Behind me a dog-walker dragged one of our colony's many pets, an obese pug, its fist of a face mewling and sputtering.

This is the type of scene that sparks disgust among middle-class Dilliwallas. In their gated colonies, served by guards and maids who may live in the very same *jhuggis,* they condemn the poor for burning rubbish, illegally occupying land, and a myriad of other environmental crimes which choke up the city's bronchial tree. They complain that the state's hands are tied by democracy, unlike Beijing's. Some citizens, though, are far more equal than others.

Further down the road was a pile of rubble and ashy dust, a few scattered bits of plastic and tattered cloth. This is where the JJ cluster had been until a fortnight before I moved in. Then, though, it had looked far less temporary: the huts had been made of bricks and mortar, with large plastic water tanks alongside and electricity posts. They had been abruptly and ruthlessly torn down. The demolition squad had deliberately shattered every brick to make the inevitable rebuilding more difficult.

Delhi *is* environmentally active, for all India's intransigence in climate change negotiations. But it is a very middle-class activism, one which does not want to share the airways. Urban beautification and middle-class 'quality of life' is all: greenness, space and cleanliness. The Delhi government has systematically closed polluting factories and evicted squatter communities—although not the equally illegal settlements of the middle classes. The pavements have been cleared of small traders, who must keep moving. Slums have been bulldozed, notably in the run-up to the Commonwealth Games (how very Beijing, you might say), and much of the seized land turned over for commercial development. Thousands of the city's poorer residents, who enable the middle classes' 'first-class world-city' lifestyles, have lost their homes and livelihoods.

At the UN's first environment conference in 1972, Indira Gandhi famously claimed that 'poverty is the biggest polluter'. But this simply isn't true. 'Urban beautification' alleviates symptoms, not causes. These symptoms particularly affect the poor, who cannot flee for holidays or the more expansive suburbs. The inverse of Indira's statement might be more correct: pollution is a cause and form of poverty.

Far more environmentally destructive, of course, are the lifestyles of rich Dilliwallas (and yes, I realize the hypocrisy of flying there to write this). Delhi's air quality enjoyed a couple of years' plateau with the metro's arrival, the daytime ban on trucks, and the switch from diesel to CNG in buses, taxis and autos. But it's worsening again. Those belching SUVs are flourishing: in February 2013, the *Financial Times* reported that 1,400 new cars are hitting Delhi's clogged arteries every day, with 6.5 million already in action. Electricity demand is rocketing, less for the *jhuggis'* lone lightbulbs than for gadgets and air conditioning. The waste produced per capita, hitherto comparatively limited, is rising as (profitable) plastic packaging and bottled water take off. In summer, the city shrivels and dehydrates. In the last decade the capital's groundwater levels have dropped precipitously, especially in the rich south, including our very own Vasant Kunj.

So, the shit's encounter with the fan is imminent. A typically reassuring Indian government response is visible at one of my favourite Delhi spots, Lodi Gardens. The Lodi dynasty ruled for seventy years from the mid-fifteenth-century. The ruins—tombs, a mosque and domes with long dark foreheads—are by far the most famous remnants of their rule. The British turfed out villagers and landscaped the place. Nowadays the Gardens combine flowers and ruins with the odd exercise pole. The tombs' etched arches, orangey stone with turquoise tiled inlays, are filled with reading passers-by and canoodling couples. Mobs of pigeons line the paths, cooing sleazily—in fact, mobs of pigeons line the paths of every city I've ever visited, as ubiquitous as Irish pubs. Occasionally Rahul Gandhi, bumbling scion of the Nehru dynasty, and his bodyguards jog the paths too. There is even an icecream stall, a bar-restaurant, and a border of expensive residential accommodation.

Swilling a dazzlingly expensive beer in the bar one day, I suddenly discovered I was in a forest. I checked: the tombs were still there, and the icecream stalls. I could hear the gentle hum of the road. It didn't look terribly like a forest, but what did I know? It contains a tiny bonsai park—perhaps the government in its infinite wisdom meant that.

With this arithmetic, nudging the goalposts closer and closer together, the state can claim that you only imagined imminent crisis. India's area under forest has been increasing for a decade and a half. Other 'forests' include orchards, parks, timber plantations, even tree-hedged cricket pitches. The number of actual *trees* might be declining, the biodiversity certainly is—but forget that. Enjoy your Lodi Garden icecream.

Speaking of the proverbial hitting the fan, I maintain that you can tell a lot about a people from their sewage arrangements, least glamorous of all the city's internal systems. The British have a complex geography of international lavatorial stereotypes. We have a rich toilet vocabulary, from the downmarket 'bog' to the upper-class 'loo'. Our opposite is the American, too paralyzed by disgust even to say the word despite their propensity to die on the can, burger in hand. The toilets of the French, Britain's historical enemy, are mere holes in the ground, which emit a terrible stench of cheese and surrender. Japanese toilets sing and vibrate and spurt unexpected jets of water; German toilets contain a sinister tray to catch and inspect turds; all Australian toilets are rusty outside dunnies full of poisonous animals. There is surely something profound to be learned from all this.

The Indian sanitation system is notable by its all-but-absence, as though the oft-cited Hindu obsession with purity makes thinking about shit untenable ('Shit is a more onerous theological problem than is evil,' pointed out Milan Kundera). Considering shit might be unclean, but shitting outside is a venerable Indian tradition: a staggering half a billion Indians do it daily. Famously, more Indians have cellphones than toilets. The sight of a row of winking early-morning buttocks lined up over the railway tracks is a travel book staple.

Eighteen months earlier, I had surged south to the rural areas just outside Bangalore, full of coconuts and fat white silkworms for the wealthy city market. There I asked strangers awkward questions about their defecatory habits. (This history was hard to shake off: at least half of my friends think my PhD is called *Shit Matters*.)

It's fine for men. They gushed about the traditional pleasures—going out with their friends to play games and chat, before taking a joyful shit beneath their favourite tree as the birds whirled overhead. As the sickly sweet smell of heat-dried piss on every Delhi roadside indicates, they are relaxed about relieving themselves all over the place; in Bangalore NGOs had even tried painting pictures of gods on public walls to discourage this. Women had a rather different stance. Thanks to patriarchal tradition, they could only go under cover of darkness, suffering pain and infections as they waited all day long. Their tales featured no birdsong, but shame and snakebites and rapes in gloomy fields of other people's shit. Some actually gave up food and water in the evenings because they were afraid of having to go. Yet very few had been able to persuade their husbands that toilets ought to be a priority.

Lest you think this is an issue confined to rural areas, recall 'Delhi belly', that inspiring mix of *E. coli, Salmonella,* and other overfriendly pathogens. Its fame is unsurprising: the city's remaining groundwater is increasingly contaminated with wastewater and untreated sewage. Almost half of Dilliwallas live in 'unauthorized' colonies and slums; until recently many were deprived of basic infrastructure. Though the majority of Delhi slum dwellings have electricity, a phone and TV, many do not have toilets or sewerage; a third of their female inhabitants have been physically assaulted while trying to access shared toilets. In non-slum areas too there is no requirement to construct houses with proper sanitation, and many neighbourhoods do not receive a reliable water supply. The sewage system is overwhelmed, drains clogged and pipes leaking. Four billion litres of raw sewage pour into the Yamuna daily, as *Newsweek* noted, turning the holy river into 'a putrid ribbon of black sludge' with levels of faecal bacteria 10,000 times higher than the safe bathing limit.

The combination of these massive infrastructural failings was malodorously evident when I tried to prove my research with tired feet. With the paranoia of the new arrival, I attempted to sneakily eye the miniature map in my guidebook. The entirety of southwest Delhi—not really on the beaten tourist track—was squeezed onto one small page. I resolved to walk from birdsong- and American-laden Vasant Vihar to the Hauz

Khas Rose Garden, which looked close and was coloured in pleasing shades of pink.

Little did I know that (a) Hauz Khas is really not that close, three centimetres on the map, three miles on the ground; (b) psychologically much longer given the route would take me along one of the varicose highways that rings central Delhi; and (c) a white woman walking said route would attract a great deal of morbid curiosity.

Cars slowed down to goggle and honk. The miscellaneous souls who haunt every Indian street followed me with blank eyes. Beyond a certain point, though, the logic of the walk talks over in a way that would horrify a rational mind. 'I've already walked so far, I might as well keep going. It'd be embarrassing to turn back now. Maybe they'll think it's a Western thing.' A lumpy bus queue stared wonderingly as I walked past. They nudged each other, but I held my chin still higher and thought British thoughts.

'And this has to be health—' The bus roared carcinogenically past, coating me in bits of gravel.

The world alongside opened up as the road began to rise. Before me R.K. Puram fell away to the left. Munirka, a busy mass of students and migrants, sprawled to the right. A few months later in almost this spot, a 23-year-old physiotherapy student and her friend would board a private bus, on which she would be savagely gang-raped. On my birthday, thirteen days after the attack and under the eyes of the world's media, she died of her injuries.

I dropped into the mapless gap between guidebook pages, and saw a different city entirely. I passed a clutch of very temporary huts, little more than tarpaulin tents, cooking fires smoking. I passed strange little shops selling furniture and textbooks, tucked into the concrete. Everything smelled like chewed cigarettes and petrol, with the odd glimmer of shit from the lower slopes. Downhill giant hogs armoured with wiry black hair were rootling in rubbish. Even at a distance they were formidable, more like wild boar. They stared up at me hungrily. I wondered whether the exhaust fumes were going to my head.

Why are Delhi's veins so sickly? 'Nobody,' a girl announced with a hair flip as we were chauffeured forth, 'walks in the city.'

The middle classes jog in Lodi Gardens; in the cooler moments buffering the day pleasantly plump women and once even a retired army general, arms swinging in military rhythm, could be found pacing around our Vasant Kunj home. They were evangelical about walking. But they weren't walking *to* anywhere. In the name of keeping fit, they would make their tiny repetitive circuits, inhaling smug lungfuls of carcinogens. Round and round, like the rhythmic second hand of a pocket watch. Then they climbed in their cars and roared off in a cloud of exhaust fumes.

Nobody walks in the city.

I looked out of the car window. I'd been lucky on my Hauz Khas jaunt: for all the shit, garbage and inadequate public transport, there were at least pavements for me to walk on, steep and cracked as they were. There were no pavements here in Gurgaon, Delhi's famously dystopian satellite city.

The road was edged with walkers, murky in the dust the cars kicked up. There were any number of them: women with shopping bags, shiny-shirted teenage boys, men in thick rubber chappals and oiled hair, customers of the little cigarette and snack kiosks that sprout on the roadside. This is 'nobody'. They are maids, cleaners, guards, laundrymen, cooks, builders, chaiwallahs, vegetable sellers. Without them the city would not function. But just as their employment is invisible to the law, they are invisible to the people with the networks and skills to be taken seriously by politicians and businessmen. Their employers take illegally tinted SUVs, taxis, the gleaming metro—why should they care if the pavement is nonexistent?

Gurgaon, a swelling southwesterly tumour just beyond the airport, is India's twenty-first-century poster boy in all sorts of ways. Even ten years ago it had only a smattering of titanic office buildings. Now it swaggers dustily across the plains, tower after golf course after mall. It markets itself as the new Singapore, a business and shopping hub plus a cluster of gated communities.

Its reputation is more Wild West: frantic expansion, violence, dirt, clots of men. A virtual gangland in the 1990s, sitting in the back of a taxi at night still feels like you're being driven to a quiet spot to be executed. The whole place was practically created by the giant developer DLF, India's largest, now embroiled in corruption controversies and suffering from the economic slump. The DLF City Court complex is even crowned by a weird spire that gives it the appearance of a church-cum-saloon on the frontier. Even the cattle are more threatening than Delhi's elusive lot, looming next to the highway with their huge U-shaped prongs.

The area is notorious for rapes and guns. In one notorious case, a tollbooth attendant on the expressway was shot dead by drunk young men in an SUV, over Rs 27 (less than 40 US cents). The authorities are nineteenth-century. In March 2012 another 23-year-old woman was gang-raped. The first remedy officials mooted was a ban on women working after 8 pm, the unspoken rationale being if women are out that late it's really their fault, and rapists only come out at night.

I stayed there for a few days in a sleek, glassy test tube of an apartment block, courtesy of a wonderful Iranian who hums Indian film songs from her childhood. Her flat was huge and the fridge empty, bachelor-style: 70 percent alcohol, 30 percent mysterious floating things in jars. This was globalized New Gurgaon at its slickest, cheaper than central Delhi and much more spacious. I pedalled next to seriously toned housewives in the private gym, and swam alongside seriously overweight kids in the private pool.

Back in the room I mulled over my electricity research, basking in the cool of the air-conditioning. The AC was powered for much of the time by a dirty house-sized private generator, roaringly guzzling expensive diesel. In its abortive election campaign of 2004, the then-incumbent Bharatiya Janata Party (BJP) famously deployed the slogan 'India Shining'. The slogan suggested the glow of a million computer screens, the gleam of the gold to be minted in the globally connected Indian market, and the polish of a twenty-first-century nation. It implied that the lights worked.

But all too often they don't. In Old Gurgaon, just a short distance away from the Iranian's ritzy flat, the power cuts last for hours a day. 'No power is as expensive as no power,' Homi Bhabha, father of the Indian nuclear programme, famously said. Lack of reliable electricity hits economic growth, education, healthcare, pretty much all the goals of a democratic government.

July 2012 revealed the scale of the problem. The largest-ever blackout in human history hit a huge swathe of north and eastern India, including Delhi. For two days an area home to over 600 million people, a tenth of the world's population, was left without power—though many of these people didn't have it anyway. Three hundred million Indians lack reliable electricity; three hundred more lack it altogether. A third of all power generated is lost or stolen.

The failure of this system is a very political one. Politicized power subsidies are the opiate of too many states. The whole sector is riddled with unviable tariffs, chronic bureaucratic disorganization, a lack of fuel, corruption, theft, and lack of cash: India's own finance minister admits there will be a US$1 trillion deficit in infrastructure investment over the next five years.

New Gurgaon is a tumour with its own privatized nervous system, anaemic as it is. It glimmers with neon signboards and glowing towers; occasional lasers carve the night sky. Many of its buildings flick their lights off for an hour too, one day a year. Not out of sympathy for their poorer compatriots—they're joining in with the World Wildlife Fund's international Earth Hour, like other world cities. Yet the streets are frighteningly dark at night, public lighting striking by its absence. The city is an archipelago of bright pools set in darkness. Some have air conditioning, laptops, high-speed internet; most do not. 'The future is already here,' said the science fiction writer William Gibson, 'it's just not very evenly distributed.'

I stared out of the window. Almost all of Delhi's tallest buildings can be found here, mostly looming apartment complexes. Its mirror twin Noida, the New Okhla Industrial Development Area, is building upwards too. Noida Wave City poster reads like an action film tagline: 'MASTER PLAN APPROVED. TIME TO CREATE HISTORY.' In reality it feels like a huge dry footnote. It is famous for a pair of brutal serial killers and a park full of elephant statues, a vastly expensive (and still unopened) vanity project by former Uttar Pradesh chief minister Mayawati. However unlovable, such subcities bubble with money—together with Faridabad and Ghaziabad, Gurgaon and Noida have received more investment than the city itself—and all lie in the neighbouring states of Uttar Pradesh and Haryana, outside the control of the Delhi government.

The view from the Iranian's window hardly screamed money, though. Just behind the fenced-in swimming pool was a wasteland of rubble. It was full of the same giant black hogs that had gazed hungrily at me on the road to the Rose Garden. There were black piglets too. They snuffled busily in piles of garbage and stagnant water, and grew almost visibly. Gurgaon is an environmental and infrastructural disaster. Outside the immaculately kept private areas, public space has been abandoned to the law of nature.

'It's strange,' said a friend thoughtfully. She was moving out of a flat complex where 'they welcomed us with a note saying we should consider ourselves fortunate to be in such a prestigious community'. In fact, she was ditching Gurgaon altogether.

'Inside, it's so lavish and spacious. Outside, the roads are potholed, the water table is falling, the air is full of grit, the electricity is from expensive generators, the police are nowhere.' And the pavements are imaginary, I thought, fingering a glass of bright pink ginger fizz.

The elites are particularly able to effect change by using their voices, articulate and well connected. Their capillary network of influence is strong. They can vocalize their displeasure—for example through the political process, personal networks, online, or media-savvy popular protest. When they can't escape the consequences, they protest the state's failures: so they complain about corruption in state monopolies, such as passports and railway tickets, and protest declining air quality.

When they can escape, though, Delhi's elites are withdrawing. Rather than provide well-aimed pressure for state improvement, they're giving up and exiting altogether. Once the articulate and well-connected middle classes exit, the people left are less able to make their case for improvements. Bureaucrats can potter along as they wish, serving out their time before their comfortable pensions. The system limps on in the same sad state. Delhi has the clotted veins of a diabetic (and a depressingly patchy healthcare system too). The pavements disappear, the schools suffer, the lights go out.

The Gurgaon defector continued, 'Public services are failing or don't exist. You have to pay so much for private everything: education, healthcare, power, water, security.' Only the richest slice of the middle classes can comfortably afford all of this, but the private-is-best ethos they espouse is ideologically endorsed by the aspirational middle tiers too. 'None of these people want to pay taxes to improve things.'

The country's pushiest citizens are silencing themselves. Instead they retreat to islands dotted across India's geography—special economic zones, corporate employment and all its perks, exclusive neighbourhoods and residential associations—and avoid interacting with the messy realities of Indian democracy altogether. Travel by car, taxi or the metro between test tube towers and malls, and you never need really leave the bubble of privilege at all. Why would you expend effort on complaining? The new citizen-consumer simply votes with his feet. He doesn't actually *vote*, though: wealthier Indians tend to vote in somewhat smaller numbers than the poor, unlike most of the rest of the world. The timing of this withdrawal is convenient, coinciding as it does with the mass entry of the lower castes and classes into democratic politics and the rise of that dreaded word, 'populism'.

Ayn Rand has long enjoyed cult popularity among business elites and students: until the rise of the Tea Party in the US in 2007, India was the world's top Googler of the libertarian author. 'Civilization is the progress toward a society of privacy,' she wrote. If this is true, then Gurgaon is one of the most civilized towns in the world.

'None of our neighbours trust the state,' the Gurgaon defector said. 'They would rather live on their little island, surrounded by gates and guards.'

She frowned. 'But strangely—despite this fear and mistrust—every morning one of the guards is charged with hoisting the national flag. And every evening he takes it down with great ceremony, and folds it away…'

6

BRAINS

> Dubeyji smiled happily and said, 'Of course we know you
> know nothing. Just write that. It's a formality. Paperwork.
> Just like a buffalo needs grass, the government needs paper.'
> —Tarun J. Tejpal, *The Story of My Assassins*

*T*he flag can ill conceal that same despised state. But Delhi would be nothing without what Jan Morris called its 'blur or slither'. I don't know whether it's innate or whether it's the result of several years of watching dons flapping their gowned wings as they squabble over Statute III Clause 2(iii)—but I *love* a good bit of bureaucracy. The verbosity, the uniforms, the repetition—it is as soothing as watching static. It was also my Delhi raison d'être, at the heart of my research. I headed into the vortex of power.

Just outside our flat I waited for the drone, doppler-shifting in from the right. 'metrometrometro metro METRO METRO *METRO!*' The caller hung half out of a door by a thin shirted arm. The van skidded to a halt, was already skittering back off again before I shimmied into a seat. The other passengers regarded me indifferently, in spite of the fact our thighs were touching in a fashion I associated with non-familial the biblical.

The Yellow Line at the southerly end of Delhi climbs high into the grubby air. Chhattapur metro station overlooks a great temple complex, dominated by a South Indian-style stepped pyramidal structure. I turned from it, though, and instead followed the comforting signs on the floor: *WOMEN ONLY*, written in cursive on pink scattered with white stars, an aesthetic which naturally lures the gentler sex to follow its arrows.

At the risk of offending the rabid men's rights activists who troll the Western internet, women-only carriages are a great and necessary invention in Delhi. It is of course unfair that the men further down the train (and there are many many more of them) must travel like sardines, but unfortunately some of them are priapic sardines who require canning for their own good.

Some hazards remain in the women's carriages, though. At any time someone can bark 'please shift', and you find yourself suddenly compressed and sitting on a humpy seat divider. I was just marvelling at the reading material of the demure-looking woman opposite—*Fifty Shades of Grey*—when the doors opened again. The lascivious striped finger of the Qutub Minar was just visible over the trees.

At the entrance surfaced an Auntie, one of India's terrifyingly disapproving older matrons. She was a particularly large example of the species, swaddled in an aggressively green and expensively silken sari. She cast a cold predatory eye over the narrow tube of the carriage. There were no seats.

I crossed my fingers, and kept my eyes fixed on the socks and sandals of Ms Fifty Shades. A question arose unbidden into my mind: why socks in this weather?

Suddenly, without seeming to move a muscle, the Auntie materialized in front of me. We regarded each other for a moment, my eyes pleading. Then she turned in a slow wordless arc, and began to reverse.

For a long moment I stared at a vast onrushing expanse of green. I had a strange sensation of falling, like a skydiver plunging headfirst towards a well-tended lawn. And then she sat on me.

The Yellow Line carves the city in two from south to north. I plucked myself from between the Auntie's buttocks and staggered, dazed, off the metro at roughly its middle. Only a few others joined me. Overhead the announcer warned us to beware of bombs cunningly disguised as thermos flasks and teddybears, and then stated our location: Central Secretariat.

Delhi has no heart—it is as disparate and fragmented as India itself—but insofar as it has a psychological centre, it lies in the iconic boulevards of New Delhi. It is a city now more associated with power than with culture, a city of bureaux and ambassadors and, at least since the big bang of liberalization in 1991, a city of kleptocrats.

It was not always so. The slow collapse of the Mughals had hollowed out the city. By the turn of the twentieth century Delhi had lapsed into a doze. It was only the seventh-largest city in India, with 232,837 recorded inhabitants—a fifth the size of Calcutta, then the empire's second city and India's undisputed cultural hub, and a quarter that of Bombay. Its non-military British population comprised only 84 individuals.

Yet Delhi continued to possess a faded glamour. The British recognized it as the heart of ruling regimes before the Raj, with all the ancient imperial symbolism that brought. They admired the best of its marble monuments—not least Humayun's Tomb, the Taj Mahal's reddish maiden aunt, now rescued from weeds to become a wonderfully serene spot for canoodling lovers. As the old Mughal capital it offered the prospect of placating Muslims, otherwise resentful of the reunification of Bengal. The city had also been a major site of action and 'British heroism' in 1857, the events of which are alternately known as 'the Indian Mutiny' or the 'First War of Independence' depending on your political proclivities. It was with these excuses that King George V unveiled 'the best-kept secret in the history of India', abruptly proclaiming the transfer of the capital from Calcutta to New Delhi, during the spectacular imperial coronation durbar of 1911.

Calcutta's inhabitants were horror-stricken at the transfer (their rivals in Bombay and Madras perhaps less so). Delhi was in the boondocks, deprived of water and full of fever. Former viceroy Lord Curzon, a Calcutta fan, felt moved to condemn it in London's House of Lords as 'a mass of deserted ruins and graves'. Even then the ominous portents for the Raj were clear, and Curzon read them like a fortune-teller's bones. Unlike the bustling 'European' port of Calcutta, Delhi presented to visitors 'the most sorrowful picture you can conceive of the mutability of human fortunes'. The city was sunken in a century and a half of melancholy 'twilight' (creative, elegiac, and perhaps even slightly self-indulgent). Some even imply that's how it should have stayed: twilit and drowsy. But of course the pesky Britishers had other plans, and Delhi has always been a poor sleeper.

So it was reinvented in the international idiom of greatness and power. The Secretary of State for India countered Curzon's criticism with a comparison. One other major transfer of capital cities had occurred in living memory. Littered with the detritus of old empire, until 1870 it too had been a 'city of the dead, like Delhi, strewn with the relics of decayed dynasties'. Now, having tellingly forced the established religion to submit, it was revivified at the head of a great united nation. Perhaps Delhi could emulate Rome.

The radial roads emanating from Connaught Place and its lesser roundabouts are strung like spiderwebs from tree to tree, stretching to the Secretariat. The politicians lurk within.

The most famous weaver of this web was the British architect Edwin Landseer Lutyens, 'part schoolboy, part great artist, part mystic'. Whilst overseeing the designs he did indeed read Edward Gibbons' famous *Decline and Fall of the Roman Empire* (as a young Churchill had a few years previously in Bombay). Just as that great empire crumbled, so the Persian prophecy has become a travel book cliche: 'Whoever builds a new city in Delhi will lose it.' Lutyens' would be the eighth city of Delhi, by most estimates. The prediction was apt. Construction was stalled by an assassination attempt, war, soaring costs, and squabbling architects. It was finally completed only fifteen years before the Britishers' final ejection. Look on my works, ye Mighty, and despair!

New Delhi was built for modern rule via the car and telephone. For all the wider city's older history, then, it shares the air of other modern purpose-built capitals like Canberra, Brasilia, and Islamabad. Deliberately selected for their more central locations, in the face of more populous and difficult metropolitan rivals, such cities have frequently struggled to carve out an identity of their own. Delhi, like Washington, D.C., risked becoming a bureaucratic enclave in a city of tombs. As Curzon had argued so passionately in 1912:

> There is serious danger that, when you have built your capital at Delhi, the Government will become more isolated, more bureaucratic, less in touch with public opinion than it is now. You are going to create a territorial enclave; you are also going to run the risk that your Government will become a political enclave.'

Few would argue against this charge now.

Some of its continuing unpopularity stems from this mechanical character, only weakly grafted onto the pre-existing organic body. A cyborg or a doll might be more human than a robot, but they are still less than loveable.

Not all planned cities were lucky enough to have a prehistory, though, or to avoid the concrete architectural psychosis of Le Corbusier. (His modernist masterpiece, the city of Chandigarh, is less than 200 kilometres away.) With his friend-cum-nemesis Herbert Baker, Lutyens would design a city perhaps second only to Saint Petersburg among planned cities—and more visually arresting, and hubristic, even than Peter the Great's painted city of bones.

The centrepiece of New Delhi was designed as an acropolis, a city on a hill to echo the Capitol in Rome. But Lutyens' Delhi refers to more than the grand area on Raisina Hill. Unlike Chandigarh or Brasilia, it is no desert of slabs, but a surprisingly green zone for all its pollution. His mentor and professional partner, Gertrude Jekyll, was a garden designer. New Delhi was landscaped as much as constructed. Lutyens takes popular credit for the broad leafy avenues, watercourses and lawn-lined bungalows that make up the bulk of New Delhi. Its trees bear fruit and flowers. His masterwork, the Viceroy's House (now Rashtrapati Bhavan), is almost as celebrated for its huge gardens as for its combination of European and Indian elements. The scheme was unashamedly elitist, enforcing the physical distance between ruler and ruled—but at least in the form of a garden city rather than a concrete jungle. It is an endangered species, however, as developers seek to move in.

On one of these leafy avenues, I met a senior politician at his home. It was disconcertingly easy to access, guarded only by peacocks and a single skinny guard. Three other petitioners and I sat in an anteroom, the rooms lined with bookshelves and portraits of Gandhi, Nehru, Tagore, and the politician himself. His reading tastes were impressively catholic and leaned towards the academic, though several of the books were his own. After only a few minutes I was ushered through into a tasteful office full of dark wood furniture. He stood to greet me, a thin grey pencil moustache in a white kurta.

The sociologist Susan Ostrander points out some of the perils of interviewing elites. They are inclined 'to "just talk"— easily, freely, and at great length, but not necessarily to the issues in which the researcher is most interested'. How true, Prof. O., how true. She recommends looking ostentatiously bored, all but tapping your watch, until they shut up and you can get on with your questions. This did not seem like an option to me: first, because it's very rude, and secondly, because it is totally ineffective.

The politician had the air of a man who said '*Enchanté*' when introduced to colleagues' nieces. He was charming, erudite, and utterly deft in evading my questions. He had an answer for everything, sweeping forwards and backwards through Indian history. Like a Victorian gentleman, he flowed with apposite quotations—Dickens! Kipling! Nehru!—and I could see why he had the ability to virtually filibuster the Indian parliament single-handed.

At the end of the hour (such generosity with his time! I marvelled), I was very gently guided back out with the promise of another interview at the time of my choice. I left with a smile and a sheaf of notes. It was only later, sitting in an auto on the way home, that I realized I had learned precisely nothing. This gloriously charming evasion is a gift, a gift that could only exist in a democracy. I felt almost jealous of the sheer skill.

❧

For all this greenery, the stony final product at the centre of the scheme still seems to embody some of the less likeable characteristics of its notorious, pun-loving architect. It is brilliant, troubled, egotistical, gripped by financial worries, and at times faintly absurd. In fact, one commentator notes that the dome of Rashtrapati Bhavan bears a striking resemblance to Lutyens' own bald, precise and 'phenomenally round' head.

The dusty surrounding tarmac is almost empty, but for a smattering of police and the yellow slashes of traffic barricades. The flat roundness of Sansad Bhavan, home of the Indian Parliament, lies on one side like a great toothy burger. Inside sit two houses, the more powerful Lok Sabha (House of the People) and the indirectly elected upper house, the Rajya Sabha (Council of States). I say the houses sit: in fact over the last couple of years Parliament has been plagued by adjournments, disruptions and walkouts, losing a third of its scheduled time. Sansad Bhavan's circular shape is echoed outside by the television vans, their bloom of satellite dishes angled to the air and lapping up every second of evasive drama.

From here it is an intimidating and lonely stroll upwards. At the top of the slope on the sweeping approach from Rajpath (the Kingsway) sprawls Rashtrapati Bhavan, the president's house and still the largest head-of-state's residence in the world. Its classical dome and spiny column are just visible through delicate ironwork, levitating on grass. The gateposts are set with elephants and little fat-kneed cherubim. It sits a little too far back for real effect, Lutyens having lost the battle with Baker—his 'Bakerloo'—to secure the prime location.

Somehow approaching heavily guarded public landmarks

always brings out the sweaty palms and shifty eyes. Never google terrorist behaviours before setting off on holiday, because the tourist ticks a lot of them off: carrying lists of major buildings, photography, backpacks, crowded areas, regular cash withdrawals, hostility to locals and attempts to aggressively avoid their questions... I tottered up the slope, trying to look inconspicuous. My bag looked menacingly swollen on my hip. Even my walk felt guilty. Maybe my sunglasses looked suspicious—perhaps I should take them off—or maybe that looked worse. I twitched with the dilemma. My camera was in my bag and it was all very photogenic, but I felt certain a red sniper dot was already hovering over my back. Should I walk faster, or did that look too purposeful for a tourist? Should I walk more slowly, or would that look like *loitering with intent*?

The thickset symmetrical cuboids of the Secretariat buildings are not Lutyens' but Baker's. North and South Blocks rear up on each side, looking strangely wet-footed in their two-toned stone. Each holds a series of bureaucrats and government departments (and, if my sources are correct, the occasional rogue monkey). Together they provide India's skull, sepulchral and oddly hollow-eyed with their lines of columns and helmeted domes. In 1929 Georges Clemenceau exclaimed, 'What beautiful ruins this will make!' (In the event, it was Clem's ruins which almost came to India: laden with toxic waste, the aircraft carrier *Clemenceau* was due to be scrapped in Gujarat. After public protest it was forced to return to France—and eventually ended up coughing asbestos at the English port of Hartlepool.)

This is isolation and arrogance institutionalized in stone,

as Curzon warned. The bureaucratic nucleus, the brain of India, is set above and apart from the rest of the city. Above, curiously, Baker's old colonial inscription has been preserved. It is a sneer of cold command which even the then viceroy found 'rather pointed':

> *Liberty will not descend to a people;*
> *A people must raise themselves to liberty;*
> *It is a blessing which must be earned before it can be enjoyed.*

The scale of this central hub is vast and pitiless—it has unsurprisingly been likened to fascist architecture. The individual citizen is left unmoored, the sun beating down on hot flat stone.

But there is something more. The politicians and bureaucrats, too, are dwarfed, the rulers themselves mere squatters in the vast monuments. Lutyens' ambition was on a superhuman scale, soaring impassively above the prosaic realities of power. There is a reason that New Delhi combines architectural concepts and motifs that reference great capital cities from ancient Rome to Haussmann's Paris, Christopher Wren's London and Mughal Delhi. It seeks to be impervious to history and the small things of men. Lutyens' vision extended even beyond the great pink-mapped empire of the British: 'The Viceroy thinks only of what the place will look like in three years' time. Three hundred is what I think of.'

Don't be fooled by Lutyens' stone edifices. He was always famous for sketching dreams and building impractical fairytale houses. Delhi is a city made of paper as much as mortar, a city of money and files.

The Indian state is a paper tiger. It is prodigiously productive in inky terms. The central government representatives I have met have been genuinely impressive, committed, knowledgeable and educated. They are attempting to build a state recognizable in Washington, D.C. and Berlin, a state based on rulebooks and rationality. The Secretariat and its ilk burst with paperwork: reports, protocols, inventories, statements, briefings, letters, laws, memos, registers, accounts, notes, schedules, charts, specifications, catalogues, programmes, orders, inspections, certificates and censuses. They build towers out of reams of paper, statistical fortifications to keep out reality.

But this castle of paper cannot support the billion-plus people who crowd upon it. Technical capacity to *develop* policies is high—but their implementation is half-fictional. Targets are set, and repeatedly missed. The ubiquitous audits and evaluations neatly quantify shortcomings and explain defeats away into blank white oblivion. The state collects information, files and orders it. Much of this paperwork is not read by anyone. But it has its own strange dystopian logic. Writing is power, especially in a country which still has high illiteracy rates and overvalues English.

The Indian state too often looks like a brain in a jar, dreaming beautiful but ineffectual dreams. In the words of economist Lant Pritchett, 'India today is a *flailing* state'. Its head remains sound and functional, but is 'no longer reliably connected via nerves and sinews to its own limbs'. Critics are divided about whether this is simply a sign of chaos, or of a more sinister indifference towards the poor which disregards the state's own hyperactive failure.

Off I set to take a look at this papery side of Delhi. A PhD student can hardly fail to sympathize with its forlorn efforts, after all.

Shastri Bhavan, home to the coal, oil and mines ministries alongside law, culture, and women's development, sprawls—but not in Lutyens' elegantly autocratic style. Instead, it's more reminiscent of the giant blocky pisspots of Bucharest and other Soviet concretocracies, a set of box files rearing out of a short layer of trees. Outside, rows of flabby white Ambassador cars loll next to kebab stands and flabby brown soldiers.

Inside was structured chaos. Piles of people clamoured for a chit permitting entry, as a woman in the corner stamped blank documents with religious fervour. I had a moment of too-British hesitation, but eventually plucked up courage and thrust myself forward. Unsmiling, a finger on an entry in a thick inky ledger, the guard made a quick phonecall. I signed, signed again, and got my paper pass.

Within the building, the ministries jumble upon one another. It is a maze of brown walls, half-broken lifts, and grey rooms bursting with dusty files. The air was dim and sticky with the faint pervasive smell of the gents'. I paced through, slowly at first and then more desperately. The room numbers were mysterious, in that nagging way that appears logical at first glance. Peons shuffled past, mustering only vague curiosity as I scrutinized sign after sign after sign.

When I finally found the right room, the office itself was pristine. I perused an accommodating *New Scientist* while the bureaucrat deftly dealt with two complainants in a mixture of Hindi and English, fielded three more phone calls, and offered tea. A silent peon brought it on a tray. It was jaw-achingly sugary. I could see how the masterfully vague politician had developed diabetes from the campaign trail.

The bureaucrat himself was unusual. No paunch here: he was lean, with a firm dry handshake and cheekbones. He had the usual affability, though, combined with a reticence that was easy to miss at first.

'Isn't it difficult working within such a big and complex government?'

He smiled. 'There are many ministries, yes, and over seventy-five ministers at the Union level. Energy policy earlier almost fell under one single ministry. Now there are ministries of power, coal, mines, petroleum and gas, renewable energy. Then the other important ones must be consulted on some such matters: the ministries of finance, railways, environment, rural development, law, fertilizers (they use gas), steel (they need coal), and tribal affairs (because of land). And, of course, the Planning Commission and the Prime Minister's Office.'

He smiled again, showing very white teeth. 'But we all work together very well.'

My eyebrows were just raising of their own accord when the phone rang. He answered in quick-fire Hindi, slotted it back. The phone rang again.

I tried again: 'What about the complications of federalism?'

A third smile. 'The [provincial] states are usually very helpful. We all work together very well. More tea?'

The bureaucrat's reticence could not camouflage the reality. For all that it aspires to be a faceless state, India has not escaped the personal. Contemporary Dilliwalas love to hate the bureaucracy, especially because of its reputation for corruption and timewasting. The police, especially the railway police, are particularly notorious.

Of course, India is far from the only Asian country with a corruption problem. In 2012 Transparency International placed it joint-94th of 174 countries, just below China and Thailand but above Vietnam and Indonesia. Some commentators believe the worries can be overstated in any case. After all, industrializing America was very corrupt, with its robber barons and grubby 'machine politics' in cities like Chicago. Corruption may not *cause* poverty; it may be a symptom of development, conquerable after but not before growth.

This, though, is not a popular line of argument with the Indian middle classes. And in 2011 the city shook with their wrath.

Jantar Mantar—the name is loosely equivalent to hocus-pocus—is perhaps Delhi's oddest sight. Just off the shopping strips of Connaught Place, it presents a series of strange and violently red-orange structures. Staircases and windows to nothing, fixed cog teeth, a sort of crap coliseum. The largest of all looks not unlike a stylized and flattened cartoon of female genitalia. Two cones prevented ascent, but teenage boys posed for photographs at the perineum.

These structures are in fact gigantic astronomical instruments, staring hopefully up at sun, moon, and planets. Jantar Mantar is also a traditional place of protest. It was here that Anna Hazare, a bespectacled 70-something with unusually fleshy ears, began a fast to demand an ombudsman—the Lokpal—to peer inside the grubby recesses of the state.

The middle classes roared with approval. End the red tape, the grasping hand in the national till! They registered their disapproval of the state on Ipaidabribe.com— disproportionately popular with the IT crowd of Bangalore, as one might expect—and imitated the activist's sleek white hat. Sales of the topi, formerly an anachronistic bit of headgear, rocketed: in the awkward phrase, it had made the transition 'from mass to class'.

There are different brands of corruption, though, and Anna Hazare's movement focused largely on only one. The middle classes agree that corruption by petty bureaucrats = bad. These low-level officials make life way more difficult than it needs to be, slowing down files and passport processing, demanding extra signatures and levelling mysterious fines. They are easy to hate.

The commonly heard call from elites is for a turn to *meritocracy*. Along with the cry to streamline the state, they have a second demand: get rid of reservations. The reservation policy perhaps is the world's oldest affirmative action programme, built into the constitution in 1950 for the most deprived and victimized sections of Indian society, the Dalits (former untouchables) and Scheduled Tribes (or *adivasis*, the 100 million 'original inhabitants' of the remotest jungly corners of the country). It was designed to facilitate their access to the levers of power, by 'reserving' quotas of seats for them in the bureaucracy, elected assemblies and public universities.

The policy was famously meant to be removed after a trial period. Instead it has been retained—and expanded. In 1989 a weak government sought to implement the earlier conclusions of the Mandal Commission, which recommended extending reservations to the Other Backward Classes (OBCs)—a vast collection of 27 percent of the population, selected more in terms of caste background than economic poverty and including some extremely large and powerful castè communities. Upper-caste students responded with protests and violence. Many continue to argue that reservations are rotten, blaming them for the divisive caste parties and corruption. Positions are sold, and the new bigshots from these formerly dispossessed groups have set about seizing the spoils of power.

Reservations have not ended the poverty of Dalits and *adivasis*—they may even have been a distraction, if an inspiring one for some. There are far, far more people than state jobs, and it is clear that meaningful change must come through improved health and education rather than the tiny formal economy. But the call for meritocracy may be misplaced.

Meritocracy can be a veil for dominance by the same old elites, smug and isolated from the rest of society—all the more so as inequality continues to grow. And let's not pretend that the opposite of reservation is open competition. After all, also widespread is a more discreet but potentially more pernicious form of corruption, a form that gets far less middle-class attention—because, of course, it's often they who benefit. I might not need affirmative action or a briefcase of cash to get my job; I may only need a phone call. Delhi is full of rich kids who rely on their parents to get ahead.

The city's slogan might be: 'Do you know who my father is?'

Squatting in the heart of New Delhi, it is impossible not to wonder: is India really the world's next superpower? For all these flaws—its size, complexity, stubborn traditions, and unwieldy head—it is common to compare India to a heavy plant-eating mammal. The shelves burst with elephant-themed books on India and other Asian beasts—*The Dragon and the Elephant*; *The Elephant, the Tiger, and the Cellphone*—all asking questions like *Does the Elephant Dance?* Delhi's greatness, its world-city aspirations, hinge on the answer not only at home, but on the international stage.

There are several crucial things one should understand about this Elephant, the gladiatorial *Elephas maximus indicus* to his friends. Without further ado, here are ten points to push this already clichéd analogy beyond its breaking point.

1. *Do not be fooled by the size of the Elephant's head*. India's foreign service is terrifyingly small, smaller than those of New Zealand and Singapore. This might help to explain why its diplomatic profile is less illustrious than one might expect.

This does not mean that the Elephant is decisive, however. On every issue New Delhi hosts a cacophony of voices, which sometimes leads observers to claim India doesn't even have a foreign policy strategy.

Incidentally, it should be noted that there are documented cases of entire elephant herds being led by blind old leaders.

2. *Elephants have very long memories.* Contrary to popular belief, the Indian Elephant is extremely thin-skinned and holds grudges. India and China are often bracketed together by journalists and by Goldman Sachs' BRIC acronym, but they are old enemies. In 1962 they went to war; the Indian foreign policy establishment still nurses humiliating memories half a century on. India shelters the Dalai Lama and the Tibetan government in exile, while China stands accused of harbouring and aiding India's Maoist 'Naxalite' rebels (after all, Maoists are often found to have goods stamped with MADE IN CHINA). Other historically unpopular targets include Pakistan and the International Monetary Fund. And Indians really haven't forgotten that whole colonialism thing either.

When old enemies insult the proud Elephant (especially Pakistan, with its dangerous habit of terrorist provocation), certain Indian males may enter a state of enraged testosterone-fuelled frenzy known as *musth*. They become extremely aggressive, make loud rumbling noises, and threateningly wave their tusks (see 4 below). However, usually such behaviour is confined to the army—which allegedly has a blitzkrieg-style doctrine, Cold Start, to unleash in case of Pakistani provocation—and to the bars I frequent of an evening.

118

The other side of this proud ability to hold grudges is that the Elephant is also an incorrigible moralizer. Indians from Gandhi on have been famously self-righteous. India used to try to depict itself as the head of the non-aligned movement, neither for the capitalist West nor the Soviet Union (and China). It purported to offer an idealistic alternative to the cynicism and power-hungriness of international relations. Even now the world's diplomats roll their eyes when they spot the Elephant in the room, and bitch over the watercooler about the faintly sanctimonious way the Elephant tends to go on in multilateral negotiations.

3. On the other hand, *elephants are not especially radical animals*, which is why they are so favoured by the US Republican Party. The pachyderm is pragmatic; as Thoreau chortled, 'Even the elephant carries but a small trunk on his journeys.'

The Elephant is a proud and hierarchical creature. He believes he is one of the biggest, oldest animals in the Hobbesian jungle and wants to be recognized for the titan he is—not in any revolutionary way, but along well-established lines. He has set his eyes firmly upon a grand prize: a seat on the United Nations Security Council. India wants to be one of the world's big boys, internationally respected with big boys' discounts on oil, trade, and the environment.

The Elephant also knows that money talks. For all the tension, India remains warily fixated on China and the example it provides for other emergent powers: if you're big enough, rich enough, and tough enough, the other big boys have little choice but to respect you. If we're honest, half of today's 'great powers' (my motherland included) are penniless aristocrats. They might be snobby about new money, but they'll hold their nose and marry it. While I was in Delhi, British prime minister David Cameron came for one of his not infrequent visits. He gushed about the 'great relationship' between the two like a wannabe stepmom, flattering Indian business leaders. My Indian friends just shrugged.

4. *The Elephant knows that size matters*. India has accordingly decided to get muscles. Despite two decades of economic growth and now officially being a 'middle income country', more of the world's poorest people live in India than in any other country. The government has priorities other than poverty alleviation, however. On 19 April 2012, the English-language newspapers overflowed with joy once more. India had successfully tested a nuclear-capable intercontinental ballistic missile, named Agni-V after the Hindu god of fire.

A decent army, navy and airforce are key, perhaps especially the latter. The Indian Ocean looks like an increasingly important arena, with Chinese bases across the Ocean and on the Pakistani shore—the so-called 'string of pearls' around India's neck—and Chinese investment and workers in Bangladesh, Sri Lanka, and Burma. In this calculus, nuclear weapons are the protein shake of international relations. Conventional weapons remain its bread and butter. India is now the greatest importer of arms in the world—something perhaps encouraged by the enormous opportunities for corruption presented by secretive, lucrative defence spending. (Shortly after Agni-V, Britain stopped sending India aid. It

continues to welcome Indian arms dealers with open arms
and award ceremonies.)

Most formidable of all the weapons of mass destruction
in India's arsenal is Rajnikanth, legendary South Indian film
star and the Indian Chuck Norris. If a million SMSs are to be
believed, he killed the Dead Sea; he once shot a man just by
pointing his finger and saying 'BANG'; and when he sneezes
there are earthquakes and orgasms throughout the land.

5. As this suggests, *the Elephant is a natural mimic.*
Fundamentally, the other big boys must let you into the
clubhouse. Perhaps the fastest way to join the club is imitation.

India has tried the odd imitative shortcut, not least to show
that it is a gentle giant despite its failure to sign up to the nuclear
non-proliferation treaty. Both it and Pakistan vie to provide
troops for UN peacekeeping missions. India has also become
a major aid donor in its own right.

In 2010 newspapers reported a particularly poignant tactic.
Spotting that the United States has the $, the Eurozone the
€, even greying faltering Japan and Britain the ¥ and £, India
decided the world would suddenly realize it had arrived if
it just had its own currency symbol. Newspaper columnists
crowed that this confirmed India was years ahead of China.
It now has its very own rupee sign, based on the Hindi letter
₹, Ra—although sadly my keyboard has yet to catch up with
this meteoric rise.

6. *The Elephant is Slow to Mate*, as D.H. Lawrence noted.
And when they do, they mate in secret at last, as the Indo-

US nuclear deal suggests. For decades relationships between India and the United States were strained, the US instead favouring military-ruled Pakistan as an ally. Since the end of the Cold War this has begun to change, though the Elephant is still sensitive.

On the other hand, the Elephant does not mate for life. Its old friends, like Iran, now shunned at the behest of the US, can testify to this. And while female and young elephants are sociable creatures, the bull elephant generally is not. India is held back by its own region, where it has tended to throw around its weight. Pakistan in particular remains the albatross around India's neck—a gigantic, nuclear-armed albatross—made worse by India's heavy presence in Afghanistan. Once upon a time it may have been possible to gain international respect through brawn alone, but nowadays respectability is key. Bullying is unseemly. Instead, you should bring your neighbours to heel through judicious use of free trade agreements and dollops of aid, as India is creakily realizing.

7. For all that the affinity seems self-evident, *the Elephant may not be a natural circus animal*. Mega-events are the scarlet sports car of international relations. They're meant either to show you've recently become a filthy-rich Master of the Universe, or to stave off a mid-life crisis. (Quite obviously, the London 2012 Olympics were the latter.) In recent years they have become de rigueur for aspirant world cities. Beijing and Rio have the Olympics; South Africa, Brazil, and even Russia and Qatar have the football World Cup. With the Commonwealth Games, Delhi settled for a slightly less shiny prize: other twenty-first-

century hosts include Glasgow and Gold Coast City.

It set about hosting with lovable ineptitude. I ended up in Delhi a week before the Games were due to start. Trench warfare appeared to have broken out in Connaught Place. I flew back to London from the shiny new Indira Gandhi International airport two days after it had opened, gleaming and full of Mont Blanc pens and spa goods. From the rear of the facades came the sound of frantic hammering and drilling, the odd glimpse of trailing wires. The newspapers were full of panic: a surfeit of snakes, collapsing bridges, 'uninhabitable' athlete accommodation, Delhi belly, deserted stadiums, rampant corruption, and the extraordinary spectacle of India's own sports minister condemning the event.

On the other hand, India recovered like Dumbo, won lots of medals, and did the ceremony thing with typical aplomb. And boy is the metro good, Aunties excepted.

8. *The Elephant needs a lot to eat.* Along with China, India gets a lot of stick for its size and its growth rate—because it will inevitably guzzle increasingly more of the world's resources, and be responsible for an increasingly large percentage of the world's carbon emissions. It has taken an intransigent line in international negotiations about its right to do so, and constantly worries about where the resources will come from. 'Energy security' is New Delhi's watchword. It lacks a large resource base of its own and is a vast oil importer, further damaging its economic prospects. Unless something radical changes, it can only grow so big.

9. *Elephants cannot really run*. While capable of fast spurts, technically their back legs can only walk. It has 'feet of clay', heavily reliant on corruptible bureaucrats and local elites to enact policy, and founded on a fractured, unequal and democratically empowered society. Torn between populism and the financial markets, with its economy faltering, India had better pray it's like Kipling's elephant, which gained its greatest asset from the teeth of crocodiles.

10. *India is a white elephant*. Forget all of this. It may come as a shock to learn that it is totally unhelpful to think of India as a giant pachyderm. There is a story, much cited by those studying India, about a group of blind men and an elephant. One touches its side and believes 'the Elephant is very like a wall!'; the second touches the tusk, and concludes the elephant's a spear; third, trunk = snake; fourth, knee = tree; fifth, ear = fan; through to the last, who touches the tail and thinks the elephant is a type of rope. It is the intellectual equivalent of the head bobble: all truth is relative, all interpretations are correct. Like the elephant India is, in the words of a longstanding foreign correspondent on his way out, 'a country easier to describe than to explain, and easier to explain than to understand'.

A similar dilemma presents itself when you're sitting in a toney Delhi bar looking out at the rest of the country. Touch the tusk (viz., the ice bar) and you might be forgiven for thinking India was like Tokyo or Stockholm. Elsewhere the picture is quite different—snakes and trees and spears abound, one might say. Delhi is far from a cipher for India as a whole. The country's centre of gravity has splintered, trickling down from that unwieldy head to the federal states.

The Indian state, too, is a mirage. Divided by ministry, state, language, generation and more, with its feet of clay precariously balanced on India's divided society, under closer inspection it disappears. Nonetheless, it will always continue producing papers, of course, shrouding its disjointed form in white prolixity. And I will continue reading them, on and on and on.

7

BOREDOM

Travel is glamorous only in retrospect.

—Paul Theroux

*F*or the first millennium after Christ, India had probably the largest economy in the world. By 1757's Battle of Plassey the British had emphatically begun the process of its annexation. There is an old colonial school of thought that provides a simple explanation for the West's world takeover. How did 300,000 Englishmen succeed in dominating 300 million Indians for so long? Forget technological asymmetry, the Protestant work ethic, scientific culture, divergent living standards, railways and guns. Forget Indian disunity, local collaborators and hungry capitalists. Forget even the answer once popular with both imperialists and young weightlifting Indian nationalists—that booze-swilling beef gobblers will always beat abstemious vegetarians.

No: colonized peoples are simply lazier. The natives slobbed around, while 'mad dogs and Englishmen went out in the midday sun' sticking flags on things.

This explanation was patronizing then, of course, and it looks all the more so today. The laziness theory does beg a question, though: what on earth does the PhD student *do* with her long sweaty days?

This question plagued me daily, especially that vast demoralizing gulf between *do* and *ought to do*. I pictured my counterpart, a more adventurous International Development student somewhere cheaper and riskier. Her life was unceasingly interesting, I was sure. She probably had a translator and her own motorbike and appropriate interview outfits. Right this second she was telling a joke to a warlord or mafia kingpin, a joke which managed to combine both cultural nuance and uncompromising ethical integrity. Over his big belly the kingpin was laughing an evildoer's laugh— *BWAHAHAHAHA*—and, shaking tears from his eyes, handing over his top-secret files.

In reality, much of fieldwork life seemed to involve waiting, watching people, musing on stuff. And then writing notes about waiting, watching people, musing on stuff. Very swiftly this settled into a routine—humans love routines, we're all budding authoritarian regimes full of arbitrary rules and rituals—disrupted only by the panic of actual interviews.

As at home, each day began with what William Gibson calls 'Internet ablutions' (though slowly: India's IT-loving reputation is belied by its creaky internet). To email or not to email? On one hand, living elsewhere demands long lightweight butterfly-net emails to capture the new place's most colourful elements. On the other hand, these take up precious Research time and suggest you're not seizing the spirit of adventure. At intervals I turned on an email auto-responder with some smug BRB message, just for verisimilitude. My comeuppance came when at night a bird took to roosting outside my window, with a squawk that sounded exactly like 'Email—email—email.'

Then I showered, and carried downstairs piles of paper and a notebook containing a list of books I've been meaning to read since 1998, where they would be buffeted by the fan. For the rest of the day, if there were no interviews, I would kill time until the sociable evening: sightseeing, prying hard-to-find books from precarious stalagmites in dusty shops, ploddingly buying the basics, and hoping big people would get back in touch.

What an idiot I must be to end up doing this, I meditated at least daily—the intellectual equivalent of squeezing pimples, or having a really good scratch and drawing a little blood.

The dust-filled air acted as a perpetual reminder of my failures. It seeped in through the mosquito screen to settle on my things, forming geological layers. In between sweepings, I padded dirt into regular tracks, like a zoo animal or a madwoman in a yellow wallpapered room. Fingerprints showed my weaknesses. A beer glass and my makeup bag were almost clean. The dust lay thickest on the electricity books, chalking them like corpses at a crime scene.

Periodically I checked to see what more successful humans do by way of routine—after all, their routines might be deranged, but they clearly seemed to work a lot better than mine. It was demoralizingly irrelevant to the failure-in-motion.

Famous writers have glamour. When they stay in bed until noon (Keynes) or hit the booze at lunchtime (Churchill), they are demonstrating self-knowledge in the face of the tyranny of socially ordained rhythms. When they survive on vinegar (Byron), tinned meat (F. Scott Fitzgerald), amphetamines (Auden, Sartre and Ayn Rand) or cigarettes and coffee (pretty much everyone), it's a sign of commitment.

But the PhD student is not glamorous. Imagine we were to declare in the university library that we could only write on top of a fridge, like Thomas Wolfe, or surrounded by snails, like Patricia Highsmith. Goodbye library card.

It was…well, a bit boring, and sometimes lonely. Just thinking that feels ungrateful. How can being somewhere so faraway and different ever be *boring*? After all, travel is often prescribed as a cure for boredom, healthier and more respectable than drugs or nymphomania.

Actually, there's a venerable tradition of not doing a whole lot in India. It's no accident that one of India's most famous exports, meditation, is basically about boredom. It means taking that grey husk of frustration and tedium and repetition, and enclosing yourself in it, exploring its corners, until it's something like bliss.

But the boredom of many Indians is not the luxurious quiet of meditation. India is a land of enforced idleness. Cities everywhere are full of commuters and isolated newcomers and queues (or milling crowds with a notable absence of queues).

In India waiting can often feel even worse. Deliveries don't show. Trains are delayed. The internet creaks. Bills are paid in person. The TV is full of the same adverts. Sending a parcel or getting a licence still takes a thousand and one steps. Important people demonstrate their power by arriving hours late. Unless you are yourself important or rich enough to get someone to do your waiting for you, you need the patience of a saint. Or a cricketer.

This is especially true for educated unemployed youths. Waiting for life and adulthood to begin, they pass time, waste time, kill time, clock watch, temporize, procrastinate. There's even an expressive Indian-English phrase for it: 'doing timepass'—complete with a plethora of timepass websites.

Much of this time-killing looks the same as it does for teenagers and twentysomethings everywhere. Lots of TV. Games. Cards. Music. Porn. Chatting. Texting. Flirting. Films. If the cult-classic novel *English, August* (1988) by Upamanyu Chatterjee—no relation, I don't think, but you never know with Bengalis—is at all accurate, marijuana and masturbation also play a central role.

My home turf, Vasant Kunj, is almost entirely ignored by travel writers. Not so by Delhi's middle classes, who nod approvingly when I give my Stalinistically number-heavy address. 'Ah!' they exclaim wizard-like—'Ambience! Promenade! Emporio!'

For I live in the centre of polysyllabic, Europhilic modernity. This is Mallsville *par excellence*: three of Delhi's finest flank our street. They loom, alien, a kilometre beyond the pat-a-cakes of dung fuel that line our local mini-slum.

Spotless, soulless, ice-cold, the malls are where the middle classes come to play. Here ladies—and the whining albino freaks that are Westerners—can hang out without being stared at. Families make a day of it. I concede they are relaxing places for those with doctor-parent-induced OCD and a financially ruinous love of imported goat's cheese.

They are also sinister, dystopian places, always too empty and heavily guarded, with feral rich kids and lab rat lighting and interrogation room chic (in fact, Indian changing rooms are Kafkaesquely called 'trial rooms'). I hold my breath waiting for a doomy voiceover from HAL.

Luckily vestiges of Indian customer service survive to recontextualise you: car parks reached only through barbed wire-filled building sites, layers of receipt bureaucracy, whitening creams. Once I tried to return some ill-advised shorts. 'Exchange?' repeated the security guard, with a sharp intake of breath. The entire mall clattered to a standstill. No fewer than seven people were required for the transaction; I signed four different documents; and finally I was forced to placate them by buying socks. Only trying to buy football boots was worse—the incredulous 'For *ladies?*'

Many observers are horrified by the rise of malls and the consumerism they signify. Pavan Varma, for example, laments *The Great Indian Middle Class* for their 'crippling ideological barrenness which threatens to convert India into a vastly unethical and insensitive aggregation of wants'. Undoubtedly there is a grain of truth in this, though not one unique to India. Yet the malls are a great place to kill time for a generation that knows and accepts that you are what you buy.

The malls are full of rich kids, who have more options in boredom as in anything else. They loiter over macchiatos and imported beers, shop, get makeovers, go clubbing, go bowling, pick at pizza and muffins, watch football and Hollywood premieres, holiday, road-trip, name-drop, blog. Crucially, the malls and upmarket café-bars are less overtly masculine than most Indian public space—so rich girls can loiter there too. The result, according the *Wall Street Journal*, is a life of air kissing and 'fancy drinks, new toys and branded clothes'. 'In India's capital,' the same article states piously, 'the children of the nouveau riche often get whatever they want, apart from happiness'.

Those a few rungs down the social ladder must make do with less, as ever. Clumps of bored young men—they are almost always men—are ubiquitous. They 'hang out', smoke bidis, snack, drink tea, drink booze, piss on walls, do odd jobs, wander around, mutter and whistle and sing to one another. At college they are loud and lascivious and obnoxious. In the parks they blast cellphone love songs and hold hands and lie in each other's laps (macho Indian behaviour is more overtly homoerotic than its English equivalent). They stand around watching their friends work, lounging against walls, sprawled over the city.

I watch them sidelong, they stare at me. These sleazy and occasionally aggressive young men, purveyors of sexual harassment, are flippantly termed 'roadside Romeos'. They

132

are everywhere, and they are threatening. Often they leer and catcall at passers-by. As a *Wall Street Journal* blogger noted, the horrific Delhi rape of December 2012 began as a form of timepass: the alleged perpetrators 'were basically lounging about partying with food and drink. And the fateful bus ride began as a "joyride"'. A recent UN study across six other Asian countries found that, after sexual entitlement, the most common reason that men rape was entertainment seeking, 'out of boredom'.

Everywhere they seek to dominate space. Boredom, anger, fear. It shapes the city's psychogeography.

As I typed one morning (an essay arguing that Foucault was either a visionary or a cretin, I can't remember which), a fly landed on the edge of the keyboard. Of course I stopped working and watched. The fly surveyed the keys with bulimic satisfaction. Clearly snacks lurked within. It tapped the Escape key covetously a few times with its fleshy mouth-trumpet, then sat back, rubbing its paws together like a corrupt businessman. How nostalgic: it was a housefly, *Musca domestica*, identical to the irritating buzzers of Britain.

I needed to get out of the house.

Bones and dignity still more or less intact despite another Auntie onslaught, I emerged from the metro in central-east Delhi. To the left sprawled the halls and avenues of Pragati Maidan. Heavy with concrete and Soviet pseudo-optimism, 'Progress Field' hosts international expos on everything from toys and bulldozers to cutlery and (yes) electricity.

It had more gates than a football stadium. I followed a couple of slick moustaches with briefcases along the path.

Everything was on the same titanic scale characteristic of depressing utopian projects. Signposts promised food, auditoriums, buses, but the few walkers were swallowed up by the size. Built in 1982, it is gradually expanding.

The main event, inside a much-celebrated building that looked like a honeycomb gritting its teeth, seemed to be invite-only. Instead I slipped inside a slightly smaller building behind the moustaches, chucking a business card into a fishbowl at the entry as proof of intent. A young coordinator, dressed like an air hostess, head-bobbled her approval.

Inside was an electricity expo. It looked like a car showroom, with pipe samples and pastel sketches of drills instead of Beemers. Only the lighting was worse, ironically. Endless hysterical placards boasted more solutions than a meth lab: wiring solutions, storage solutions, finance solutions, solutions to all your multifarious power needs.

The vocabulary of electricity lends itself to manic self-promotion. How could we even talk about modern politics and business without it? Power and networks and dynamos, crossed wires and live wires and short circuits, flux and fuse and juice and high voltage. Feeling plugged in, amped up, electrified, recharged. Making connections, pulling the plug. Even our selves are explained through such analogies, from the 'hardware' of our bodies to the 'wiring' of our brains. (Of course, man is literally electric too—'a mass of electrified clay' in the irreligious phrase of Percy Bysshe Shelley, himself intrigued by electric experiments and one of the inspirations for *Frankenstein*.) Our ideas ping like lightbulbs overhead, and our emotions feel electric: headaches like an electric shock,

that lightning jolt when he touches your hand. The chugging
rock of AC/DC notwithstanding, it's the language of speed
and interconnection.

Suitably recharged, I left utopia and continued walking
south. Once again, my tiny map proved a reliably unreliable
aid to distance, and my tongue threatened to loll as I walked.
I stopped and asked a pair of idle construction workers where
I might find Purana Qila.

'Purana Qila? The Old Fort? Never heard of it,' the first
worker said.

I tried to describe it thoroughly. As usual, my Hindi failed
me. 'It's a fort. And it's old.'

Nothing. I tried again. 'It is not far from here, from my
opinion. It is old. Ancient. A big building, old and very big.
Many white people'—or I might have accidentally said 'horses';
gora and *ghoda* are far too similar for comfort—'want to see
this.'

'Oh!' his eyes lit up with recognition. 'You mean the Jew
Gate!'

Between two arrow-slitted watchtowers, the terracotta
entrance to Purana Qila did indeed turn out to be graced
by six-pointed Star-of-David lookalikes. It is not, of course,
Jewish. According to most guesstimates, this is the oldest part
of Delhi. Beneath it allegedly lie the remains of Indraprastha,
the legendary Pandava brothers' great capital, enshrined in
the epic *Mahabharata*.

It appeared to be an unlikely centre for timepass. Yet people
paddled aimlessly around the bathing lake, slumped on the
grass in each other's laps, even resorted to zorbing. Close, too,

only a little further south again, is one of the more profoundly depressing theatres of boredom I have had the misfortune of visiting: Delhi Zoo.

Zoos are always depressing. Nice Western liberals aren't meant to enjoy them anymore. Delhi Zoo is PETA's dystopian fantasy. It's a shame, because it has an excellent menu of animals. India has long been admired for its wildlife: in the 1610s the trustworthy English travel writer Thomas Coryate praised the Mughal emperor's menagerie of 'Lyons, Elephants, Loepards, Beares, Antlops, Unicornes'. At least some of these are on display.

Unusually, it was the small animals near the entrance which looked more appealing. Virtually all the zoo's cages were small and exposed, heavy on concrete and chicken wire. The larger animals appear to have succumbed to lassitude or mental illness. An alopecia-stricken lion paced the smallest corner of his enclosure over and over and over. A chained African elephant rocked to and fro, ears flapping in a terrible rhythm. Several tigers have died there. But reptiles always seem pretty lassitude-stricken anyway, so it's a bit less tragic to see them slumped in a corner.

'Madam! Madam!' It was the reptile house guard, gesticulating wildly with a stick. 'Snake! I will bring you snake! You will put it on neck, click photo!'

Have a large comatose serpent slung on my neck, get papped by every passing teenage boy, and pay for the privilege? I politely declined.

Further in, timepass materialized in all its worst incarnations. PUT YOURSELF IN THEIR PLACE, a cartoonish signboard ordered, DO NOT TEASE ZOO ANIMALS OR ANY ANIMALS. It was futile. Groups of young men were blasting tinny music from their phones. A couple of men, their children watching, were throwing rocks at a gharial to make it move. At last they hit it full on the snout, with a terrible hollow *thwock*, and it shuddered and slipped into the water. At least where the animals were utterly exposed the crowd seemed satisfied simply by shouting.

I'd met up with the ever-noble Persian, my Gurgaon chum, and some boys from a home run by Tara, an NGO—all around twelve years old, very self-possessed and curious as they explored the zoo's endless winding paths. They were polite, charming, and unfailingly kind to the animals.

And then up swaggered some older timepassers: 'Oi, shorty, is that white bitch your *girlfriend?*'

You bastards, I thought.

Yet it is difficult not to sympathize—*very* grudgingly. Many of these young people have little option but life in limbo, watching indefinite tracts of time flutter by. Like me they often are or were students. Waiting forlornly for a middle-class job to open up in a phenomenally competitive labour market, as Oxford's Craig Jeffrey has shown, they collect endless degrees from fourth-rate colleges—the sort of places notorious for scandals, like the entrepreneurial registrar who subcontracted postgraduate examination marking to schoolchildren, and the student campaign for the right to cheat in exams because cheating is so widespread.

There aren't enough jobs, and those that do exist are often dull and humiliatingly menial: endless delivery boys and tea-bearing office peons (from the same root as the word 'pawn'), the security guards who slump outside offices and shops in shabby uniforms, maids sweeping leaves off the driveways only for them to blow back a minute later. That this is often quasi-work, not un- but *under*employment, is obvious: the seemingly unnecessary fifteenth waiter, the miscellaneous hangers-on and odd-job-men around family shops, the eighth man holding up a ladder or a paintpot and watching the others work, that superfluous guard in the mall who stamps receipts as you exit.

The result, as in so many other countries, is a dangerously large and disaffected group who are really, really bored with the status quo. And prices are rising. There are considerably more young men than women around. Cities everywhere tend to attract more men, and in North India's patriarchal rural regions women are scarcer still. And all the time, Delhi's wealth is in their face.

Today's celebratory India storyline is not irrelevant to these young people. Worse: it's raised their expectations and left them hanging. India's population may be surprisingly unrevolutionary—but as *The Economist* wrote recently, perhaps the country's rich 'might want to pay their security guards a little more, though. Just in case.'

Be afraid. Be very afraid.

8

FEAR

Hungry Joe collected lists of fatal diseases and arranged them in alphabetical order so that he could put his finger without delay on any one he wanted to worry about.

—Joseph Heller, *Catch-22*

*I*t was my very first Holi. I'd been invited to a genteel, gin-and-tonic-fuelled event at an insulated elite mansion. But instead I was spending it with my permanently beaming French housemate, who was saving India through the medium of rugby—and so we were celebrating with half the Indian rugby team.

The Frenchman and I prepared with all the seriousness of a *Rocky* training montage. We loaded up with weapons: cans of coloured foam, packets of pink and lime and orange powder, tins of water-soluble pigment, Barbie® water balloons, and giant submachinegun-style water pistols. I picked out some old clothes (white is for attention-seekers and masochists), carefully moisturised ('Colour only sticks forever on dry skin', I was warned), and generally got into the samurai psychological space.

In the same way that Spain has a handy way with bulls and America with portion sizes, Indians excel at festivals. They might be *too* good at festivals, in fact: virtually all Indian households spend huge amounts on celebrations like weddings and religious festivities, averaging 10 percent of poorer households' entire annual budgets. They are an iconic component of India's international reputation. Tourists flood to watch the lamplit diabetes-fest of Diwali, the vast watery Kumbh Mela (the world's biggest religious festival), and the great regional highlights: Ganapati in Maharashtra, dunking the goddess Durga in West Bengal and, er, camel trading in Rajasthan.

No festival is more iconic than Holi. It is one of the most memorable—and it turns out, frightening—moments in the Indian calendar.

The Hindu 'festival of colour' is celebrated increasingly madly across North India, most notably a couple of hours southeast of Delhi in the grubby sacred towns of Mathura and Vrindavan. Here the god Krishna, an avatar of Vishnu, was born and grew up. Krishna is one of the more exciting deities, with his dashing blue skin, populist cowherd background, flute, and penchant for pleasuring milkmaids. His name has been spread across the West by ISKCOM, a.k.a. the Hare Krishnas.

From these heartlands Holi has expanded rapidly across the top half of India in recent years. In the UK, too, Oxford students gather in the rain to throw watery colours. South

India largely tries to ignore it, but undoubtedly the colours will seep downwards. The festival's enormous popularity today across the country and the world probably owes much to Bollywood. Just like the 1990s fetish for white convertibles and inexplicable Switzerland scenes, shots of white-clad superstars gambolling flirtatiously through puffs of colour have been a Bollywood mainstay.

Holi looks a lot like the Roman Saturnalia and Feasts of Fools celebrated across medieval Europe. To ring in the new year, social norms are briefly overturned, or at least relaxed, and the old year is consumed in a brief carnivalesque period of fire, anarchy, and debauchery. People light bonfires and paint each other with less regard for seniority, caste, and gender than normal (although young men still sometimes bent to touch their seniors' feet, and some were very wary about powdering me). Women get to beat men with sticks. And many people quaff booze and bhang—an almond or pistachio milkshake laced with cannabis, or served in laddu or samosa form—and sway blank-eyed through the streets.

The celebrations started early, around 10 am. All the rugby players were from the same village, as the old unplanned quasi-rural settlements that the modern city has guzzled are still known, and indeed almost all shared the same surname. We headed there for the carnage. The few autos plying their trade charged an extortionate Holi premium, but it was worth it. The driver obligingly veered us towards passing pedestrians and cyclists so we could catch them unawares and strafe them with colour. I felt quite the hooligan.

All this good clean sociopathic fun went a little to my head.

'Did you see that skill, Jean-Nicolas? Sod the PhD, I should have been a sniper!' We ditched the auto and swaggered along the street. I kept making strange chopping arm signals like I'd seen in the films.

'Target at twelve o'clock!' Heading straight for us was a motorbike piled high with young men. 'At my signal, unleash hell!'

Ride of the Valkyries blasting in my mind's ear, the two of us opened fire.

'Ai-ai-ai-ai-ee-ee-eee-aiii!' A jubilant infidel-slaying cry, last seen on *Xena: Warrior Princess* circa 1999, burst from my throat. The bike shot past us, its brood of young men now pleasingly Krishna-coloured.

The outbreak of vowels died on my lips. The bike screeched into a U-turn. The young men's eyes were holes inside blue masks, like vengeful Smurfs.

They chucked eight gallons of what looked like bona fide squid ink all over us, and roared off.

The Frenchman muttered an imaginative Gallic obscenity. We smudged our way into the village. I think under all the ink I was successfully passing as a man: at a couple of houses we were offered fly-strewn snacks and vast tots of whiskey by respectable Uncleji figures. Their respectability was signalled by their own war wounds, which were confined to decorous little stripes. I've seen more war paint on the average Delhi clubber.

The rugby players led us to the team's clubhouse for a brutal initiation ceremony involving colour, waterpistols, and a hose. Once they ran out of colours, the players grabbed handfuls of mud. I don't care what they say: you don't '*play*' Holi—it's far too perilous. It's fun as long as you're on the winning team, like all sports. But when one person turns on you the others follow, aiming savagely for eyes and maximum saturation.

Suitably baptised, the players paused to pose in their dripping vests, assiduously cultivated muscles bulging like melons in a paper bag. Then we took off over the wasteland, full of delinquent puppies and giant pigs and people bathing in a filthy plastic-filled pond, into the village proper.

The pack started to hunt. Whooping, faces daubed, grinning mouthfuls of white teeth. We pelted through the narrow dung-caked streets, accompanied by a motorbike brought along solely for its mistuned roar. We sprayed anyone who looked like they wouldn't actively burst into tears. Most victims just stood and took it with a resigned expression, before smearing us with more powder. The entire village was left dripping with fuchsia and vermilion and lime. I thought: Crikey Moses! being an antisocial menace is *fun!*

Suddenly women and children pelted us with water grenades from above, vanishing out of reach of retaliation. I do wonder why the most popular Indian festivals simulate being in the Green Zone. Diwali had been even more terrifying, with improvised explosive devices detonated every few metres. We hurried away, shaking muddy pistols at the sky—only to walk into another ambush.

Out leapt a feisty group of Aunties. They covered their faces with saris to protect against the gunfire and launched themselves upon the yelping boys, beating thighs and buttocks with until their thick sticks snapped. For once I thanked God for my ovaries.

Our reign of terror was over, and the mood abruptly turned serious. There was work to be done. Without explanation we piled into a car and drove a short distance.

Out in the yard a ring of older men were sitting, all solemnly chewing mutton curry in perfect rhythm. In the centre sat a man with all the trappings of local power: three phones, a thick gold chain snaking through a thicket of black chest hair onto his paunch, and the same smiling vicious eyes as Stalin. The others fell silent when he spoke.

The Frenchman and I were ushered to meet him. He was a local politician, and might offer the team sponsorship. He stood, and we dipped our foreheads so he could swipe us with gritty yellow powder.

'Click photo,' he said, snapping his fingers.

We obeyed.

'*Khana*,' he said, with another finger snap.

From nowhere two bowls of curry arrived, mushrooms bobbing greasily on the surface. The two of us thanked him and ate and made appreciative sounds. All eyes were on us.

'*Bilkul lazeez hai*,' I said in my threadbare Hindi. Everybody laughed, and my heart jumped. Was it wrong? Was it too Urdu-Muslim? Was it four centuries out of date? I kept smiling and took another huge swallow and thought, *And* I bloody hate mushrooms.

Then we were back off, beers and bhang flowing. The rest of the day passed in a colourful blur, because someone sprayed me in the eye.

As the afternoon died and the players got drunker, it became clear that being the only girl in the gang has a sensible upper limit. I went back home, looking like a patchwork quilt, and tried and failed to scrub off the colour.

With time to kill, I squinted through the purple film encrusting my eyes at the computer screen, and idly searched 'Holi India culture' on Google Scholar. This was a grave error. Instead of pleasant slices of anthropological whimsy, the results all seemed to come from the *Journal of Hazardous Materials*. With oozing eyes I scanned 'The "Holi" dermatoses: annual spate of skin diseases following the spring festival in India' and 'Ocular hazards of the colors used during the festival-of-colors in India—malachite green toxicity'. And finally: 'Bilateral periorbital necrotizing fasciitis following exposure to Holi colors: a case report'.

I lay awake that night worrying that my flesh would start gangrenously eating itself while I slept.

It is not only the traveller and the Holi warrior who tremble in Delhi: the whole city is on edge every day of the year. Middle-class Dilliwallas, especially (and unsurprisingly) women, speak as though they are under siege.

'Of course, you won't go out after 6 pm,' my recently discovered relatives nodded, 'seeing how it's such a dangerous city.' They hadn't ventured north to Old Delhi for years, or ever visited my southwestern area, half an hour away on the outer ring road. Another older friend hadn't even braved the metro. Each day they go to the same shops, do the same daily commute, keep their eyes averted from the rest of the city, and exchange rumours: 'Someone got shot at those lights. She was just sitting in her car, stopped at the lights. They drove next to her and shot her in the head. The police have not caught them. Blood everywhere at the lights. The police will never catch them.'

But what are the middle classes—and here I must include myself, with my gated life—afraid *of*? In its choice of bogeymen, Delhi is a dedicated follower of global fashion.

Terrorism is a consistent fear, though it isn't greeted with quite the same hysteria as in Boston or Bradford. The Global Terrorism Index claims India has witnessed the third-highest number of terrorist incidents of any country in the decade since 9/11, after only Iraq and Pakistan. Delhi has been attacked several times, and is periodically prone to spates of hoaxes and panics. As in America, the terrorist is seen as a bearded, goggly-eyed Muslim madman. Islamists with links to Pakistan claimed responsibility for bomb blasts in 2005 and 2011, and for December 2011's dramatic attack on the Indian Parliament.

The difference is that India has possibly the second-largest Muslim population in the world—*possibly*. WikiLeaks revealed that the US government thinks India has underestimated the number. The 2001 census put the figure at 138 million. As I write, the ever election-minded government has held off releasing data from the 2011 census, but the Pew Research Center gave an estimate of 176 million (14.4 percent) in 2010. Delhi itself had a distinctly Muslim flavour until Partition, from seven centuries of uneven Muslim rule and habitation. Islamophobia is a lot more dangerous in such a context: the country has also seen 'saffron terror' bombings, allegedly committed by Hindu fundamentalists.

The insurance market appears to think the risk is declining. Nonetheless, scanners, soldiers and security guards are ubiquitous, especially in locations frequented by tourists and the middle classes, like the entry to malls, monuments, the metro, and big hotels. You might think there is nothing less reassuring in the metro than the sight of an archaic-looking rifle sticking out of a sandbag emplacement, but for the lonely fieldworker the security caress is a rare and overstimulating moment of intimacy. Sometimes I went in and out of the metro just for the human warmth.

But the procedures are slow and awkward and unaccountable too. Dilliwallas are pumped with enough X-rays to cut the subcontinent's fertility rate. At the Taj Mahal , two months after Holi, guards would confiscate my brother's playing cards, of all weapons of mass destruction. The prodding and probing goes hand in hand with an intensifying censorship regime. For all India's democratic claims, Reporters Without Borders ranked it 140th out of 179 countries for press freedom in 2013, below Afghanistan and Zimbabwe. Their shameful verdict:

the [Indian] authorities insist on censoring the Web and imposing more and more taboos, while violence against journalists go unpunished and the regions of Kashmir and [Maoist-'infested'] Chhattisgarh become increasingly isolated.

The second bogeyman is ubiquitous in cities, especially those with striking levels of inequality: the rampaging poor. Big cities are precarious places, vast and dynamic but always on the verge of hysteria. Streets are not controlled solely by force, but by social norms. I remember the strange eerie hush of affluent disbelief during the London riots of August 2011. So this is what would happen if we stopped believing in authority and law all at once: smoke, destruction, bonfires of designer trainers. Delhi, like many other Indian cities, has also had its violent and lawless moments. 1984 is the most famous: murderous mobs targeted Sikhs in revenge for the assassination of Indira Gandhi, with the not-so-tacit approval of the authorities.

The fear is concretized in Delhi's geography. Mughal-era Indian cities were composed of insular neighbourhood clusters, *mohallas*. These were typically internally homogenous— through shared regional, caste, occupational or religious lines—and largely self-regulating. This segregated spatial logic was only reinforced after independence as Delhi increasingly became a city of administrators. Clusters of residential housing were built and allocated to government employees. This survives in place names, which often tellingly retain the imperial terminology of 'colonies' and 'enclaves': Defence Colony, Railway Colony, Press Enclave, State Bank Colony, Engineers Enclave, INA (Indian National Airways) Colony. There are others with weirder names: New Friends Colony, Sunlight Colony, even a Nasbandi ('Vasectomy') Colony out in the eastern suburbs, where a programme in 1986 reportedly offered plots to anyone agreeing to a sterilization.

Today's middle-class neighbourhoods face towards their own local markets and parks, effectively shunning the outside. The insularity, the resultant fear, has been taken to new levels: 'Folks with plenty of plenty, they've got a lock on the door.' Our own flat was perfectly on trend: secured inside walls, fences, fistfuls of locks, wandering nightwatchmen, and bored guards jotting down vehicle registrations and (I always suspected) our late-night comings and goings. Swimming in a morass of roads and oh-so-many people, the wealthy inhabit an archipelago of guarded mansions and gated communities.

At present the patrolling *chaukidar* generally carries nothing more threatening than a whistle and a stick to clack around in circuits through the night. Yet reports are on the rise of heavily armed Aunties, well-built trigger-happy women packing Glocks under their saris just in case. India allegedly has the second-largest number of privately owned guns floating around in the world (after the US), and even its own National Rifle Association-style lobby group. One German anthropologist writes of a quasi-militarized 'Fortress Delhi'.

Other fears are disease-related, again bearing with them a fear of the poor and their packed and squalid slums. In Britain the most dangerous thing is the lesser spotted office stapler. In comparison India seems violently dangerous, a Pandora's box of dengue, malaria, giardia, TB, cholera, Japanese encephalitis, an alphabet's worth of hepatitises, diphtheria, dysentery, typhoid, HIV, and the disgusting-sounding chikungunya, which I'd never even heard of before arriving in Bangalore. Oxford insisted my Chennai-born friend got fourteen vaccinations before she returned to her own hometown. Every itch might be leprosy, every spot bubonic plague—though nobody ever warned me about necrotizing fasciitis. A plague fear struck in 1994, dengue fear in 1996, and again in 2013, and in lower-grade incarnations throughout the monsoons, capable of striking fear deep into the heart of the American embassy with its huge mosquito-magnet swimming pool.

Together fears about crime and disease reinforce calls for increased security and slum clearances, never mind the destruction of homes and livelihoods this might entail. India has always been segregated, but this trigger-happy paranoia is something different. This *is* the twenty-first century. Private security and weapons are everywhere, while rent rises and heavy-handed governments drive the poor further to the margins. The elites hole up in similar gated communities in Capetown, London, Dubai, Buenos Aires, Guangzhou, Mexico City, and virtually every urban agglomeration in the United States.

Delhi is positively fashionable.

Finally, there is the fear of nuclear apocalypse, something that seems very remote but probably is a lot less unlikely in Delhi than in, say, the pretty Cotswold village of Little Barnacle. India has an illustrious nuclear connection. Robert Oppenheimer, father of the atom bomb and Sanskrit fan, famously (mis)quoted Krishna's line from the *Bhagavad Gita* after the world's first successful nuclear test: 'I am become Death, the Shatterer of Worlds.' (Beat poet Allen Ginsberg used the same chapter to describe the effects of LSD. Apparently God looks a lot like a mushroom cloud.)

I hadn't thought about this much until I had to teach a class on the undying nuclear-powered hatred between India and Pakistan. Several times in the heat of almost-war, parties within the Indian and Pakistani states have allegedly contemplated nuclear escalation. Under its nuclear shield Pakistan eggs on India with its terrorist proxies in Kashmir. How patient will India be? The optimists think that all parties are too rational to risk nuclear war. The pessimists prophesy doom.

By the end of the class the students were pale and shaking. John Hersey's classic 1946 essay 'Hiroshima' outlines what the apocalypse might look like: just a 'sheet of sun', a 'noiseless flash'—and then 'a sort of twilight'. It makes me wonder about my parents' generation, when everyone seemed fairly resigned to instant senseless death. I'm not sure how anyone gets out of bed, let alone goes out and roams the city.

Why was I dwelling on all this scary stuff? Might the secret be that travelling makes you just a bit mad? Not only that: heat sends the mad blood stirring. By May, it was homicidally hot in the urban jungle. The weather forecast showed a line of tiny, unblinking 40°C+ Saurons. The temperature had replaced bowel movements as the expat topic of choice. The whole city looked badly cremated.

For the first couple of weeks everyone seemed to sink into lethargy, glassy-eyed in the dust. Stuck in our foolishly un-air-conditioned flat, we had tacitly agreed to ignore each other's increasing near-nudity. Showering three times a night in pyjamas and sheet, my bed gathered brown outlines like the rings of a tree or the police outline of a corpse. I quickly became unable to talk about much else, even though I realized that admitting you don't have AC in civilized circles is as incomprehensibly eccentric as admitting you have a phobia of buttons (a phobia my Australian housemate really did suffer from, so at least the heat-enforced nudity was helpful on that front). People were mildly intrigued, but mostly a bit disgusted.

In the freezing Decembers of my teenage years, we used to stuff wrapped-up burgers up our tops to keep warm while waiting for a late-night taxi home. Now I found myself slipping bottles of iced water inside my T-shirt. I lay back on the scalding plastic of the autorickshaw and fantasized on Patrick Leigh Fermor's description of England—'like living in the heart of a lettuce'. He meant it as an insult, but just think of it. The bland watery crunch, the green-white coolness. Delicious.

Then, like the flick of a switch, it suddenly became intolerable. The heat lay like an iron dome across the sky. The air was hotter than blood. That the apocalypse was nigh was confirmed when I was caught in a hailstorm. Out of the boiling May sky, golf balls of ice thundered onto North Delhi's corrugated roofs. They melted in seconds.

Some argue Europeans colonized Africa not through some devilishly rational imperial scheme, nor even in Seeley's 'fit of absence of mind', but in a fit of madness. The men on the ground were riddled with disease, booze, opiates, fatigue, fear, jungle fever, delusions of grandeur—the dark hot madness of Kurtz in *Heart of Darkness* and *Apocalypse Now*, or the fire-starting madness of *Jane Eyre*'s Mrs Rochester, far from home and crazed by confinement.

I simmered at inanimate objects in perpetual lethargic rage. If you looked closely there would be sweat patches on my skull, under the hair. I tried to drink water Indian style, pouring it into waiting lips without touching the bottleneck, but it splashed all over my face and left me angrier than ever. I started going a little bit mad too.

My interviewees' offices were still Alaskan wastelands of air-conditioning and office chairs. But outside the city was a hothouse of unease. It is well known that violence increases with higher temperatures: summer is murderous. Adrenaline courses through the blood and tempers fray. Delhi's famous and terrifying road rage escalates, especially with the rapid, rainless rises of April and May—tens of people are killed for minor scrapes or slights—as does sexual violence. Like me, the city seemed in the clutches of some sort of urban jungle fever.

The most famous contemporary outbreak of Delhi heat hysteria was the 'Monkey Man' panic of April and May 2001. It is not just the wealthy who are afraid in the city. In April and May 2001 fear swept through the narrow winding lanes of poorer areas from the eastern outskirts into the city itself. Monkey attacks are not unusual in Delhi, but the Monkey Man was something else. Generally appearing on balconies and scratching people (rather erotically), he first appeared in witness accounts as a black half-monkey, half-man. He evolved into a mutant cyborg with glowing eyes and metal claws, able to jump four storeys, or even morph into a cat. The panic escalated, with a four-foot-tall monk beaten up and handed over to police in the suburb of Noida, while at least three others leapt to their deaths to evade the beast. Vigilante groups instituted patrols and the police offered a reward for the Monkey Man's capture—though he was never caught.

The diagnoses were as interesting as the panic. Middle-class Indian columnists lamented the irrationality of the lower orders (never mind that in 1995 the 'miracle' of Ganesh statues drinking milk, first witnessed in New Delhi, had relied heavily on middle-class support and spread to the diaspora in the UK, US, Canada, and beyond). The virulently Hindu nationalist party Shiv Sena blamed Pakistan for unleashing an army of cyborg monkeys. Conversely Bollywood immortalized the Monkey Man in *Delhi-6*, a paean to national integration in which the *kala bandar*, the black monkey, represents the sectarian evil in all of us, or something. Writing in the *Wall Street Journal*, the anthropologist Lionel Tiger compared the phenomenon to *The X Files* as part of a ubiquitous urge for 'the ghoulish and disastrous'. He suggested citizens were recognizing that 'everyone from New York to New Delhi lives on the edge'.

The eventual consensus was 'fear psychosis'—exacerbated by heat, mass communications, and pranksters. The attacks all took place within half an hour of blackouts. The postcolonial theorist Aditya Nigam evoked labourers 'living through prolonged spells of power cuts and darkness, sweating it out' on joint terraces in gossipy high-density areas. Like Frankenstein's monster, the Monkey Man is electricity's dark side.

In the feverish nighttime, the bogeyman thrives. If Delhi gets a little hysterical in the heat, what chance do I have?

On the road the great travel writers become skinny, blistered, even peeved—but very rarely afraid. Most come in two colours, as old as colonialism. There are the intrepid, hypersexual, and permatanned explorers—T.E. Lawrence, Wilfred Thesiger, Patrick Leigh Fermor, Robert Byron, the self-appointed Bruce Chatwin—thumbing the *Odyssey* with one hand, penning witty letters to duchesses with the other. They're always climbing things and making sweeping architectural pronouncements. (Admittedly their own friends and biographers call them fantasists; his friend Evelyn Waugh even called Byron a 'dangerous lunatic better off dead'.) Then there are the self-deprecatingly bumbling amateurs—Bill Bryson, Eric Newby (actually a hardcore military man)—who might occasionally fall over and commit unspeakably awful cultural faux pas. But they don't seem afraid either. All wear hardy footwear and enjoy satisfying amounts of male bonding.

Their books are brilliant. But the myth they propagate is not. The Mothership has not gone too far from her semi-permanent moorings in Yorkshire: Australia seems intimidatingly distant, so she is saving India for when she's 'more experienced'. When I'm away, she ends each Skype call with the ritualistic words 'I'm just not as brave as you.' Well: bollocks.

I maintain that everyone (bar a few madmen and delusional hippies) feels the fear. Travel is a scary, and occasionally boring, business. There is a lot of waiting around, for planes and buses and people and electricity. The waiting is alleviated by moments of abject panic, and occasionally hunger. There is much musing on bowel movements, and on what book to read next, and on whether you are going to run out of clean knickers. There is much paranoia about whether people are talking about you, or whether you're inappropriately dressed, or your guide is going to kidnap you. The word intrepid doesn't feature much.

Travelling alone is a particularly strange and intimidating experience. New cities, with their size and guarantee of anonymity, are both liberating and lonely. Male travellers often wax lyrical about the joys of wandering the city, the joys of being on the verge of lost. 'The crowd is his element as the air is that of birds and water of fishes,' Baudelaire famously wrote of the flâneur, the wanderer. In India wandering is generally the preserve of young men. 'His passion and his profession,' Baudelaire continued, 'are to become one flesh with the crowd.' As a lone woman I have the impression that the crowd would quite like to become one flesh with *me*. Women surge through public space with a purpose, not pausing or looking around too much. (Young Western men travelling alone also tend to attract a surfeit of lampreys, offering postcards, girls, and drugs.) If you're not a heroic explorer type, if you're not a man, if you are alone—you experience every street and site differently.

It can be too much. It's OK that it's too much. Take a deep breath, steel yourself, *be safe*, and go back out there. 'We must travel in the direction of our fear': it's worth it.

Admittedly in my Indian travels around I have encountered a crocodile, cobras (twice), giant venomous spiders, moonshine, wild dogs, a scorpion, a convicted stalker, homemade guns, angry monkeys, angry bulls, angry camels, a Mach 6 earthquake, and a short circuit that exploded a lightbulb and sent fan blades whirling at my head. I have been escorted by the military through an armed uprising, and drunk tea with a group of opium-addled headhunters—skull-collectors rather than especially extreme corporate recruiters—who had facial tattoos to show they'd succeeded in carrying off a head or two. (They were friendly enough, but their children threw rocks at me.) I've also been given warnings of varying degrees of plausibility about the dangers presented by to me personally by black bears, Islamist terrorists, tigers, fake gurus, wildfires, striking transport workers, leopards, bandits, corrupt policemen, bull sharks, wild elephants, Maoists, tsunamis, Pakistan, disgruntled cricket fans, and the metre-long flesh-eating turtles released into the Ganges to help dispose of half-burned corpses.

I have encountered precisely one of these in Delhi: the earthquake. We lived on a flight path and I mistook the quake for a passing Airbus.

Delhi has a disastrous, and worsening, reputation. It is the Scientologist of cities. Some of this is justifiable—but let's put it in perspective. Delhi is not actually all that dangerous. The worst injury I've had from months of roaming, inspecting toilets, and Delhi life has been from a very small pothole. What's *really* most likely to kill you?

First, as I watch an unhealthy amount of TV crime dramas, let's look at murder. Other countries challenging India as new emergent powers on the global scene include Brazil, Mexico, South Africa, and Nigeria. Big cities in all four of these are far more dangerous than Delhi. Latin American cities are in an entirely different league of violence. A widely covered study published in early 2013 showed that five of the ten cities with the world's highest murder rates are Mexican, and fourteen of the fifty worst are in Brazil. Four cities in South Africa and the United States also feature in the top fifty, but not a single Indian city. In 2011, the homicide rate per 100,000 residents in Delhi was 2.7, versus 20.7 in Philadelphia and 58 in New Orleans. That's a rate not so different to London. Reassuring conclusion: you're *extremely* unlikely to be murdered.

Second, what do most Dilliwallas actually die from? The real causes of death are more prosaic than terrorists, the nuclear 'noiseless flash', or Victorian-sounding diseases. In fact, they're remarkably similar in Delhi to other cities. Overall, there's been a transition from 'developing world' diseases to mimic the rich West. Like his British counterpart, the average Dilliwalla is likely to die not of malaria but of prosaic, noncommunicable 'lifestyle diseases': heart disease, stroke, diabetes.

The elephant in the room is Delhi's reputation for hating women. So what's likely to kill you if you're a young Indian woman?

In 2012, the United Nations announced that India was the most dangerous place in the world to be born a girl: you are twice as likely as a boy to die between the age of one and five. Even with the likely huge underreporting, a woman is raped in India every 20 minutes. Delhi's rape figures are the worst of any large city, and reporting has (thankfully) rocketed in the aftermath of the 'Nirbhaya' case of December 2012. 'Nirbhaya' means 'the fearless one', an unnecessary and oxymoronic title. Every report makes it clear how terrified the young woman was.

The Global Burden of Disease report recently confirmed that, nationwide, some old suspects are still in the top five causes of death for 15-49-year-old women: 'maternal disorders' related to pregnancy, tuberculosis, and diarrhoea. But heartbreakingly the top cause of death is suicide, especially for well-educated young women in wealthier areas. And also in the top five is fire, frequently associated with domestic violence and dowry murder. Countrywide in 2010, and again likely an underestimate, a bride was burned every 90 minutes.

The most dangerous things for young women, then, are not tigers or motorbikes or malaria. They are discrimination, social pressures, the continued stigmatization of mental illness, and violence. Violence by strangers—and by women's own families.

It's dangerous to be female and Indian. It's dangerous to be from an upwardly mobile family, hungry for dowry and obsessed with *izzat*, honour. It's even more dangerous to be a poor woman, a minority woman, a migrant woman—when your pregnancy is marred by poor nutrition, when you are legally all but invisible, when your rape case cannot raise middle-class protest but is laughed out by the police.

I count my blessings every day.

9

HEARTS

He used to call me thirty times a day. It stopped for a few months, and I found out he'd moved overseas. I breathed a sigh of relief, but as soon as he came back, he started calling again…

He called so often I had to change my phone number. He used to send me SMSs calling me all sorts of terrible stuff: bitch, slut, whore. I had no idea what he was trying to achieve… We'd had coffee once.

—Friends

*I*ndian men—and, dare I say it, especially Delhi men—are notorious for their stalkerish tendencies. Rare is the woman, Western or Indian, who has not been pestered far, far beyond the point of flattery.

Further south, the metro surges back through the earth and into the hot air. It carves an arc—as serene and soaring as tons of moulded concrete can be—over the quiet bustle of Kailash

Colony and the Roy residence. A short swoop away are the four orangey segments of Lajpat Nagar, still famous for its cheap clothing even as it rapidly gentrifies.

Delhi's house-numbering system, at least in slightly older areas, perpetually baffled me. Block letters are haphazardly arranged, at least to my untrained eye, and E-24 is nowhere near E-23. Here, looking lost in the middle of a subdued and dusty little park in the centre of a housing estate, I encountered one of these young male tormentors.

He turned the corner, ambling in the opposite direction. He slouched, with a gluey crest of hair that lent him the appearance of a Portuguese man-o'-war.

The young man popped out his headphones with a big white-toothed grin, and asked me in slightly awkward but very confident English whether I was OK. I eyed him suspiciously, and he flicked a glance over his music player: 'I'm so happy to meet you. Most of my real friends are Westerners. My best friend is an Australian girl.'

I was early, and lost, and convinced I had to embrace all the city had to offer: so here goes. We started chatting.

Nicky was from a large town in the sprawling state of Uttar Pradesh. He had moved to Delhi to study, and might have become one of India's vast army of unemployed graduates, but his grades were good enough to escape to Australia. There he spent six years, acquiring a business degree (the much-coveted MBA), a comparatively lucrative job, and an anglicized version of his name. He had even—he told me wide-eyed—had gay friends: 'even a lesbian!' Now he was back, and currently worrying about finding a suitable boy for his sister.

'Do you want to get coffee?' he said, already walking. I was still early, still embracing stuff, so I nodded, and we set off on a disconcertingly roundabout trip: quiet residential streets, the hum of the main thoroughfare, an unplugged security scanner in the middle of the street, dodging traffic, and up the stairs of a weirdly empty mall, all gleaming and dark grey.

We ordered coffee: black for me, something sickly and cream-covered for him. He let me pay.

Then Nicky began to speak, almost compulsively, palm hugging his downturned phone throughout. He wanted me to understand why I should be his friend—because he understood how to treat women *now*, especially Western women, after a long painful journey.

Almost as soon as he arrived in Sydney, Nicky fell head-over-heels 'in love' with an Australian girl: let's call her Sheila. She was green-eyed and relaxed and kind—the couple of times they'd exchanged words. Encouraged, he set out to woo her.

Here Nicky paused, drummed the back of the phone, looked away. His floppy hair—conspicuously oiled, a last vestige of the provincial town—fell over his face. He began to speak again, more quickly.

He began to woo Sheila in the ways he'd been honing since he was a wide-eyed Indian teenager. He kept lists of all the dates and times he'd seen her and what she was wearing. He wrote her streams of emails declaring his undying love in his (at the time) rudimentary English; she replied only twice, to ask him to stop. He texted her endlessly. He had friends approach her. He sent her expensive gifts: a gold necklace, an iPod.

Finally, Nicky followed Sheila home from work, pursuing her onto the train after she had shouted at him to leave her alone.

You can see where this is going. Nicky shook his head as though something bitter was in his mouth, pushed away his coffee. He was arrested and told he would be deported by a series of increasingly foulmouthed policemen. He ended up in court—'that was the first time I heard the word: stalking'—was kicked out of university, and served a community sentence.

By this point, my murmurs of sympathy were becoming somewhat less convincing.

Nicky pressed on. He had tried to see Sheila again—'just to say sorry, yeah?'—and ended up back in court. (The conviction was not enough to put Nicky off Australia, though. Not until he had been beaten up three times in 'curry-bashing' attacks, the racist Australian pastime of choice, finally being stabbed in the arm, did he decide to move back.)

We left the coffee house and paused on a corner.

He acknowledged that what he'd done was wrong and scary—'now I understand'—but insisted he hadn't known better. When he was growing up all the boys, and all the girls (he was sure), thought that a surfeit of attention was the only way to prove your interest was serious:

You see it in Bollywood and on the TV. Indian girls always say no, they have to say no, they have to stay modest, but they expect you to keep chasing them… They want you to keep calling, calling, calling, sending SMS, gifts, following them every day, checking what they're doing and who they're seeing. That's how you show it's *real* love.

Nicky barely dates Indian girls anymore: he finds the expected process of pursuit confusing and risky, 'though it wouldn't even be a crime in India'. He resents the fact that they explicitly demand expensive gifts, and that they are hurt and confused when he suggests splitting the bill 'because I know men and women are equal, yeah?' or when he stops texting them after not hearing back.

He shook his head forlornly. 'How do you know when no means no?'

That evening, another friend corroborated: 'A friend of mine from work was getting older, and her family thought she'd never marry. One day she noticed a man on the metro, staring at her. The next day he was there too, and the next and the next, standing closer and closer. Finally he followed her home and asked for her number. They're still dating a year later.'

Admittedly the man has married someone else in the meantime, but ah well—it's the romance that counts, isn't it?

Many young metropolitan Indians find themselves in an awkward middle ground. They lap up Bollywood love songs and stories (men just much as women), gossip about dating and sex, swap tales of passionate affairs. Unlike their parents they want a degree of individual choice, not a dictated ritual arrangement. They believe in something more than duty and the love that grows from familiarity: they want marriages that bring emotional closeness, intimacy, and friendship.

In Delhi's public spaces, the parks and monuments, young couples furtively snuggle, half-hidden in nooks and bushes. (Many pairs of boys do something similar.) Even if they are not having 'full sex' but just 'fooling around', they like to talk about it. Another PhD researcher, with a good deal more fieldwork stamina than I had, carried out research in the South Indian IT hub of Hyderabad ('Cyberabad'). 'Of course I know what sex is,' one of her interviewees said impatiently. 'An orgasm? Um…is that a kind of condom?'

A journalist friend kindly filled me in on what I might expect from dating a Rich Delhi Boy. 'He texts you from his expensive phone: *hi babez. u wnt to go 4 dinr.* You don't reply, so he calls two hundred times. He arrives in his Black Honda Accord, Punjabi music blaring. Swaggering out, he's wearing jeans and a tight T-shirt covered in graffiti, or maybe a shirt open to show his chest. He keeps his designer sunglasses on indoors.

'He takes you somewhere in Lajpat Nagar for your date, followed by a "partay" at a "lounge bar" in GK1. He drinks a lot (expensive Scotch with Coke) and hits on the waitress. They don't have a table. His witty reply: "Do you know who my dad is?"'

The Rich Delhi Boy might think I was an easy date, but certainly not marriageable. A surprisingly number of the young people I spoke to were sceptical about pure 'love marriages', seeing them as fragile and frequently ill-advised. This is perhaps not surprising given that 'falling in love' seems two young people, often from very different social backgrounds, are fiercely sexually attracted to each other so they elope after two impulsive weeks. They also noted the West's high divorce rates, though, not something to aspire to.

'I don't want to make my parents unhappy,' a long-limbed and elegant friend told me, 'and I trust their judgment. They know what to look for.' She shrugged. 'Plus I'm shy. There are loads of one-night stands at JNU'—Jawaharlal Nehru University, the huge leftwing safari park for students near our flat—'but the dating scene's not for me.'

She argued that family consent and involvement in conflict resolution is the best foundation for a stable and long-lasting marriage. 'Our families will make sure we work on it.' She certainly did not intend to live in a joint family with her husband's parents, though. The majority of Delhi households have already converted to the nuclear family: data from 2011 shows 69.5 percent of the city's households include only one married couple, even if household sizes still remain larger on average than in the spinsterish West.

At the same time, she said, 'I will have some choice.' Half-laughing, she used to point out the wealthy young men and women on awkward dates in the city's upmarket coffee chains, à la the talkshow *Koffee with Karan,* sometimes with a watchful chaperone just out of earshot. The pairs darted looks at each other's angles when they thought the other wasn't looking. They had the nervous energy of two strangers discussing how many children to have. 'If we don't click, if there's no chemistry'—a popular word—'then I can say no.'

Something else is emerging, then: the 'arranged love

marriage'. It means intimacy and chemistry, celebrating wedding anniversaries, and sharing confidences. It means that the hallmark of marriage for women, 'adjustment' to a new life and new demands, applies at least somewhat to men too. It even means dating—but largely in the safe confines of the engagement, with the family's endorsement.

How durable this unusual combination of family facilitation and individual choice will prove versus the seemingly unstoppable sweep of Hallmark Valentine's cards is anyone's guess. The institution is undoubtedly modernizing, though. Another friend told a horror story about her brother's search for a wife. The family of one prospect hired a private detective to check them all out and hack into his phone records. A progressively minded marriage counsellor had only this advice: 'You must make your prospective spouse undergo a full medical examination. Blood tests. Swabs. Urine samples. Etcetera. So many have AIDS nowadays.'

Who said love is blind?

For all his claims of revelation, Nicky did send me first one, then three, then tens of texts. The first were friendly, the next angry, the later ones full of vitriol and obscenities. This, as he himself recognized, is the dark side of Delhi men, made all the more frightening by its wide acceptability.

In ancient Hindu tradition women are the libidinous, uncontrollable, lustful sex. Men are meant to be able to keep it in their pants, something scholarship on sex in India has perhaps reinforced through its weird obsession with famous celibates (like Gandhi, who famously used to test his powers of control by sleeping naked next to his nubile great-niece) and semen containment. Within two minutes of arriving in India this would seem ludicrous to all, male and female.

The Indian-English term I most detest is 'Eve-teasing'. It is a viciously coy term that obscures the spectrum of fear and woman-hate beneath. 'Teasing' spans everything from whistling to sexual jokes, obscene gestures to physical assaults. 'Eve' suggests that it is always Woman, that lascivious red-lipped apple-plucking whore, who is to blame.

True to form, Delhi never stints on victim-blaming. Without improvements to its overstretched and unrepentantly prehistoric system of law enforcement, it is impossible to see how the city can alter its culture of sexual violence. The police are perhaps the most grimly inadequate of all India's many institutions, permanently dogged by accusations of misogyny, corruption, torture and even illegal executions through fake 'encounters'. The Delhi police's famously sinister slogan is *With You, For You, Always*. A sting by the campaigning magazine *Tehelka* in 2012 revealed some characteristic statements by the capital region's police officers. *Tehelka* summarized: 'She asked for it. It's all about money. They have made it a business. It is consensual most of the time.'

Despite the speed with which the attackers in the 'Nirbhaya' rape case were found guilty and condemned to execution, an estimated 23,000 rape cases are stuck in the judicial system. In 2011 its chief justice reported that of the Delhi High Court was lagging 466 years behind schedule, despite the fact that it considers each case for an average of only four minutes and 55 seconds. 'It's a completely collapsed system,' the prominent advocate Prashant Bhushan was quoted as saying. 'This country only lives under the illusion that there is a judicial system.' Given this, is it reassuring that India has revived the death penalty after an eight-year unofficial moratorium? Or does this, as *The Economist* warns, mark part of a broader 'illiberal turn'?

Poor treatment of women is all the more shocking and outrageous given India's plethora of women leaders. Most famous is Indira Gandhi, who virtually dominated Indian politics from 1967 to her assassination in 1984. Despite her uneasy reputation—she led independent India's only brush with dictatorship, during the 'Emergency' of 1975 to 1977—her white shock of hair continues to flash from postage stamps, green like the Wicked Witch of the West. When asked where the centre of Indian power lay, my interviewees agreed that (1) India is deeply dysfunctional at present, and nobody is in control, but (2) insofar as power rests anywhere, it rests with a woman: Sonia Gandhi, the Italian-born widow of Indira's son Rajiv and president of the ruling Congress party.

Delhi itself has had a female chief minister, Sheila Dikshit, since 1998. My interviewees in the Delhi power sector spoke highly of her for her willingness to listen to business and her technocratic inclinations. In this she is very different from two of India's other high-profile women politicians, Mamata Banerjee and Mayawati, both renowned for their cynical populism, patronage politics, and enormous egos: 'Didi' painted swathes of central Calcutta her party's vivid blue, whilst

'Behenji' lost the Uttar Pradesh elections in part because of her tendency to blow public funds erecting gigantic statues of herself. Misrule is gender-equal in India.

'Hinduism respects women,' one of my interviewees said, in yet another of those answers that seems puzzling in retrospect, given our interview was about pylons. 'We have Durga and Kali, for example—goddesses with necklaces of skulls who ride tigers and crush men underfoot.' Yet such powerful female figures have not necessarily led to improvements for most women. How could they, when everyone—especially their families—feels the city is so scary, so risky, for women? Far better to control the movements of the women in your family than risk her dishonouring herself and you. Sympathy too often seems reserved for a select and idealized bunch of 'good women'. A recent campaign against domestic violence showed Hindu goddesses covered in bruises under the title *Save our Sisters*. Similarly 'Nirbhaya', as the journalist Jason Burke noted, could be 'neatly slotted into one of the three legitimate categories allowed to women in India: mother, spouse or child'. But what about women who aren't goddesses, or your sister?

Foreigners have already made up their minds about how all this applies to them. In 2012, 6.6 million international tourists visited India, the vast majority safely. In December of that year, the 'Nirbhaya' rape case hit headlines across the world. In the following months companies reported that foreign tourist numbers had fallen by 25 percent, and female tourists by 35 percent. Really, though, it is worse for Western women in some ways—but much, *much* easier in others.

Indians are fond of highlighting the differences between

the dissolute, materialistic West and the spiritual East. This contrast is perceived to be especially strong on the terrain of women's bodies. Western women wear short skirts, bikinis, and turn up in pornography around the world. Indian women of course come in a multitude of varieties. But the ideal Indian woman is modest, demurely dressed, and chaste even in the twenty-first-century megacity. Bollywood makes this clear: for all that heroines may dance in skimpy clothes and drape themselves over the heroes' pneumatic torsos, they finish the film in traditional wedding saris.

Foreign women—and my delicate brother—frequently complain about constant violation by hundreds of goggling strangers. Some beaches now even have signs imploring locals not to harass visitors. On one hand, Indians (some themselves internal tourists) have an inexplicable urge for pictures of dreadlocked albinos holding their unamused babies. On the other, young men—and often less young ones too, wearing suits and with their families mere feet away—are clearly interested in something else.

I don't deny the staring grows wearing. But gradually you become inured to it, just as you stop seeing the dirt. After a while your skin becomes hardened, callused, by the roving eyeballs, and you barely notice it anymore.

Except for the most egregious instances. There are moments when it becomes almost intolerable. My friend and I were wearing deliberately baggy, modest clothing for a nightbus. Yet for hours we suffered a creepy guy poking his fingers through cracks in the seat, trying to fondle our arms, backs, buttocks. We protested increasingly loudly, but the rest of the bus ignored us avidly. Around 5 am I lost it. '*Tu janvar!*' I shouted: you animal. Everyone just stared, muttered, even looked disgusted. At me.

But Western women get a free pass in other ways. For example, Indian women never, ever call in at local 'English wine' shops, those faintly embarrassed purveyors of beer and spirits. Even respectable men do it away from home. My ability to buy booze means narrowed eyes from the neighbours and the nightwatchmen and the men in the ice bar, but it does mean I get my own lady queue. Smoking, too, is permitted (just barely) for Western women. It means you're a slut, but well, everyone could see that anyway.

Western women can also embrace their promiscuous reputation in ways denied to Indian women who must preserve their modesty. Indian neighbourhoods are notoriously gossipy. My flatmates and I frequently crashed elsewhere to milk acquaintances' air conditioning, turning up panda-eyed in the morning. A young man even came to stay with us (awkwardly, nobody realised that Feckless Brother and I were related). Alas, the gossip surrounding our flat—where pretty young foreign women come and go every month or so, occasionally having flings with the downstairs people—was so epic in proportion that the neighbours decided it must be a brothel. The landlord called in to check, but unfortunately only a blonde Russian monoglot was home.

There are news reports of assaults on Western women almost every week. Statistics are difficult to come by: the government does not release crime figures for tourists. But for all the staring and groping, we are simply too high profile a target much of the time. Even the police cannot simply sit by and let Delhi's international reputation fall into even more tattered tatters. It is Indian women, at least the poorer or less 'sisterly' ones who cannot inspire huge elite protests, who bear the brunt of massive, institutionalized hatred of women.

India's population continues to grow, and by 2028 is likely to overtake China's to become the world's largest. So, when confronted with the results of a study claiming most internationally sized condoms are too big for Indian men, the former editor of an Indian men's magazine quipped: 'It's not size, it's what you do with it that matters. From our population, the evidence is that Indians are doing pretty well.'

For most of the chattering classes this is no laughing matter. The black-clad spirit of the Reverend 'Pop[ulation]' Malthus, himself for decades a professor at the East India Company College, is alive and well here. When asked what would solve India's energy crisis, one bureaucrat leaned forward and dropped his voice as though trading gossip. 'The population must stop growing. I am not advocating Sanjay measures'— Indira Gandhi's widely despised older son, who led forced sterilizations in Indian slums in the 1970s—'but something serious must be done.'

This is an old argument. In 1968, Paul and Anne Ehrlich produced their flawed but enormously influential book *The Population Bomb*, which quickly became a classic of the misanthropic 'survivalist' genre of environmentalist writing. In their vision, the world is 'Spaceship Earth', a small contained body hurtling through the blackness with clearly limited resources to support life. Consequently they treated the developing world and its endless breeding with unconcealed horror and contempt. Chapter 1, 'THE PROBLEM', opens with 'one stinking hot night' in Delhi, full of fleas and smoke and, worst of all, 'people, people, people, people':

> People visiting, arguing, and screaming. People thrusting their hands through the taxi window, begging. People defecating and urinating… [D]ust, noise, heat, and cooking fires gave the scene a hellish aspect.

This image of India, perhaps with the valiant Mother Teresa thrown in, is one that haunted American and English minds at least until the 1990s. The Ehrlichs' solution? Alongside incentives for voluntary sterilization and research into mass sterilization chemicals, cut food aid to India to force population control.

In fact, one of India's great underreported achievements is its falling birth rate. The Ehrlichs' apocalyptic predictions have not come true. Unlike China's brutal One Child Policy or the Ehrlichs' own authoritarian recommendations, this declining fertility rate has relied not upon heavy-handed government intervention but on the power of urbanization, rising wages and female education to incentivize naturally smaller families. The most recent figures show that in several of India's wealthier, well-educated states, including Delhi, the birth rate has fallen below 2.1, the natural rate of replacement, and stands at around 2.3 nationwide. It is still uneven: the rate of growth is fastest in the enormous, poor states of the North, nicknamed BIMARU (for Bihar, Madhya Pradesh, Rajasthan, and Uttar Pradesh) after the Hindi word for 'sick'. Nonetheless, it is an impressive and promising development, which improved economic growth, healthcare, and education could spread across the subcontinent.

The belatedly falling birth rate is not an unmitigated good, for all the fond talk of a 'demographic dividend' as China and Europe rapidly age. First, this sprawling young population lacks skills and opportunities, confined to frustration, waiting, and 'timepass' in a growth trajectory that neither educates the masses nor provides enough employment. Second, it is complicated by Islamophobia. The average birth rate amongst Muslims remains high—and I have lost count of the educated Hindus who prefer to view this as some sort of conspiracy. 'They intend to outbreed us,' one toilet correspondent informed me, his hand closing into a fist. In large-scale studies there is no relationship between religion and birth rate. There is, though, between poverty, insecurity and fertility rate. Muslims remain by and large one of India's poorest and most marginalized groups, even (or especially) in international business's favourite state, Gujarat.

Third are India's missing women. In this brutal logic, if you must pay a dowry to marry off your daughter, and she will then leave to keep house for another family, it does not make much apparent sense to have a daughter at all. While increasing wealth and its dispersal led to the decline of dowry in medieval Europe, pressures to marry within caste groups keep prices high and rising. So with falling birthrates comes preference for sons, and illegal sex-selective abortion. Dowry itself has been technically illegal since 1961, though you wouldn't know it: payments are rising rapidly throughout the social hierarchy, stretching well beyond its earlier roots in the upper castes of the North. One friend described going to dowry viewing parties in which the 'generosity' of the bridal family is on display, from scooters and jewellery to Victoria's Secret underwear.

Scans and abortions are expensive. Keeping a woman in the home, foregoing the income from her work, isn't cheap. Dowries rise with your ambitions for a rich, higher-caste husband. These women are not missing from the poorest, but from the ranks of the rising, increasingly wealthy classes. Depressingly, a wealthier India may not automatically be positive for women. Despite Delhi's conspicuous wealth and conspicuous greed, money cannot cure all.

10

SOULS

I thought India was pretty jammed with poor people and cows round streets, witch doctors and people sitting on hot coals and bathing in the Ganges…

—US President Harry Truman

*A*nother month, another friendly if terse message from a relative: *WE ARE INVITING YOU TO TAKE A LUNCH WITH US*.

Yet this brought the dreadful dilemma: which gifts to bring? A swift spot of websurfing suggested some 'culturally appropriate' gifts. Alcohol seemed a bit risky for hitherto unknown family members. The internet suggested you cannot go wrong with sweets, but I have an unerring eye for bringing them to diabetics or, like the last relatives, dieters with weak willpower.

'Indian giving' is of course named not for the subcontinent but Native Americans. Most *Indian* Indians I have met are extremely generous as both gift-givers and hosts. Some are also the worst recipients of well-intended gifts imaginable, especially when the gifts are from younger relatives and overseas guests. Gratitude is an awkward attitude to display to your juniors.

Uncle unwrapped the gifts. He was a dapper elderly man with an impish smile, rarer nowadays. First, some dental glue to secure false teeth, as per transnational request. This met with a grunt of approval, a slight head wobble—Indians do not distribute pleases and thank-yous with the same wantonness (and insincerity) as the British. Second, a crisp shirt from Marks & Spencer, a reassuringly prim British brand now making inroads into metropolitan India, seemingly in part as a purveyor of luxury underwear. Their Indian advertising campaigns seemed to feature a lot of scantily clad women; I'm not sure which demographic it was targeting.

Uncle's eyes darkened. He cast the shirt down. 'I will not take this.'

'Why not, Uncle?' Oh no. Maybe he'd seen the advertising campaign.

'It is very bad for you to give me this. There is no point. I will not wear this shirt,' he said gloomily, 'because I am not long for this earth.'

Another gift failure. Lunch was more successful, though Uncle didn't eat himself, but simply sat and watched. It was a Bengali feast: bowls of rice, cubed potatoes, deep-fried airy *luchi* breads. Dishes of the choicest seafood: prawns with coconut, fish with mustard seeds, fried fish, smoked fish-head daal, fish in a thin garlicky stew. The flavours were wonderfully clean and light after the heavy ghee-filled Punjabi stuff that dominates Delhi. The capital does have Oh! Calcutta, a chain restaurant loveable not only for its food but because (a) it is named after a nudity-filled musical with a title (unwittingly?) based on a French pun, *O quel cul t'as!* or 'Oh what a luvverly arse you have!', and (b) in the bathrooms was an oh-so-Bengali sign offering to provide key supplies for your dinner: 'reading glasses, sewing kit, woollen shawl, ear buds'.

The only unwelcome arrival was a plate of bitter warty *karela*; I discreetly hid it under the rice. Having eaten my fill, at last I let out a sigh.

Error. Family love is expressed through quantity of food. Out came second helpings.

'No really, Uncle, I'm fine.'

His eyes darkened again. 'What is this? You have eaten nothing. We have made this for you only!'

Under the table I loosened my belt, and set back to work.

The Bengalis have a famously sweet tooth. Out came dessert. I braced myself. *Mishti doi*, an almost caramel yoghurt. Sweet and crumbly *sandesh*. *Rasgulla*, round spongy balls in syrup, and *rasmalai*, my dad's favourite, scattered with crushed pistachios. They were individually delicious, but together they set my pancreas groaning. And then finally a large glass of Fanta, presented proudly. I felt the elastic in my knickers give way.

I must have lapsed into a short post-food coma under the fan for a moment. Uncle coughed gently.

'I shall show you the family tree,' he said, rising from his armchair and propelling me deeper into the gloom. A chunky yellowish desktop took pride of place in the room. He flicked the switch and it made a strange noise like an old tree about to fall. The screen flashed once. We waited.

Eventually the computer released a series of froggy croaks. He opened the files: three giant spreadsheets, one each for Clans Chatterjee, Mukherjee, and Ganguly. Each contained a long string of names, a thin erratic string at first, flaring into a broad tree in the nineteenth century when there seemed to have been a profusion of brothers. (A long tenuous sidestream attempted to prove our relationship with Bankim Chandra Chatterjee, the famous nineteenth-century author of India's slightly sectarian national song *Vande Mataram*, 'Hail to the Mother(land)!') It was at this point that I realized my father's proud middle name 'Hari' was in fact pronounced 'whorey'.

'We have astrology reports for all the recent relatives, so we can tell what their personalities are like. Here is my father, for example,' Uncle explained.

'But you *knew* him. Wouldn't it make more sense to write down your own memories of his real-life personality instead of using the star chart predictions?'

Uncle's smile didn't waver.

Each sheet went back roughly forty generations—'to 942 A.D.,' Uncle confirmed. A short and erratically written paragraph informed me that this was the year when a king brought five Brahmins over from Uttar Pradesh to perform a ritual.

'The Aryan invasion!' Uncle said brightly.

I bit my tongue. Prehistory is a sensitive subject in India, where pseudo-archaeologists claim the Taj Mahal is a Hindu temple and that Indians invented most things ten thousand years ago, from toilet paper to bicycles (more on which in a second). Even so, the old 'Aryan invasion' theory is pernicious. It claims that a fairer-skinned race of Ubermenschen swept in from the northwest, bearing Sanskrit, and conquered the subcontinent's existing, darker-skinned inhabitants. This racial story was overlaid upon the caste system. The theory was disproved a long time ago: linguistic evidence suggests slower, older waves of migration, and genetic evidence shows much admixture took place between the two populations. Even its old proponents dated it two millennia before 942A.D, but the theory seemed to survive within my family.

'This is why you find so many Chatterjees everywhere, even in Germany!' Uncle continued, mistaking my bitten tongue for awe. 'It is the most common family name in the world!' (It is not. That honour almost certainly does belong to Asia, although reliable statistics are rare, but is probably Chinese: Li, Wang, or Zhang. 'Chang!' Uncle exclaimed when I suggested this—'that's the Chinese version of Chatterjee!')

'Look!' Uncle pointed with a blunt clean nail at the very bottom. 'Here you are. And here are your brothers, David and Boris.'

'Uncle, please let me update that. My brothers are called David and Thomas.'

'Are you sure?'

The computer froze, again. We settled back to wait, my back slurping sweatily against the rubberized chair back. The fan thwacked through the hot juicy air.

I glanced around. Prominently displayed in one corner was

a calendar. The page said DECEMBER 2008, with a gaudy border of clipart images: the iconic sacred syllable *om*, flowers, planets, Ganesh's elephant face, Krishna wielding a flute—wait a minute, was that bearded figure Jesus? Dominating the page was a man with thunderous eyebrows and enormous staticky hair which trebled the size of his head. His palm was raised in a gesture of benevolence, and he seemed to be wearing an orange prison jumpsuit.

It was Sathya Sai Baba, the late, great symbol of middle-class Hinduism in the global age. India's 'teeming urban spiritual supermarket', as one scholar has called it, is a highly competitive place—and nobody was more successful than Sai Baba. The Jimi Hendrix hair was no accident. He was a spiritual rockstar with followers all over the world, and controlled a fortune calculated in the billions of dollars. Half a million people attended his burial, including the prime minister. His photo had smirked at me from many a taxi dashboard.

While some modern gurus' reputation rests on their business philosophies and some on their yoga skills, Sai Baba's appeal was perhaps more old-fashioned: it rested on claims of divine reincarnation and the performance of miracles. In many pictures he is shown brandishing a statuette or a golden trinket that he had materialized from the ether. He combined this with a far more modern style of influence, carrying out good works on a spectacular scale—schools, charities, canals, drinking water provision, flood relief. His message was carried through digital radio and the internet as well as more traditional posters and cassettes.

'But why is Jesus on the calendar too?'

'All religions are one,' Uncle said. Sai Baba had a nice line in contemporary aphorisms—'follow the innernet, not the internet'—not least of which was a very modern-sounding cosmopolitanism. He began with the claim that he was the reincarnation of a yogi who had died in 1918, and whose Sufi-tinged claim *Sab ka Malik Ek* ('One God governs all') can still be found painted on autorickshaws.

The second Sai Baba's claim expanded. By his death Sathya Sai Baba was variously an avatar of Krishna and Ram (Vishnu's most famous incarnations), Shiva and his female consort Shakti, and even (he implied rather controversially) Jesus—although he had dropped his predecessor's Islamic hue like a hot *aloo tikki*. Pursued by financial, religious and sexual controversy, at Christmas 2000 he noted that Jesus Christ, too, 'underwent many hardships and was put to the cross because of jealousy. In those days there was only one Judas, but today there are thousands'. The money continued to flow.

'Enough,' said Uncle. It was time for another Bengali tradition. 'Now you must take a nap.'

Sloping back from an interview a week or two later, I ran into a tourist. He was instantly recognizable: a crust of beads and henna and dreadlocks atop a pair of violently coloured dropped-crotch pants, looking lost in the middle of the anti-pedestrian embassy quarter. Guards eyed him from a white turret.

We were walking in the same direction, but at first ignored

each other as tourists are wont to do. Of course, after nightfall we huddle together in backpacker cafes and Irish pubs, eating hummus and bitching about mosquito bites and Machiavellian locals. But out on the streets and around the monuments, at least when we first arrive, we pretend the other tourists don't exist, ignoring the fact there are several tens of thousands of us wandering about at any one point, all following the same guidebooks.

Eventually the silence became awkward. I introduced myself with some weather-based small talk. He told me his name but I didn't catch it—something like 'Jerd'. The moment passed and I couldn't ask again.

'I *love* India. Really,' Jerd said. 'Apart from all the tourists, of course. Everywhere is so crowded.' And apart from the pesky Indians.

'And why,' I asked in what I hope was a level and neutral tone, 'do you love India so?'

In the thicket of his brand-new beard, his face creased with an expression that I mistook for gastrointestinal trouble. It was in fact spiritual profundity. 'Because it is a land of ancient timeless wisdom.'

Oh no. He was an *Eat, Pray, Love* type.

It was inevitable that I would pick up *EPL* at some point. I too like eating and loving, and have nothing against praying. I too was *One Woman Searching for Everything*, or at least *Something*. I too had slept on a bathroom floor, though inadvertently while in the throes of sickness. I even shared the author's name, Elizabeth.

But on India we must disagree. For Elizabeth Gilbert,

India is *the* place you go for a dollop of divine transcendence and spiritual awakening. To me that's a three-hundred-year-old stereotype, and not much more sensible than travelling to Ireland and expecting to become funny. I don't deny that India has a proud religious heritage, the cradle of four world religions (Hinduism, Buddhism, Jainism and Sikhism). Nor do I deny that religion and the sacred permeate Indian public life in a fashion utterly alien to the West. I do protest the idea that this is an unadulterated blessing. In India, as elsewhere, spirituality suffers as money and politics and prejudice creep in.

(It probably didn't help that I already had my own guru: the Supervisor, a capricious half-god(dess) with a sceptreful of red ink. As with any other guru, we were instructed on the first day of the PhD that 'this should be the most important relationship in your life'. Sometimes when I work I open her webpage so that her face stares down on me, her eyes kind but always faintly disappointed. I imagine she can see me across the leagues of Eurasia, and shoots off cryptic missives—'Eh?'—at the moments of my greatest weakness. My university provides 'How to Manage Your Supervisor' courses, as though supervisors are household accounts, or grief.)

'Of course Delhi isn't really India anymore, it's just too Westernized,' Jerd continued sorrowfully. 'And expensive. In *real* India, people are poor but they're so happy. It really makes you think. Do we really need so much *stuff*? Such *crude materialism?*'

He paused to haggle over two rupees with an auto driver, and drove off towards nirvana. Or, more probably, some shady new avatar of Sai Baba.

It's not only bead-encrusted New Agers who believe that India is a land of spirituality. Indian nationalists have long made the same argument: the West might lead on material comfort, but India is the conscience and soul of the world. Three hundred million gods—the commonly quoted figure, plucked from the sky by some long-dead sage—permeate the very air. The Harvard scholar Diana Eck argues that the whole of India constitutes a 'sacred geography', a network of pilgrimage places.

In such a geography Delhi is something of a backwater. With a few notable exceptions—the murky Yamuna river, the shrine of the Sufi mystic Nizamuddin Auliya—it is not an especially holy city. Its historical fortunes were revived more by Islam than Hinduism. Until now.

One sultry September afternoon, I travelled east over the oily-roily holy river to Akshardham. This isn't just any Hindu temple: it's the world's largest. The Guinness certificate is proudly on display, though its South Indian rivals argue that IMAX theatres and food courts shouldn't count towards the world record.

I nearly gave up. Security is draconian, forcing customers— sorry, devotees—to leave bags, phones and cameras outside; only wallets are exempted. I'd thought this was a transparent excuse to extract Rs 200 from us for official photos, but the ban even extended to my notebook. The security guards carefully examined each page (shopping lists, book titles, other such subversion):

'This diary is not allowed.'

What are you afraid of, Swamishri? Your ever-plucky author

persevered, though, with merely a few muttered curses (also banned). It was worth it.

You couldn't invent Akshardham. The place makes Muhammad Ali look self-effacing. A representative line from my glossy brochure: 'The sheer magnitude, beauty, and experience of Akshardham simply puzzles and amazes all as to how it was accomplished in record time.' It hums with ambition, dwarfing the small crowds that afternoon. It would remain 'for millennia', the same brochure announced breathlessly—no, not mere millennia: it will *forever* remain etched in the annals of history'. There is an eerie internet consensus that it is 'the eighth wonder of the world'.

Planned and executed by an organization that rejoices in the acronym 'BAPS', the complex is a strange hotchpotch of architectural styles, all adorned with a frenetic crust of sculptured stone. The sculptures look almost too crisp and numerous, giving the whole a faintly plastic air; much was carved in Rajasthan and later assembled, which might explain this. The construction was amazingly ambitious: it took 32 years for BAPS to acquire the land, in typical Delhi bureaucracy style, but only five years to build the complex: 7,000 artisans worked on 300,000 stones for 300 million man-hours. As this suggests, Akshardham is obsessed with numbers: 100 acres, 1,070 feet of elephant carvings, 300 x 300-foot step-well-cum-musical fountain, 45,000 extras in the child-yogi film (shown on an 85 x 65-foot IMAX screen), and so on, until you are numbed into a sort of Stalinist awe.

At the heart of the complex, surrounded by hypercoloured paintings and donation boxes, sits a giant gold-plated statue in an eye-watering cavern of green, shell-pink, gems and gold. This is Swaminarayan, former child-yogi and founder of a reform sect that has been carried all over the world by successful Gujarati migrants. Whilst retaining a strong Gujarati emphasis, the sect—or rather the BAPS splinter—has proved an adaptable and aspirational brand of Hinduism, taking to the internet far more adeptly than almost all its rivals.

As I walked around the little 'holy water body' surrounding the main temple (water from 151 sacred rivers and lakes, flowing from 108 spouts), the inspiration became clear. A white-clad man with blue age-rings in his eyes greeted me. 'When we were planning, we visited great monuments around the world to study the secrets of their success. See those elephants? Angkor Wat. The boat ride? Disney World.' We might add: the illuminated musical fountain? A Vegas casino.

The Disney analogy feels right on the money. The anthropologist Christiane Brosius, perhaps Akshardham's closest student, can only bring herself to call it a 'temple' in eye-rolling inverted commas. As the *New York Times* said shortly after the complex opened in 2005, 'The crowds here aren't pilgrims; they're day trippers.' The whole place is a grand theme park.

The temple is supplemented with fee-paying exhibitions. First up was a 50-minute series of animatronic extravaganzas inside something called 'the Hall of Values'. The guru-child robot—an eleven-year-old with a rolling bass voice—creepily looked me right in the eye every time. (Akshardham, if you're reading this, that little guy is firmly in the Uncanny Valley: a little *too* human-and-yet-not and therefore utterly chilling.)

Then there was the aforementioned indoor boat ride, unashamedly modelled on Disney's 'It's a Small World'. In 14 minutes the boat swept us through 10,000 years of Indian history, during which Hindu mannequins invent everything: gravity, astronomy, Pythagorean geometry, aeroplanes, plastic surgery, embryology...

For Akshardham isn't just about Hinduism. It's a nationalist pageant too. Witness the garden filled with statues of 'patriots', in which, incidentally, Gandhi is dwarfed by the more authoritarian 'Sardar' ('Chief') Patel, 'the Iron Man of India'. (In the Swaminarayan movement's home state of Gujarat the state government is planning to build a far larger monument to Patel, a 'Statue of Unity' double the height of New York's Statue of Liberty.) Akshardham presents a compelling vision of India: a spectacular, clean and emphatically Hindu India, unified by its glorious past and all set to conquer the future—because, well, it invented all of modernity ten millennia ago anyway.

This is a decidedly middle-class vision, erasing dirt and diversity. Instead it offers a strong nation, family values, schoolwork, vegetarianism and scripture. The other visitors were notable for being almost exclusively Indian—for domestic tourists it's one of the capital's most popular sights—and all sleekly dressed, dispensing money with aplomb.

This vision is not only for domestic consumption, though, for all the funny looks the Indian tourists gave me. Akshardham aims at the world stage. I was chatted up, formally surveyed ('Which country, madam?') and repeatedly reminded that BAPS is transnational. With, of course, more statistics: 700 temples and 3,300 centres worldwide, attracting 45,000 youth volunteers and 34.5 million visitors; London's Swaminarayan temple was, at least until recently, the largest Hindu temple outside India. More than us irreligious *goras*, Akshardham eyes the huge Indian diaspora, offering deep-pocketed international migrants a pristine and proud version of India.

No culture is timeless or impermeable, for all the claims. Hinduism has evolved in conversation (and conflict) with the West, Christianity and Islam. It continues to adapt to new technologies and audiences, often with great fleetness of foot. Swapan Dasgupta, a prominent advocate, speaks proudly of 'evangelical Hinduism' and compares it to the showy mega-churches and preachers of American evangelical Christianity.

Strikingly unusual, though, is twenty-first-century Hinduism's primary audience. In most of the world the poor are more religious than the rich. In India, and in an interesting selection of other countries (China, Brazil, Turkey, some of the Arab world: all aspirant powers), the reverse is true. As Akshardham shows, the emerging world's middle classes are not necessarily becoming disenchanted with science and the market. Instead, science is absorbed by religion, à la the boat ride and its many inventions; the market tapped for snazzy new temples; and the socially mobile realize that they ought to get in on conspicuous religion too.

The real coup for Hinduism comes with the internationally popular idea that it is fundamentally peaceful and benign, a lifestyle choice rather than an expansionary religion. As one of the bureaucrats I interviewed claimed: 'Hinduism is not a religion. It is a way of life.' (Yes, regardless of my questions, somehow the interview breadcrumbs always led back into the forest.) He continued, 'All paths eventually lead to the same God, though Hinduism is the oldest and purest.'

This is the subtle genius of contemporary neo-Hinduism, and a claim I would hear repeatedly from Indians and tourists alike. Across the West, Hindus have become a model minority, the antithesis of Muslims. They work hard, they integrate, they get rich, and they don't bomb anyone. Of course, this picture focuses on the middle-class migrant, not the poor Indian in Saudi Arabia or the illegal worker in London. It is a cleansed and narrow ideal, which conveniently ignores the fact that Hinduism too has chauvinistic and intolerant strands (though, like other religions, it is not reducible to these). The modern atrocities committed in its name—in Ayodhya and Mumbai in 1992, Gujarat in 2002, even Delhi in 1984—deservedly received huge amounts of attention in the 1990s.

The worst excesses of the 1990s recede into memory. Perhaps equally concerning today, as Meera Nanda's plain-speaking book *The God Market* (2009) argues, is a creeping Hinduization of public space in India—and a Hinduization that is less tolerant than Western myths suppose. As I interviewed the bureaucrat, a red thread upon his wrist, his Hinduism was discreet but insistent. The idea it might be inappropriate in his profession was seen as a Western anachronism. Nanda describes a 'state-temple-corporate complex', in which politicians, businessmen and Sathya Sai Baba-style mega-gurus increasingly collaborate. Gandhi has been accused of bringing the Hindu idiom into popular politics, but today the place of religion in public life is conspicuous and unashamed to a degree never seen previously in independent India.

191

Perhaps the only surprise is that it took the majority religion in a religious country so long to assert itself conspicuously. In the post-1991 new India, tradition and national identity become key resources in the fight against the crushing force of Westernization. The equation of Hindu = India is almost too tempting to resist.

I mulled over several theories as to why shiny new Akshardham is so enthusiastically visited, while far older Delhi sites stand virtually empty, like the tombs of enigmatic slave-kings in Mehrauli. Appreciating ruins is a fairly recent invention: given they smack of decay's inevitability, perhaps it takes an especially confident or especially philosophical generation to start the habit. Perhaps Delhi the prospective world city wants—*needs*—a big, glossy, self-congratulatory monument like Akshardham to position itself in the world. Domestic tourists flock to other relics, though, from Hyderabad's Golconda Fort to the Ajanta and Ellora Caves, so maybe Delhi simply has too many ruins already. Perhaps, like me, everyone was just searching for answers that seemed elusive in the money-grubbing city, and found them in Akshardham's shine.

Or perhaps Dilliwallas just really, really like indoor boat rides.

11

TONGUES

Hindi? Hindi?! It's not even a real language! Why would
you want to learn that redneck tongue, when you could learn
beautiful, glorious, poetical Bengali?

—Uncle

'Oh, ah, India.' A typical British conversation. The
woman, I remembered, had said it in the same way
you might say 'newt collecting' or 'sebaceous cyst', nodding
a little too heartily, fingers whitening around her wineglass.
'It must be warm out there.' English weather-speak, the
anthropologist Kate Fox reminds us, is the human equivalent
of chimpanzee grooming. I swear introductions back home
were easier when I could say I studied toilets.

And then the classic question: 'So, do you speak The
Language?' Or, as one old and dinner-encrusted Oxford don
once wince-inducingly put it: 'Do you speak Hindoo?'

The answer would be complicated even if I had a crumb of linguistic facility. Stand on the streets of any global city and you will hear a host of different tongues. In this, as in everything else, Delhi boasts a mixture of the familiar, the foreign, and the unsettling new twist on the known.

It stands at the head of a gigantic Tower of Babel. India has no national language. The constitution lists a host of languages for government development: 22 at present (English does not make the list), though that number is likely to rise again. The country boasts perhaps four hundred more outside this official list, plus thousands of dialects. Many of India's states have their own official languages, though at the federal level the main official language is Hindi (*not*, I stress, 'Hindoo'). It's now a true world tongue, with perhaps half a billion native or second-language speakers in India and several hundreds of millions more around the world. Stage #27 (approximately) of my journey to Dilliwallihood meant attempting to join this vast group.

Bollywood has done much to bolster Hindi's expansion. One such international movie hit, the internationally acclaimed historical cricket film *Lagaan* (2002), contains much to send the eyebrows twitching. Aamir Khan casually whittles a perfect cricket bat; the fielders practise by chasing chickens; the bastardy British display worse muttonchops than a battery sheep farm; a man with a withered arm unwittingly invents spin bowling; et cetera. But for the expat monoglot, by far the most ludicrous and irritating scene of the entire four-hour experience is linguistic.

'Madam! You have learned Hindi!' exclaim Aamir's muscled pecs.

'Oh,' the British heroine says airily, twirling a parasol, 'my faithful manservant taught me over the weekend.'

She's also called Elizabeth, to rub salt in the wounds. Theoretically Hindi should indeed be an easy language to learn, as it stems from the same delicious-sounding mother language (Proto-Indo-European or PIE) as Latin and its progeny, including English. But when I tried to learn Hindi, I rapidly discovered that *Lagaan* wasn't the piece of hard-nosed documentary realism I'd thought.

My faltering studies took me to Mussoorie, self-proclaimed 'Queen of the Hills', and now a faintly demoralizing honeymoon spot above the celebrated military town and schools of Dehra Dun. It's a little north of Delhi and freezing in the winter—even in the early autumn I wore pink camouflage earmuffs against the morning chill—but close enough that on summer weekends it can feel like an outer suburb.

I stayed in the bungalow of another self-proclaimed Queen, the hawkish and gracefully ageing 'Rani Ji'. She looked rather like Indira Gandhi—the same cruel eyebrows and aggressively starched saris—and indeed claimed to have been a close friend of the twice prime minister/sometime dictator. (She also claimed that Mahatma Gandhi had dandled her on his knee, and that poppet-sized cricketing legend Sachin Tendulkar had slept on her floor: 'Such a polite, grateful little man'. I hope she's writing an autobiography.)

The bungalow was damp, and at night spiders the size

of ferrets shimmered onto the curtains. During the day Rani Ji ruled. She sat on the porch to survey the town below, and dispensed her wisdom. 'India has gone dreadfully to seed,' she assured me. Mussoorie was being ruined by swarms of Dilliwallas, who scattered chatter and piles of plastic over the hills, throwing rubbish from their cars and cigarette ends into the forests. These intruders she lampooned as 'the *paratha* crowd', because they brought their own greasy flatbread lunches up from the city.

Rani Ji herself knew the correct hill station etiquette because she was the estranged wife of an Indian prince. Her father had been so rich that he buried Rolls Royce cars in the Rajasthan desert. High in the clouds, she advised us of the best animals to keep in a royal menagerie: 'Tigers are infinitely superior to lions; their coats are more manageable. Elephants are prone to the most grievous flatulence, sometimes fatal. Anacondas are disloyal.'

The language school sat above the honeymooning town. The other students included several unsettlingly smiley American missionaries and a woman exploring polyandry in hill tribes. The trees speared the fog to give occasional flickers of the Himalayas. Gangs of langurs hissed at us, all black faces and black homicidal eyes in a froth of grey fur and tentacular limbs. The monkeys especially hated Sukrit-slash-Sukriti, the black-brown puppy who followed loyally behind, a little nippy creature of never-determined gender who was later kidnapped.

Unfortunately, my Hindi could not keep pace with my new menagerie-based knowledge. The textbook appeared untouched since the nineteenth century. I learned how to hail a tonga (a small two-wheeled cart, apparently), and how to bark commands like German offizieren in old war films: 'Sit down! Speak! Faster!' An entire chapter focused on a class of verbs for feudal overlords: to cause a third party to do X for you, e.g. 'I'll have the carriage brought round, old fruity', 'Philomena had the man shot'.

I mastered just enough to sound like an imperialist, but still not enough to be remotely interesting—nor, critically, enough to understand the responses. Back down in Delhi, my yearning for practice was frequently thwarted by the fact that 50 percent of speakers became instantly dispirited by my ineptitude and switched to speaking English. To borrow from Mark Twain, I 'never did succeed in making those idiots understand their own language.' The other half were chewing paan and their speech was unintelligibly mangled by a mouthful of drugged red spittle. It's like trying to talk to a bunch of drunken vampires.

Each morning I attempted to 'chat' with Kamala. We reached a working equilibrium. I bellowed incoherently, she did a mocking impression of my bellow, and then we waggled heads at each other until her phone rang. This was punctuated only by the occasional clash of civilizations. The worst of these involved a sanitary towel. Unfortunately, she pronounced it so that it sounded exactly like the Hindi word for 'tree'. I was bemused until she did a Michael Jackson-style crotch grab.

For all the power of Bollywood, Hindi's dominance is far from unchallenged. India is living proof that languages probably did not evolve to spread Miss World-style messages of peace and love across all humanity, but to pass around scurrilous rumours and attack plans against other groups. Its many dictionaries are bloodstained.

Since independence, the subcontinent's new countries all struggled to manage linguistic diversity. India's neighbours showed how high the cost could be. Pakistan's selection of Urdu, mother tongue of only a tiny elite refugee minority, as its national language eventually led to civil war and the loss of half of its population, as East Pakistan broke away to become Bengali-speaking Bangladesh. Discrimination in Sri Lanka (as Ceylon was nationalistically renamed) against the successful Tamil-speaking minority helped fuel a vicious terrorist insurgency—the Liberation Tigers of Tamil Eelam, true pioneers of suicide bombing—and a 26-year-long civil war, put to a brutal end only in 2009.

India, which had a finger in both of these pies, has also seen blood spilled over languages. The early years of independence witnessed mass protests and suicides, demanding new states on linguistic lines. But it has generally accommodated its immense linguistic diversity better than its neighbours, redrawing state boundaries on linguistic lines in the 1950s.

Delhi itself now has three official languages, with Punjabi and Urdu alongside Hindi. To a European the linguistic picture looks curious. European languages, at least in the west of the continent, largely share the Latin alphabet: it's easy to pretend you can read French or German or Romanian.

But visually India is a graffiti wall. Across the country different languages have different alphabets. Gujarati is crimped and hatless, Bengali has gnarled runes, while the east coast's Oriya (Odia) appears to made up of cartoon Cubist faces. The South, with its own distinct Dravidian family of languages, has particularly resisted Hindi's imposition, arguing it amounted to a thinly veiled attempt to secure Northern dominance. Southern scripts have more curves than Aishwarya Rai: Tamil is all jalebi whorls, Kannada whorls with eyebrows, Malayalam McDonalds logos. The speakers of some of these may be able to chat together awkwardly, like Portuguese and Spanish speakers, but they probably wouldn't exchange postcards.

Most striking is the case of Hindi and Urdu. The two languages began almost as one: both were birthed from the same Delhi dialect. Here it is obligatory to point out that Urdu is a cognate of 'horde', and its name came from the Muslim occupiers' *ordu*, camp.

They share syntax and many everyday words of bazaar chat (though not some of the most commonplace, like days of the week or family relations). My first teacher was a very kind and devout Pakistani woman with big feline eyes. She spoke Urdu, but was perfectly at home chatting with her Hindi-speaking friends on the phone. Yet she could not read Hindi: the two languages' scripts are totally different. Urdu has the sensuous *nastaliq* gliding from right to left, a fluid Persian-Arabic calligraphy liberally scattered with dots. Hindi instead uses the Devanagari script, which looks like the laundry of a big-boned family: thick square sleeves, starched collars and blocky socks, all dangling from the washing line in familiar left to right fashion.

This difference in scripts is more than a historical inconvenience. It's toxic. The twin languages have as bloody a history as the twin countries they are most associated with, India and Pakistan. From the nineteenth century the battle between the two became bound up with the nationalist movement. English was understandably rejected as the future language of independence. Instead Gandhi called for a happy marriage of Hindi and Urdu, 'Hindustani', although he paid little attention to the key question of actually writing it down. But as Hindu-Muslim strife grew, Hindi increasingly became associated with Hindus and Urdu with Muslims. With the country's partition in 1947, the two languages were bloodily wrenched apart.

Outside the bazaar, Hindi and Urdu increasingly diverge. They look to different symbolic worlds. Highbrow Hindi draws upon Sanskrit, venerable ancient language of the Hindu scriptures, for its vocabulary (such as the replacement of 'toilet' with the wonderful *shauchalaya*, 'abode of cleanliness', echoing the porcelain-white 'abode of the snow' of the Himalayas). Highbrow Urdu instead looks west to the Islamic world, deploying increasing numbers of Persian and Arabic words. Today's upmarket registers, found in literature and official media and the speech of the pretentious and/or hyperreligious, can be almost mutually unintelligible. They are most different in the words with most resonance: dignity, reason, hope.

In the first years of independent India many of Bollywood's great lyricists were Muslim. Urdu could be found tucked in the corners of film posters (hand-painted) and in the mouths of on-screen princelings and courtesans; many of its Persian loanwords remain Bollywood standards. But now Urdu has been pushed to the fringes, conspicuous only in the great former centres of Mughal culture like Lucknow, Agra and Old Delhi. Hindu-Muslim violence broke out when Uttar Pradesh, the gigantic state that includes Delhi's eastern suburbs, made Urdu its second official language in 1989. Bollywood today prefers dabs of Mumbai *tapori* slang in its Hindi, and Punjabi for its bumbling Sikh stereotypes. The language has been ghettoized like much of India's Muslim population.

There is another linguistic valve to let off pressure, one much favoured by contemporary Bollywood. India has a second countrywide official language besides Hindi, a lukewarm compromise which was to have been phased out in the 1960s but instead expanded like a virus: English.

'To the Bahai Lotus Temple.' The auto driver nodded, and coaxed the engine to life. We zipped past a sluggardly truck with its ornately hand-painted 'HORN OK PLEASE'. The roadside sprouted with adverts for English classes. The driver was humming a Bollywood 'item number' (low on plot value but high on bosom-thrusting raunch, an 'item' originally being Bombay *filmi* slang for an attractive young lady) in a pretty plausible falsetto. 'Am too sexy for you…'

He paused his crooning for second to ask a question: 'Madam, *yahaan se* left, no?'

English isn't just visible in Delhi. It's *everywhere*. Part of this is technological. People SMS or email using pragmatic English transliterations of Hindi words. Part of it is social. Once upon a time India's language of high culture was Sanskrit, later Persian. Now English has become the language of aspiration.

We stopped at the traffic lights on Africa Avenue. The auto driver turned off his engine and resumed cleaning out his ear with his little fingernail, lovingly sculpted into a long ear shovel. (As further evidence of personal transformation, my earwax seemed to change texture in Delhi too, from candle to turmeric.)

A trader materialized next to me, brandishing a sheaf of cellophane-clad magazines with a vaguely piratical air. His eyes gleamed like coins. 'You want magazine? Very good magazine.'

More English. He flashed news magazines, *Business Today*, jowly industry magazines, women's magazines: Indian editions of *Cosmopolitan*, *Vogue*, *Grazia*. Some whitened celebrity gave me a sharky smile from the glossy cover. My auto driver eyed her with interest, humming under his breath: 'Am too sexy for you...'

India might just be the one big place where the internet has yet to vanquish the power of print. At a time when British and American newspapers are closing, India's continue to grow. It boasts more paid-for papers than any other country, aided by rising literacy rates and insanely cheap prices—though they are consequently very dependent on advertisers and backers with deep pockets. The *Times of India* is already the world's largest-circulation English-language newspaper. Regional-language papers are growing even more quickly.

'No, madam?' The trader shrugged his face, and flashed one final set. Beneath the cellophane were what I first took to be golden mangos. No: they were several giant pairs of Caucasian breasts, as comforting and pneumatic as airbags.

The auto driver started the engine again with a couple of gasoline coughs. I shot the trader a feminist glare as we whined off into the city.

Several lung-pummelling minutes later, we arrived at the Lotus Temple, a glorious set of white swan's wings rising in a southeastern suburb. It looks something like the Sydney Opera House, something like the mediaeval European pictures of six-winged, bodiless angelic seraphim—actually, it looks quite a lot like a lotus when I think about it.

Despite being persecuted across the Islamic world, the Bahai faith welcomes all of humanity and its religions as spiritually united. The temple is a popular local destination, and crowds throng its walkways and blue pools. The queue and access is controlled by guides who all seemed to be American gap year kids, combining earnestness and military precision. But inside the vaulted space is wonderfully tranquil.

It was there at the temple that I suddenly realized I'd forgotten how to speak English—or at least British English. Gesturing towards the shoe storage hut with a pair of leopard-print pumps, I said brightly, 'Shall I do the needful?'

It had finally happened: like Rudyard, my mind had been Kippled by the effort to look towards two countries at once. Kipling went from a boyhood of dreaming in Hindustani to high priest of imperialism. I went the other way. I went native.

The phrase wasn't Hindi, but it wasn't exactly English either—at least, not the English spoken in Oxford or New York circa 2013. This was a whole new beast: Indian English—or

'Hinglish', as it's somewhat pejoratively known. It is evolving at high speed and in different directions like some precocious elephant-headed toddler. After all, we've all got to adapt to these days of globalization, when we're all packed into the same crammed world cities. We've all got to learn the art of give-and-take, a little reciprocal *lena-dena*. *Thoda* adjust *kar lo*, my friend.

Hinglish is a language for all occasions. Let me leap to some ill-informed and over-hasty conclusions for you. Here is my short guide, though it's probably already out of date.

Are you trying to sell something? Better use English. It suggests class and trustworthiness—so you'll buy booze from the 'English wine shop', 'English drugs' from the chemists, and biscuits advertised by depressingly white-skinned people laughing about dogs. There is even a terrible cheese variant—a country of cow-lovers obsessed with dairy products, and yet the main non-cooking option is strange rubbery stuff, like tofu in a cuboid condom—rather insultingly named 'Britannia'. Sure, the Brits might have sneakily partitioned the subcontinent and carried out the odd massacre and forced famine, but they're just so lovable when they look up at you with their big wet overbred eyes, unlike your sly bobble-headed countrymen—and you can be sure the products are safely made in Guangzhou.

e.g. 'Coca Cola…*yehi hai* right choice baby!'

If you're selling yourself, consider mixing it up. Remember that Hindi is a 'magpie language', and has been picking the pockets of unassuming others for their diamonds and rust for quite some time. Luckily this means that it is now très romantique, with many different words for love: the standard *pyaar* or *prem*, the romantic Persian-Urdu *muhabbat* and passionate *ishq*, the mother-love *mamta*, the Sanskritic *sneh*—though Bollywood scripts today are just as likely to say 'I love you'.

Hindi is also full of repetition and rhyming-chiming, a feature made famous by Salman Rushdie's 'writing shiting'. For emphasis, broken can be *toota-phoota*, quiet *chupchap*, upside-down *ulta-pulta* and (my favourite) naked *nanga-panga*. Ergo, it is a language made for wooing via the amorous medium of limericks and film songs.

On the other hand, just as the auto driver had realized, English has provided three words whose glorious lyricism is recognized all over the world: 'sex', 'sexy' and 'fuck'.

e.g. '*Zara zara* touch me, touch me!'

And if no English phrase covers the concept you're trying to sell... invent a new one!

e.g. 'Don't take tension—try latest timepass. Search the matrimonials: Girl, 26, Traditional with Modern Outlook, convent-educated, foreign-returned, homely, wheatish complexion, seeks suitable boy, caste and creed no bar.'

Do you want to sound posh and authoritative? If in doubt, go for the Queen's English. By queen, of course I mean Victoria; Elizabeth II really has cheapened the lingo with her ridiculous txtspk and constant gangsta namechecking.

> *e.g.* 'Piffle and poppycock. Kindly do not pluck or pilfer the flowers outside our bogey and that laundry-cum-guard carriage, or any such tomfoolery. I must bathe.'

You may also consider arbitrarily capitalizing some of the nouns in your writing to give an air of gravitas. The only problem is that British English does not contain enough registers of formality. Hindi has three words for 'you', from the respectful *aap*, to the chummy *tum*, and the intimate, rude or Bollywood *tu*. Fortunately you can customize English to permit this.

> *e.g. Business email 1*: 'Dear esteemed Professor, I would like to felicitate you on the Publication of your cogitations on today's Culture of boredom…'

> *Business email 2*: 'k thx for rply Professor. C U there :) tc… bye'.

Are you trying to count? Go English. India's much-celebrated invention of zero becomes understandable when you try to master Hindi numbers, as freakishly difficult as learning to poach eggs. It is astonishing that the country has produced so many great mathematicians. Perhaps it's the algebraic practice provided by abbreviations. These are everywhere, making everyday conversation a cross between alphabet soup and cryptography.

Are you hanging out with relatives? Family ties are incredibly important and only Hindi can capture the specificities of your relationships. There appear to be hundreds of variations of uncle and others. You can affectionately extend respect by calling non-relatives 'Uncle', 'Auntie', and *didi* (older sister); even certain popular politicians are blessed with this honour. The word *bhaiyya* (brother) has a strange power to wheedle and coax—try extending it into a long bleat in auto negotiations—though it's also a Dilliwalla's insult for migrants from Uttar Pradesh and Bihar. And be careful: if an attractive young man calls you a *behenji* (sister), you should probably revisit your fashion choices. If he calls you 'Auntie', with a respectful tip of his coiffed cockscomb, you might as well pack up the knitting needles and head for a nunnery.

One other word is crucial for these family encounters: *bas*. Enough. Please, no more food.

Do you want to sound modern and go-getting? You have two options:

(1) Spice up that Queen's English with some sexy businessisms. They may be the aesthetic equivalent of bludgeoning to death a Corgi, but hey, that's capitalism. Maybe throw in some acronyms for that corporate *je ne sais quoi*.

> e.g. 'Please revert the letter for updation of information, and we'll prepone the meeting then and there itself while you deboard the train, isn't it.'

Probably best to schedule your meeting in English, too. As Rushdie pointed out, 'No people whose word for "yesterday" is the same as their word for "tomorrow" can be said to have a firm grip on the time.'

(2) Swear like a trooper. (Options 1 and 2 are mutually exclusive, unless you're a Bombay gangster.) Like everywhere else, many insults involve incest, genitalia and/or your mother.

> e.g. No, I'm not going to provide you with a list. Shame on you.

As well as a whole store of the aforementioned English naughtiness, there is the intrinsic *filmi* coolness of the Mumbaikars' dialect, which is so awesome that the word for 'awesome' sounds just like 'jackass'.

> *e.g.* 'So that hot online lady turned out to be a 40-year-old man…that's first-class KLPD, yaar.' (This slightly crude abbreviation is unfortunately shared by the Netherlands national police agency. Let's say it refers to a snafu: the polite American English translation might be 'My expectations were raised only to be cruelly thwarted, leaving me ruefully shaking my head.' The less polite one involves a stick and a male appendage.)

Indians also mysteriously hate spoons: a spoon, *chamcha*, is a toady, a sycophantic minion. To which you might reply '*Bhains ki aankh?* buffalo's eye?'—which means, aptly, 'WTF?'

Are you in trouble? In this case, use Hindi. It's full of little blame-dodging techniques. Strong and unruly feelings like regret, love, hunger, and diarrhoea often happen *to* you in Hindi (*mujhe dast hai*, etc). We humans are mere ants facing a powerful and hostile world/our passions/loose bowels. And rather than admit a lack of knowledge, perhaps you just don't remember: 'It's not that I don't know where the hotel is, madam,' the auto driver always says. 'Of course I *know*, hahaha, the memory just isn't coming to me—*mujhe yaad nahin.*'

Consider supplementing your Hindi evasions with the little English word 'sorry'. Not only is there no Hindi equivalent: as Rupert Snell says, sorry is 'unmatched as a social disclaimer—a perfect blend of concision and insincerity'.

Are you reporting on India? India is special, with advantages and problems utterly unlike those in the rest of the world. This must be linguistically stressed in the Anglophone media whenever possible.

Indian politics are particularly exceptional, with all its melodrama (*tamashas* and *filmi*-style *dramabaazi*). Newspapers overflow with the country's own special varieties of strikes and protests (*bandhs, hartals, gheraos, dharnas*), useless bureaucrats (*babus*), and dodgy demagoguery (tax sops for *aam admi*, 'the common man').

The crime world overlaps heavily with politics in India, where a huge number of MPs have criminal records and are surrounded by gangsterish minions, *goondas* and other *badmashes* (English also gets its word 'thug' from India, after the murderous robber cult of Thuggee, suppressed in the 1830s). Unsurprisingly crime too enjoys special Hinglish vocabulary. Theft is far more innovative than the poor old

Brits could manage, as we see from the news story 'Frequent dacoities and looting of fish from bheris in the Sonarpur area; Sleuths nab their man'. English is also inadequately visceral for paying a bribe (*hafta*) or taking out a contract on a hated enemy (*supari*). The scale of all this crime and politicking is such that Hinglish requires its own numbering system. English hundreds and thousands are mere trifles: instead Indian journalism requires the *lakh* (100,000) and the *crore* (10,000,000).

Much of this is euphemistic. There is no sexual harassment in India, only 'Eve-teasing'. New university students aren't savagely tortured by their contemporaries, but given a traditional welcome 'ragging'. Police violence is usually confined to the charmingly rustic 'lathi charge', which sounds like a variant of the Harlem Shake; a *lathi* is actually a five-foot-long metal-tipped stick hungover from the colonial police. And I can confirm that against all appearances there are no blackouts or electricity theft in India, but mere 'loadshedding' and 'heavy AT&C losses'.

At other times Hinglish can reveal the brutal truth. There is a problem I never realized I had before I arrived—one so terrible that advertising girls have tears in their eyes and transnational corporations are forced to step into the breach. I am talking, of course, about 'Hair Fall'. Previously I'd laboured under the misapprehension that the human head naturally shed 150+ hairs a day, but now I understand that I am in fact part of a feral, balding underclass.

As the above suggests, the traffic is far from one-way. English is the greatest magpie language of them all. It's 'about as pure as a cribhouse whore,' said the sci-fi guru James Nicoll. 'We don't just borrow words; on occasion, English has pursued other languages down alleyways to beat them unconscious and rifle their pockets for new vocabulary.' Tangy words it has shamelessly nicked from the subcontinent include shampoo, jungle, cheetah, dungarees, bandana, verandah, bungalow, juggernaut, cummerbund, mongoose, catamaran, yoga, pundit, polo, avatar, chit, loot, dinghy, doolally, coolie, pariah, cot, typhoon, atoll and nirvana. Even Britain's nickname 'Blighty' is bastardised via the Indian army from the Urdu *vilayati* (foreign). Remember that next time you pukka nationalists don your cushy khaki swastika-covered cashmere pyjamas.

Unsurprisingly several of these words are food-related—curry, chutney, toddy, punch. The wine critic and fundamentalist New Yorker Bill Marsano has said, 'The British Empire was created as a by-product of generations of desperate Englishmen roaming the world in search of a decent meal.' This colonization of British English is continuing via the curryhouse (albeit usually run by Pakistanis and Bangladeshis). Into the mouths of Britishers the Hindi is discreetly slipped: naan, daal, biryani, aloo gobi, chana masala, lamb '[with] two onions' (dopiaza), chicken 'roasted' (bhuna) or 'bucket' (balti)… The average curry-munching football fan probably understands more Hindi than his elite English equivalent.

The allure of both Hindi and English is down to this promiscuity. They are able to accommodate, more or less, the requirements of the non-fluent. Linguists call them 'bridge' or 'vehicular' languages, which enable non-native speakers to communicate with speakers of a third language. Hindi is probably the world's third most widely understood language, while perhaps two billion people around the world have some degree of competence in English. Throw in Hindi's twin, Urdu, and you can make yourself at least vaguely understood by almost half the world's population—maybe not to perform a sonnet or ghazal, but to order a beer.

India's languages are perhaps especially open to outside influence. There is no real tradition of translation. Instead, everyone simply grows up speaking three, four or five tongues. It's extremely impressive. It's also Hindi and Hinglish's great asset and weakness.

There is a school in every country that disapproves of their language's magpie tendencies. Hindi has been perhaps too keen to kick out its own vocabulary in favour of Englishisms, diminishing the world's store of charming words. Grumpy old Indians sigh that the Youth of Today have forgotten their heritage and can only talk in informal txtspk, expletives, and a bastardized foreign half-language. Grumpy old Britishers sigh that the Youth of Today can only talk in informal txtspk, expletives, and Americanisms.

Part of me eye-rolls at these snooty oldsters, of course. Languages always have and always will expand and evolve, and it's not as if in the pre-English era all Indians walked around reciting Ghalib and musing on Sanskrit's finer poetic nuances. But there is a very real difference between the two tongues. English is the indisputable lingua franca of today's world. It connotes modernity, business savvy and class—spread, of course, by the superpower America and before it the British Empire. Hindi lacks this prestige.

Hinglish is not yet a real solution. English has many dialects. All can facilitate social interactions, all can be creative, all are valuable. Not are all equally respected. The fact is that English, like globalization, is far from democratic. All too often Hinglish appears in literature only to be mocked: *Are you writing a novel? You are having much of luck. Yenithing and yevrything in Hinglish sounds first-class hilarious only! Quickly, fut-a-fut, throw in a few descriptions of bubbling chutney, stir in family life, and watch the awards roll in for your zabardast prose. Wah, wah!* It doesn't (yet) bring enough authority and credibility to the table. Not all dialects are created equal.

Now I've lured you through the chapter, I'll be honest. There's no need for you to learn Hindi, or any other Indian language. Yes: it's time for the obligatory section on India's most famous and beloved gesture. Throw out the phrase books, the capricious software, the overpriced and suspiciously non-native tutor. You don't need 'em. All you need to do, citizen of the world, is to master one simple yet profound gesture: the Indian head bobble.

The bobble's effect is something between a nod, a shrug, a dog's tail wag, and flipping the bird at someone when their back's turned. Observation suggest that it means:

'Yo, homies'

213

'Yes'

'No'

'Thanks'

'I understand'

'I don't understand'

'I acknowledge your existence, underling'

'I shall give the impression of doing your bidding, madam, but I would like to register my extreme lack of enthusiasm. In fact, I'm not even sure your request is possible, but I'm damned if I'll tell *you* that.'

'Meh, whatever'—or more precisely, the sense of profound existentialist ennui contained in the French word '*Bof*'.

There are many variations: dangerously rapid wobble = probably a good thing; slow waggle accompanied by closed eyes = ominous. Just to make it more interesting, many people—the same people who otherwise deploy faces of extreme joy or hysterical sorrow to accompany everything from Bollywood dance moves to haggling—deliberately keep their faces entirely impassive while wobbling to avoid giving away any clues. Because clues just complicate communication.

This ocean of meaning gives rise to some minor ambiguities in social interactions. My favourite dubious history of the head bobble was put forward by an Indian management consultant:

For well over 400 years, Indians were ruled by the British Empire and before that it was all monarchy. And people were afraid of saying no as an answer…

Is it a yes or a no? You decide. One TEDtalker has called the head bobble the archetype of Indian recognition of 'the power of subjective truth in decisionmaking'. That is to say,

Indians, as my (Indian) friend generalised wildly, hate to say no. Is the hat shop that way? Yes, madamji, if you want it to be that way. Do you still have train tickets left? All truth is relative, madamji, and we are but motes of dust in the timeless eye of the Universe. Not for nothing does the waggling movement resemble ∞, the eternal loop of infinity.

What I'm trying to say is that the head bobble is a cunning and sublimely useful manoeuvre: imagine its potency when deployed against an unfairly nosy supervisor or when caught indulging in some light bigamy. I am frankly amazed that (British) English hasn't already stolen and trademarked it. Americans might think straight talkin' is a virtue, but every Britisher knows that this is a misconception characteristic of a nation with too much roadkill and not enough doilies. A Chicago-born friend was recently horrified to discover that 'very interesting' in British English actually means 'perfectly blithering, you gormless old berk'. The head bobble shows equal sensitivity to the relationship between hierarchy and honesty.

You too can become fluent in the bobble. Imagine your head is ludicrously gigantic, like that of a Thunderbirds doll or James van der Beek. Keep your face entirely expressionless (resigned eye-closing optional): we're talking reluctant subordinate 'tude here, not African-American diva. Relax your neck and dip your left ear precisely 15° and then precisely 15° for the right ear. Repeat smoothly for several minutes. Practise in all social situations for the rest of your life.

12

STOMACHS

Of course reading and thinking are important but, my God, food is important too.

—Iris Murdoch, *The Sea, The Sea*

YOU MUST COME TO OUR PLACE FOR DINNER. The text came out of the blue, from a newly discovered cousin of unknown genetic proximity. I wrote back instantly: of course, delighted, where & when.

Then I turned and examined the condition of my younger sibling. He was lying facedown with his head in a bucket.

Three years younger and eight inches taller than me, Feckless Brother had very sweetly wangled his way into our parents' pockets and come to visit. He now sells wine for a living in a much-maligned part of southern England, where everyone is small and tangerine, and had never travelled anywhere before that didn't sell full English breakfasts on every corner. He also looks much more Indian than I do. In Delhi this proved confusing to everyone, most of all him, and led a creepy number of people to assume we were married. Nonetheless, for the first few days he had coped admirably.

My phone rang. It was the Mothership, who never called. 'Your brother says he's wasting away.'

Yes: the only problem was feeding the poor wee mite. Feckless Brother is one of life's natural Atkins Dieters. In Britain his usual meals consist almost entirely of pigs-in-blankets, an obscenely fleshy dish of sausages wrapped in bacon. Sadly for him, he was staying with a sadistic vegetarian in a primarily vegetarian country. For a couple of days he managed to restrain the carnivorous urges, although with much cursing and complaining.

At last he cracked, at the worst possible moment.

We took a bus out of the malevolent bubble of Delhi heat and headed a little northeast. After a painful juddering night on wheels, we arrived at some low hills near the hill station of Nainital. There by Naukuchiatal, the Lake with Nine Corners, we were to spend a couple of days at a music festival, complete with floppy-haired high-kicking boyband, turbaned rock guitarists, and Lou Majaw, an obsessive sexagenerian Bob Dylan devotee from Shillong, who wore long silver hair and Daisy Dukes.

If you manage to look at all nine corners of the lake at once, you vanish in a puff of enlightened smoke. It was a lovely spot, all red soil and surprisingly puffy trees and little thatched storage huts. The sky was cool, at least in comparison with Delhi, and unbroken except for the odd paraglider and staccato flutter of tuning instruments. Beside the lake a rusting green sign appealed:

> I smile when you smile at me
> I feel you touch my waters…
> But I hurt so much
> When my shores are scattered with your litter
> AND NOW
> I, your Darling The Lake
> LOOK UGLY

The festival was quiet. We set out to liven the place up with a misplaced sense of patriotism. We were merrily headbanging to a heavy-metal group, occasionally falling into a large hole in the ground just in front of the stage, when Feckless Brother suddenly stopped and drooped.

'I'm wasting away, I'm wasting away…'

I looked at his eyes, round and blurred as salami slices. He'd had a beer or two, and it was clear the bloodlust was raging. At a trot he set off towards the food stalls, sniffing the air. I followed.

The meat stall would have given the Borgias pause. It was deserted except for a vast number of obese flies, all busily feasting. Even the bored youngster manning it looked reluctant to touch his produce. But my brother thrust a clutch of rupees over the stained counter and seized a chicken leg. Holding it like a microphone, he tore in. It was a pleasant shade of salmonella pink. He looked guiltily over the bone.

The scythe of food poisoning struck four hours later, with clockwork predictability.

Delhi belly is an Indian rite of passage—so much so that Kipling owes another verse: 'If you can heave—and not spill out your innards…' Feckless Brother did not appreciate this attempt at consolation. So I will repress my verbal diarrhoea on the subject of sanitation, and spare you the details and him the burning cheeks. Suffice to say, as we buzzed at the door of our relatives' house he looked distinctly forlorn.

Cousin turned out to be a kind, impatient woman with sensible hair and two little daughters. Gifts dispensed—once again sweets had proved a bad idea; they were dieting—we all thronged around the sitting room. Feckless Brother gingerly seated himself, wincing. I perched on a hard bed and smiled at the two little girls. They shrank back silently with terrified rabbit eyes.

As Cousin disappeared into the recesses of the house, things got off to a bad start. 'Are you enjoying the school holidays?' I asked, sounding very English and a little too loud.

The two little girls burst out crying and hid.

Cousin re-entered at speed, bearing bowls. 'Here is food. You will like it. Amma has been *slaving* away *all* day preparing it for you with her own hands.' The grey-haired lady in the corner nodded vigorously.

India's cuisine—or rather cuisines, given its vast and delicious regional range—is more than a practical business of refuelling. It's more even than a concrete manifestation of culture. In India eating is *moral*. It has *consequences*. Particular people do and don't eat particular things, offer food to the gods and receive back the leftovers. Weddings are vast and elaborate multi-course feasts, sometimes for thousands of guests. On the other hand, there are strict traditional rules about who should and shouldn't share food: competitive and humiliating exclusions are the other side of generosity. And it is a vast and labour-intensive cuisine, requiring hours of (almost always female) effort, whilst the best morsels go to the men and boy-children.

This moral marination also means that India is probably the best country in the world to be a vegetarian. Vegetarianism is so common that you can relax knowing that there will be a number of delicious, varied options available as a matter of course. It would be suicide to serve pork to a Muslim or beef to most Hindus, so you are not likely to find your veggie dinner spiked with that well-known vegetable, ham, unlike in much of Europe. Many upper-caste Hindus, especially older women, are punctiliously vegetarian: no fish, no eggs. My only criticism is that 'wedge' restaurants tend to be rather pious and nonalcoholic, but otherwise India is my stomach's natural home. Joyous, joyous Veggiestan!

Not today, though. My stomach did a slow flip of social horror. Before me the bowlful of chicken curry glistened pleasingly, red and pocked. In true Anglo-Indian style, a pair of boiled eggs lolled in the sauce like eyeballs, ringed with a delicate layer of orange grease.

Feckless Brother had turned an ominous shade of yellow. 'I'm so sorry—I'm sick, I can't eat that. *Really* sick.'

'Nonsense,' Cousin said, '*nonsense*. I am a doctor, and there is nothing wrong with you. Now you *must* eat it or Amma will be so *very* disappointed. She worked *all day and night* with her *own hands*.' The old lady's eyes filled with tears, and she nodded so vigorously that her bracelets rattled.

My little brother emitted a gurgle.

I could see a couple of bits of bone, some sinew. It couldn't have looked more chickeny if it was wearing a feather boa. There was no way to pretend this was a plant. Perhaps there was a nearby plant pot or handbag I could secrete it in. I cast around—but the relatives were watching, militant pleasure giving way to a scowl as the seconds ticked on. If only the meat-and-two-veg reputation of the British hadn't tracked us here, five thousand miles away from England's overboiled grub.

Feckless Brother looked pleadingly at me with big brown Labrador eyes. I could hear the Mothership's phone voice echoing through my head, like a lady version of Alec Guinness: 'Protect your brother—he's only twenty-two and ever so delicate. Be a good big sister, and go to the Dark Side.'

I took a deep breath. Down went the meat, the delicious evil meat, and six years of vegetarianism. 'Mmmm…'

Cousin brightened. 'There is much more in the kitchen!'

Like our father, Feckless Brother returned from his Indian voyage only half the size he started at, and possibly harbouring a parasitic new friend. Rites of passage often include physical changes to mark your transition to adulthood: scars, tattoos, muscles, piercings, sensible haircuts, a new air of dignity. Yet against all the odds, each time I go to India I become fat.

There is a myth in the West that the entire developing world finds fat women attractive. Just as Botticelli's Venus proudly displays a bit of a tummy inside her medieval seashell, countries with major malnutrition problems are supposed to like voluptuous curves. Unfortunately for me, this is no longer true (apart from in the world of South Indian pornography, I hear, but this could be scurrilous gossip). Delhi has wealthy pockets enough to have begun the transition to an obesity epidemic, especially among the screen-loving middle classes. One 2012 study—admittedly sponsored by a cooking-oil maker, the rival of traditional ghee—found that three-quarters of Dilliwallas were overweight or obese. The city has correspondingly begun the transition to skinny girl love. My physical expansion was not socially acceptable.

Nor will Indians let you discreetly wallow in your newfound corpulence. It's not just foreigners who attract eyes: anyone even vaguely weird-looking or even vaguely female does. This is coupled with a famous nosiness—the classic 'how much do you earn?' quizzing—and a frankness hideous to British ears. 'Your personality grows larger every year!' a typically brutal Auntie said to a friend's cousin, by which she meant: 'Fattyboomboom, you are expanding at the same rate as Delhi.' I've eavesdropped on brutal conversations that basically went 'Woah, porky, lose the monobrow'. Equally when people say I 'look like a Punjabi', I slap them and burst into Bollywood tears. When this comes from anyone who isn't a Punjabi, it's unflattering. Our Bangalore landlady took to patting me on the cheek and saying joyfully, 'You are getting so fat!'

The newish and perhaps more ruthless idea of beauty comes

222

with natural consumerist bedfellows, of course. A stroll of the nearby malls saw shop assistants pounce on me with hunger in their eyes. 'You need a manicure, madam. And a haircut. And a good moisturizer. And a facial peel. And an eyebrow tweeze. And—' This is a generational shift: the Indian state is still dominated by comfortable paunches, straining under white shirts. But the pressure applies to both men and women.

As ever, Bollywood was ahead of the curve. Though earlier stars had already begun a trend for male cleavage, curls of hair licking out from low-cut shirts, in the early 1990s Shahrukh Khan could still be lean and boyish. Salman Khan ushered in a whole new era of exhibitionist ab shots and toplessness. Fluffy hair was out(ish), bad boys in wifebeaters were in. Never mind six-packs: the best of them have *eight*-packs. By the end of the decade SRK had muscles; even effigies of the god Ram were bulking up. The stars' exercise regimes are now discussed in India's vibrant and increasingly raunchy gossip magazines—Pilates, celebrity trainers, protein shakes, steroid abuse—and actresses' post-pregnancy weight gain is treated as a national scandal. India opened economically to the world, and the Hollywood physique swaggered in. Its neuroses scuttled in behind.

Gyms have sprouted over the country like muscular mushrooms in the last decade. Previously working out was a niche activity, largely confined to the macho wrestling of young male nationalists. Now it's aspirational. In our distant suburb of Bangalore in 2010, the brand-new local gym was proudly advertised on the local high street. Its proximity to Electronic City meant groups of IT workers graced it at odd hours, tubby and miserable in their shirts. Despite this, sign-in was manual, in a thick penciled ledger. My coworker Alicia and I were the first women to join, much to the undisguised creepy joy of certain older members. It was a novel experience, fiendishly humid, and prone to power cuts that hurled leg-pumping patrons from the suddenly stalled machines. But it was inspiring, too: soon other women could be seen trailing their saris dangerously over the treadmills.

Forget power cuts and sari workouts. Although local gyms dominated as late as 2008, Delhi now boasts an array of options, from the nostalgically cheap and sweaty to sleek multinationals. No mall is complete without a gleamingly expensive gym complex, priced like London. They have juice bars and Western soundtracks and rows of Apple desktops for checking your emails. Their clientele wear designer sports brands and play golf. India might still be plagued by malnutrition–one in every three malnourished children in the world lives in India, says Unicef—but Delhi does everything fast. Already, and in the face of endemic poverty, thinness is becoming a status symbol.

India looks unlikely to imitate California in all things. For all my physical disappointment, I have unwittingly got one asset that is unfairly overvalued: fair skin. Giant billboards displayed the pristine visages of Bollywood stars, male and female, in blatantly Photoshopped before and after shots. Buy the cream and you too can look, well, non-Indian. All the big brands are implicated. You can even buy whitening cream for the, ahem, intimate feminine areas, advertised with videos of husbands shunning wives until they bleach their unspeakables and happiness is restored.

Beyond this, ideas of beauty are very much conditioned by class and location. In the Bangalore suburbs my old boss was scandalized by my long wavy untied hair: 'It is not tidy! Why don't you tether it up? Then I think it will look'—he paused for sleazy effect—'*very* good.' Many women wear theirs tied back, oiling it sleek and straight. The city's elite women, though, proudly wear theirs au naturel, or rock bold short haircuts which would be attacked as 'childish' elsewhere in the country. In smaller towns good girls are unlikely ever to wear a short skirt. Even wearing jeans and a tight T-shirt is an emphatically middle-class statement. But Delhi's wealthiest young women—those who need never take public transport—shun baggy *shalwar kameez* combinations. They are more likely to be found in power suits, taking bikinis on their foreign holidays, and stalking Delhi's nightclubs in skimpy dresses and stilettos worthy of California's finest.

Unlike this last group, I had resolved to Keep It Real in Delhi. This came with some downsides. Food shopping in India is an exhausting experience. I am part of Europe's millennial lot, credited with a culture of narcissism, entitlement, flibbertigibbetism and, I might add, supermarket shopping. The old system of actually going to all the different vendors and sorting through their produce seemed to me a full-time job.

Option 1: I lay in a puddle of my own sweat, apathetically flicking through *Power Insider* or an equally rambunctious electricity magazine. Under the bawl of a jet overhead, there came a faint jingling clop. A pause, then: '*Sabzi!*' And a machine-gun rattle: '*Aloo lo, gajar lo, mattar lo, bhindi lo, kele lo!*' It was time.

I flicked open the blind. The sabziwala had parked his placid bony horse a little up the street. He whipped back the canvas for a fat suspicious woman to reveal his wares: the promised potatoes, carrots, peas, okra, bananas, and a few others. She poked and squeezed and prodded. The sabziwala's boy, who looked distinctly school-age, tossed handfuls of small onions into a small basket to weigh. The woman eyed him suspiciously, argued briefly, and handed over the money. She gathered up her enormous armful of vegetables, a small brown paper packet of chillis and coriander wedged on top, and waddled away.

Another everyday ritual: another minor challenge to overcome. Deep breath.

I threw on some ill-matched if suitably discreet clothing, stubbing my toe on an electricity textbook, and rushed downstairs. Out on the road, I looked at the vegetables with what I hoped appeared a professional eye. Most I recognized, some I didn't. I was sure the sabziwala and his boy exchanged glances. A curtain twitched.

For all its strengths in Stalin and Shakespeare, the British education system does not teach you to estimate weights. As a result I would either order four times too many carrots for the flat, or be left holding a single sad potato. Western education also is a little thin on haggling skills. I would find myself acquiring unneeded piles of ladies' fingers and, most foolishly, extravagant (but gorgeously juicy) mango purchases. Most mornings began with the faint bitter feeling I'd already been scammed six different ways, although probably at a combined cost of Rs 10.

The other shoppers checked and rechecked the prices rigorously. The city was filled with woeful tales of inflation. Rumours swirled: that onions were being hoarded to push up prices, that potatoes are going to Bangladesh, that the state allows half of all India's food to rot in warehouses. (Conspiracy theories are extremely popular in India. Alas, some of these food-based rumours may be true.) The government is very sensitive to this, fearing riots and demonstrations, and until very recently has tried to keep inflation under control even at the cost of growth.

Kamala arrived again in the evening with a clatter. I steeled myself and presented her with my vegetable purchases. She laughed throatily, picked up her ringing phone and chortled into it. She did manage to whip them into a simple but delicious meal. Our kitchen boasted only what looked like a temporary campstove to my eyes, but is in fact a common arrangement: a bench-top gas burner which ran on red dusty bottles of cooking gas. (The poor continue to use charcoal.)

Gradually I gained confidence and decided to experiment a bit more with my purchasing choices. Alas, I realized that perhaps some vegetables haven't broken out of the subcontinent for good reason. I reserve particular hatred for *karela*, bitter gourd. Karela looks like a wrinkled warty green dildo. Like many phenomenally nutritious foods, it tastes even worse, like watery earwax. Alpha Housemate demanded this on a regular basis, as (a) it's meant to be phenomenally nutritious and (b) there seems to be something uniquely masochistic about Bengali palates. In the fridge she would also store vials of a strange anti-diabetic home brew that looked terrifyingly like urine.

Option 2: I crossed the road to the local market, admittedly a poor specimen versus the larger neighbourhood bazaars. It was a sleepy two-layer collection of stores. Alongside an array of takeaway options, a barber's sign promised 'Rich Man Hair Cut'. A battered pharmacy with viciously short opening hours peddled piles of medication and vitamin pills. Out of the corner of my eye I could see our local 'English wine' shop, its grimy counter packed in the evenings and Fridays with men clamouring for tiny bottles of cheap desi spirits.

At random I selected one of the *kiranas*, the small convenience stores. The owner was a big man with a haughty moustache. The tiny store, about the size of an American walk-in wardrobe, nonetheless managed to sell a vast array of items, from shampoo to eggs to Nestlé's ubiquitous Maggi noodles ('this is a traditional Indian lunch!' my newfound cousin-brother told me, spooning them out). They were densely packed into the shelves, so that a young man had to scale boxes to reach the highest items. So far, so good: it was very convenient, had a decent range of goods, and appeared to employ at least ten relatives and hangers-on alongside the haughty moustache.

There was one major and growing obstacle to my *kirana* love, however: water. Rather than an expensive purifying pump, our flat relied on huge 25-litre canisters of water. We called the haughty moustache, who dispatched an impossibly skinny young man with the 25kg load upon his shoulder. Only the haughty moustache did not necessarily do this. The bottle would arrive an arbitrary number of hours, or days, after we'd made the call. We would appeal in person, parched and desperate, offering to roll the huge canister down the road ourselves. The moustache, stroked, looked haughtier and more Stalinist each time this took place. I'd known monopolists might raise the prices of scarce goods to cream off extra profits, but I hadn't realised they would take so much pleasure in it.

Option 3: I strolled down the road, waving off overpriced auto ride offers, to my local mall. This was a weird and depressing place, like a normal mall after a zombie apocalypse. Most of the lots stood empty. There was a KFC—the chicken chain and Pizza Hut, both owned by the same American corporation, can be found across the city—with a consistent reputation for food-poisoning my housemates. There was a Toyota showroom that never had any customers. And then there was Big Bazaar, sprawling over three floors.

India has been called supermarkets' final frontier. They are already beginning to conquer China and Latin America, but outside our quarter, a great political showdown was taking place in New Delhi. The government had promised to allow foreign firms into 'multi-brand retail', hitherto the preserve of the local. The prime minister and his allies argued foreign investment would reignite India's economic growth rates and counter inflation through improved food supply chains, claiming somewhat implausibly that farmers otherwise allow up to a third of their crop to rot in the fields. The opposition, and some key coalition partners, were raising a stink, backed by the 40 million Indians whose livelihoods depend on small stores. They in turn claimed the rise of supermarkets would drive up unemployment and exploit small farmers. The reform was eventually forced through in autumn 2012—after a year of wrangling—although it relies on the federal states to take it forward. Perhaps unsurprisingly, Delhi is keen.

After being searched and forced to leave my shopping bag with a guard, I set off inside. Big Bazaar, the 'Indian Walmart', is the largest supermarket chain so far in India. It sells toys, electronics, kitchenware, and dispiriting clothes. On the top floor I found the food: pasta, American brands of cereal, endless tins. Everything got piled into cheap cloth bags that left a strange ashy substance on my hands. If this is the future, I disapprove.

Periodically I took the more exciting **Option 4**, and ventured further afield to INA Market, a sprawling claustrophobic mass of stalls where everything is on sale. I came home with four tins of tuna covered in Arabic script, two cushions, and a seriously out-of-date jar of Marmite which bubbled alarmingly in the heat and then abruptly sealed itself, never to reopen.

Just over the road from INA Market, the paparazzi struck. Something about my face appeared to attract young journalists. I like to believe my eyes look wise but kindly, that even strangers recognize that they flow with wit, profundity and carefully curated insights about India. Or maybe I just walk less purposefully than other passing women.

I'd already been interviewed twice. Admittedly I never knew whether they'd actually been broadcast, but I believed they'd gone well. The first was on the future of gas pipelines, the second on what I assured the interviewer was the wonderful flowering of Indian rugby. Now in the regulated souvenir market of Dilli Haat the greatest intellectual challenge arrived—the moment when my knowledge of Indian food, that pillar of Delhi life, was put to the test. Very publicly.

'Madam, can we interview you?'

Alongside its carefully arranged handicraft stalls, Dilli Haat also periodically hosts small events and conventions. Early in my trip I had gone to 'Comic Con', to find various Batmen, Darth Vaders &c. under a giant poster of a formidable woman with a bindi and round Harry Potter spectacles, who is perhaps called Superauntie. Now I stumbled into an exhibition of fruits and nuts from all over India, centred on the national fruit, the mango. A local TV crew, who seemed to be student journalists, was gathering responses on this breaking news.

It was unclear why exactly they would want to interview someone from a country where the sum total of mango knowledge is that (1) they exist and (2) they are vulnerable to use as a comic euphemism. I still don't know why I said yes.

The cameras whirred. The young interviewer pounced, eyes glittering under a thick layer of kohl. It was investigative journalism at its best. 'What is your preferred variety of mango? How do these compare to the mangos of our international mango rivals? Which Indian state's mango policy do you believe has been most successful in rejuvenating agriculture, that great neglected bastion of the Indian masses to which in the end all our futures are tied?'

'I like… those orangey-green ones. You know, those sort of round ones. About this big. Um. Orange.'

The whirring stopped. They left, shaking their heads.

Like most gluttons, my geography is mapped in hunger. And boy had I come to the right place. Wealthy Dilliwallas—at least those not on a diet—seem to navigate the way I do. Their monuments are kebab stalls, their boulevards lined with laddoos. And Delhi, once a culinary backwater, has become a foodie's city. It's a whole culinary universe, expanding fast just like our own.

You can stumble to its old centres of gravity, now left darkened and shrunken like dying stars, or to strange outposts of other culinary cultures. Here you may find some of the most celebrated of Delhi's food. The positive side of the not-entirely-coerced end of my vegetarianism was that I got to try it. In fact, I decided to introduce a clause in my vegetarianism that seems to annoy carnivores far more than even the most zealous vegan: the 'When in Rome Do As the Romans Do' clause (optional: the vomitarium, inappropriately timed imperial fiddling, sodomy).

The Red Fort is one of the world's more discouraging

heritage sites, because its earlier opulence is not in doubt. Built for the great emperor Shah Jahan as the palace of his new capital, it has seen better days. The British used it to garrison troops, and it has never really recovered. It still boasts corners of opulence and beauty, and hosts India's Independence Day celebrations on 15 August. But now the complex is faded with too much sun and exposure, unable to compete with the better-preserved examples at Fatehpur Sikri and Agra.

A short hop away, the candy-cane-coloured Jama Masjid retains the magnificence of its sheer scale. With Feckless Brother's presence to guarantee I wouldn't become lustfully overwhelmed by its phallic shape I was finally able to ascend one of its minarets. The view was spectacular: the pigeon-flecked grey petals of the mosque's domes, the motley orange and blue and brown of Old Delhi opened up like a tablecloth, fading to a musty horizon.

In the Masjid's shadow Feckless Brother and I gorged ourselves on Old Delhi's famous food: thick greasy parathas, melt-in-the-mouth kebabs, and Mughal curries swimming in ghee, all wonderfully, illicitly meaty. Around us the streets were dark and loud. The great thoroughfare of Chandni Chowk was once a 'moonlit square', the nighttime glow of its canals—now long gone—reflecting the glory of its lavish *haveli* mansions and silver (*chandi*) merchants.

Today many areas in the walled city of Shahjahanabad have been designated slums. Tourists persevere, even when many richer Dilliwallas have given up visiting except to have wedding outfits copied. It's the sort of place that says 'You want authenticity? I'll give you goddamn authenticity. Have some spleen, and giardia.' One of my housemates *literally* cycled over a bleeding heart on one of its side-streets.

South Indian food may be the best of all. Breakfast: take a wee pot of spicy sambar broth. Dip *vada*, crisp savoury lentil doughnuts, or swap them for the healthier *idli*, white flabby dimpled discs that soak up the soup (though Auntie used to feed me six, rather than the usual couple). Or try dosas, pancakes left to ferment overnight and served with coconut chutney, as long as my arm. Back in Oxford I mourn the fact that the United States nabbed most South Indian migrants, and their grub.

But fear not: Delhi's tastes are far from parochial. You can blow your ill-gotten rupees on dim sum, sushi and Italian fare with equal ease. In the big hotels and South Delhi's lavishly appointed restaurants, Sunday brunch is multi-cuisine, many-dollared, cocktail-spattered affairs, full of bright young things and glamorous couples and awful children bullying their nannies (who are not permitted to eat). 'Asian fusion', that mysterious concept, is popular too. Delhi is plugged into to all the great international fads: bubble tea, frozen yoghurt; you can even get your hands on a cronut, the bastard offspring of croissant and doughnut.

Hey, you might even be able to get hold of beef. Hindu respect for cows is legendary. (Recognizing this, the British Council has gone so far as to paint its Indo-friendly building with the black-on-white patches of a Friesian heifer.) Cow slaughter is banned in several Indian states, including Delhi, more or less. The infrequent beef of Delhi is killed on legal technicalities, sneakily imported—or more often substituted with 'buff', the less controversial water buffalo meat (and a little chewy but OK to my turncoat vegetarian tongue).

This is a universe best experienced through your hands. There is nothing more sensual than eating with your fingers. Suddenly food is three-dimensional, a mass of textures and caresses, squishes and slickness. I could feel every arc and whorl of my fingertips embracing it. For someone brought up under the tyranny of silverware, it's another illicit thrill. Try it. First, wash your hands. The restaurant might not have soap, but this modicum of hygiene is the reason why India's population numbered in the hundreds of millions while Europeans were still sewing themselves into rotting furs for the winter. Take your right hand (your left does unspeakable things). Playing with your food is positively encouraged: mix rice and wetness through with your hand, until you can form it into pellets. Form the fingers into a shovel, and scoop. Flick the food with your thumb into your waiting maw. Do not insert your fist.

Now all you need is good company, and something to wash all that deliciousness down.

13

LIVERS

What's the use of a great city having temptations if fellows don't yield to them? Makes it so bally discouraging for the great city.

—P.G. Wodehouse, *Carry On, Jeeves*

*F*ieldwork, that swirl of boredom and panic, is a thirsty business. On this front I discovered my new home was both a blessing and a curse. Delhi today is a city of gin.

Academia has its own version of the intrepid explorer: the old-fashioned anthropologist. He's a more scientifically minded version of Indiana Jones—in fact, Susan Sontag actually called the species 'the heroic anthropologist'. Wielding his notebook, he is a fearless martyr to the cause. He is utterly committed to documenting the Truth, monk-like in his self-control.

More recently, anthropologists have belatedly conceded that

they, too, are people. But still the good anthropologist is meant to be above ordinary mortal temptation. In my pale map-lined room before Delhi, I read solemn paragraphs about this and nodded wisely. The good anthropologist eschews fear and lust, tolerates discomfort without a murmur, and spends the evenings writing fiendishly detailed field notes. She certainly does not accidentally schedule interviews for ice bars, or spill beer all over the field diary.

Unfortunately for my aspirations, Feckless Brother brought with him a litre of good Scotch. It was a big peaty devil from Islay, an island as empty and sodden as Delhi is dense. Fittingly, whiskey brings together the two sides of my family history. The Mothership's grandfather was an exciseman who marched sternly between Scotland's famous distillery sites, from Islay to Knockando to Aberlour. Now India is the world's largest whiskey market: *The Economist* reports that Indians drink almost as much of it as the rest of the world put together. It makes a good gift for professional men, with Indian drinkers favouring spirits over beer or wine. Big international brands like Johnny Walker are popular with the rich, who flash it about at posh social gatherings. Most of the stuff drunk is not Scottish, though, but much sweeter Indian varieties. Many are produced from molasses rather than malted barley; purists dismiss them as mere rum. They still have hearty Scottish-sounding names—Royal Stag, Bagpiper, McDowell's, Imperial Blue.

Indians aren't big drinkers on average. Early on I stumbled into a pub quiz, an über-British tradition given a viciously competitive Indian twist: the whole thing was like a gameshow, with one team in the public spotlight at a time. I remember looking disconsolately at the tiny glass handed to me: '*This* is a pint?' In Britain the pint—or to use its awkward full name, the *imperial* pint—is 568 ml. This looked about two-thirds of that. Not girly enough to be a half-pint, not as satisfyingly diuretic as the real deal. (Whiskey, meanwhile, comes in a mysterious old measure called a 'peg'.)

I could have done with something more substantial. Humiliatingly, *all* the questions seemed to be on Britain. 'Which popular British sitcom contained the catchphrase "Good moaning"? What is the name of the Duchess of Cambridge's puppy? Who was the first male voice of the UK's Speaking Clock?'

I felt all the eyes on me, and scored a resounding zero points. Unsurprisingly, the prize money was won by a bespectacled group from IIT, the prestigious Indian Institute of Technology. They weren't drinking.

Traditionally, religious and caste norms discouraged alcohol consumption. Islam formally proscribes it, while Hindu Brahmins are similarly deterred by classical texts. Gandhi was a staunch opponent of drinking; this survives in the strict prohibition in his home state of Gujarat.

This is slowly changing. Legal drinking ages are barely enforced, and elite youths are beginning to drink ever earlier in life. While the provinces suffer from the effects of toxic illegal hooch, Delhi is full of drunk drivers. Female drinkers are particularly stigmatized in much of India, and the vast majority of Indian women are what the World Health Organization calls 'lifetime abstainers'. In Delhi, though, wealthier women and students emerge to drink and dance. Some clubs even have

'Ladies' Nights' in order to try to improve the gender ratio.

This novel booziness is fuelled by big brands. The state monopolies inherited from the colonial regime have given way in much of the country to the triumph of the market. Most forms of alcohol advertising are banned. But the big liquor companies have proved themselves capable of beating the threat of the traditional liquor lobby and surviving foreign competition—a pesky little law isn't going to stop them. They sponsor sports events and awards, extend the brand through new products like mineral water, and use word-of-mouth and internet marketing. Bollywood stars on and offscreen knock the hard stuff back. The government largely tolerates this. After all, alcohol taxes and licences are a useful source of revenue for them too.

Feckless Brother's Scotch was dark and tasted of fishing boats, even at blood temperature. The liquid's level moved steadily down night after night—well, it hardly seemed sensible to cart it all the way home. I could generously give the empty to Kamala: the prestigious bottles are refilled with cheaper stuff and resold. And a dose of self-abuse is all part of the romance of the travel experience. The less wholesome expats through the ages have had a tendency to pickle themselves in alcohol. Just look at the seductive list of wandering authors who turned whiskey priest: Mark Twain, Lord Byron, James Joyce, Graham Greene, F. Scott Fitzgerald, Truman Capote, Ernest Hemingway, Jack Kerouac and, er, Winston Churchill.

Delhi evenings are intoxicating in any case. Night falls with tropical speed, dropping a shutter over the city. It is an ambivalent darkness, simultaneously threatening and tempting. The city's geography shifts subtly. At dusk the polite world strolls around the grand blocky hoop of India Gate, a war memorial made oddly festive, families eating and posing before suddenly vanishing back to their quiet suburbs. The grand embassy-lined avenues of Chanakyapuri, empty at the best of times, become a vacuum. Elsewhere everything is flashing neon promises in pools of black.

As ever, I had evening plans. Delhi is an intensely sociable city and anyway, being away from home forces you into good behaviour around strangers. So many people, Indian and non-, can't guarantee how long they'll stay here before they move on to better jobs in Bangalore, Bombay, Singapore, London. Everything is always in a gentle state of social ferment—you've got to keep your complement of friends up.

Tonight would be a particularly sociable night.

Back in Blightistan, I'm more slumdog than millionaire. My potential career options (academia? international development?) have been strongly influenced by the fact that being badly dressed is part of the uniform—gown, fermented tweed, sola topi. Yet one febrile May night I found myself trying to extract a semblance of civility—nay, glamour—from my dusty wardrobe.

Alpha Housemate had temporarily unplugged herself from her *Matrix*-like symbiotic relationship with *Sex and the City* reruns, and snared us tickets to a 'fashion-show-cum-IPL afterparty'. A designer friend of hers, an improbably leggy ex-model in Dame Edna glasses, was featuring. In attendance would also be—I quote—'hunks'. I refused, started to warm up to the idea, found our companion would be a blonde Russian model, and refused again. Still, I was tempted.

'Alpha, I'll see you there,' I said, twitching the blinds. (It felt wonderfully like espionage. I could see why the downstairs neighbour liked it so much.) Time to head off out into the night.

The streets outside lay deserted. Vasant Kunj suddenly shed its hum of traffic, except for the odd uniformed taxi driver drinking in the back of his car. The street was almost unlit, leaving pools of black frustrating for the female night owl. Faces reared suddenly out of the gloom.

Dogs prowled, tails up, the females with rows of teats nearly to the floor. Instantly my hackles rose. India has tens of millions of strays, Delhi alone probably quarter of a million, and they often travel in packs. The country has a strong animal welfare lobby, so New Delhi has resorted to sterilizing them—slowly. The world's first rabid dog was probably Indian; tens of thousands of Dilliwallas are bitten every year. I debated throwing my useless smartphone at them if they attacked. Luckily on the corner Fortis Hospital glowed like an ocean liner at night, all crisp white lines and corporate rude health.

Across the world darkness has traditionally meant danger, a time of violence, chaos and nightmares. Doors locked and bolted, the good people are all tucked up in bed, asleep and dreaming of filling in their tax returns. God has put his feet up to watch Netflix: as Jesus said, 'But if a man walk in the night, he stumbleth, because there is no light in him.' The bad people are loose.

As dusk fell I felt increasingly unsettled, even more conscious of being female. Women virtually disappeared from most streets: 96 percent say they don't feel safe in Delhi after sunset. Throngs of young men emerged. The city, already overtly masculine, became an unashamed boys' playground.

There are so many joys of city life that are next to impossible for a woman in Delhi (and might even give some men pause for thought). London's night was documented on foot by an insomniac Charles Dickens; Gladstone paced the same dark streets rescuing prostitutes; Teju Cole narrates similar nocturnal wanderings in post-9/11 New York City. It's addictive, seeing a city's dark side. But night walking was, or felt, too dangerous even for me to really contemplate (just as it does in some areas of London, admittedly). Sometimes I did explore alone—don't tell my family—walking to auto stands and being motored buzzily around the city. In the half-deserted muttering streets I would be on high alert, keys sticking out between my fingers like a budget knuckleduster and mentally unspooling horror films at high speed.

But darkness means much else too: leisure, revelry, rule breaking. In the nineteenth century Dickens contemplated 'the restlessness of a great city, and the way in which it tumbles and tosses before it can get to sleep'. Even more so, today's global cities are meant to be 24-hour affairs, so aggressively confident that they can take on the night. This is one of my favourite parts of the adventure. Oxford is a crusty old man of a town, a teatime city. Its watering holes stand out for the high quality of their toilet graffiti and the pleasant laxative effect of their many murky ales rather than their all-night frolics. It's virtually asleep by 11 pm.

Delhi, by contrast, is a *proper* city. It certainly has its share of nocturnal action. It begins to ebb earlier than many European cities, but fantastically outperforms several other Indian competitors. We were unable to properly celebrate our toilet conclusions in Bangalore, India's self-proclaimed 'Silicon Valley', because Hindu nationalist violence had compelled an 11.30 pm closing time. (Dancing was also banned between 2008 and 2011.) A fellow fieldworker described nice university girls in Chennai going out clubbing in the afternoon to be home in time for their 7 pm curfews. Compared with this, Delhi is *jhakaas*.

So it was with defiant excitement, and just a tinge of fear that I went out into the darkness. As wary and night-loving as a cat. Squinting into the blackness for an auto, arms waving frantically, heart beating just a little fast. A driver pulled up, only to utter the twilight curse: 'Madam, night charge.'

Like a good researcher I'd done my cricket homework in advance of the afterparty, sort of. Early one morning, before the dome of heat had sealed the sky, I visited Feroz Shah Kotla, ruined fortress of the fourteenth-century Muslim sultan Feroz Shah Tughlaq. As ever, the driver had only the most approximate conception of the fort's location, and kindly offered to take me to an arbitrary second location instead, but using call-and-response we gradually homed in on the fort, off a large newspaper office-lined street to the east of Connaught Place. The tour group was waiting—Delhi has any number of excellent historical walking tours, perfect for scholarly timepass.

'Keep quiet,' my friend hissed as we passed the ticket booth. I belatedly realized I had been mistaken for an Indian, for the first and only time. 'They must have thought you were a Punjabi.'

I scowled, white liberal guilt forgotten.

Above us inky showers of birds periodically spattered against a sky the colour of an old manuscript. The fort was dishevelled but still recognizable, a crumbling mass of squat formations and domes in misshaped orange and grey stones. Sections seemed decapitated wholesale, a couple of feet from the ground. A clay-coloured dog watched from the fragments of a wall. It was mirrored by a couple of guards in sky-blue shirts and berets and shiny high belt buckles, twitching bored moustaches. The lawns still retained faded patches of their spring green, and the bushes flowered pink. Below the fort the industrial east unfurled; bridges, eyeless concrete, the cigarette-shaped towers of power plants along the river's edge.

The highlight of the fort's remains is its Ashoka pillar, a thirteen-metre-high polished sandstone phallus set atop a three-tired crumbly pyramid. It is over two millennia old, though it has not always belonged to Delhi: in the fourteenth century Feroz Shah Tughlaq appears to have had it lowered on a bed of silk, and dragged hundreds of miles to his capital. It still bears the worn letters of the emperor Ashoka's edicts, in a surprisingly open and curvaceous script. They proclaim an iconic message of Buddhist virtue and tolerance, plus a smattering of detail about taxation. Ashoka, a great conqueror too, is still celebrated for this message.

In the fort's dark recesses, under its squat arches, are discreet signs of worship—petals, a few messages. Genies or djinns lurk here.

A little further down the road was another place of worship: the cricket stadium. Named after the fort and now far more famous, it is the home ground of the Delhi Daredevils, in celebration of whom the fashion-show-cum-afterparty was being held. From djinn to gin.

The C-word is the one conversational topic that almost never fails—I just wish I knew something about it. 'Cricket,' the postcolonial critic Ashis Nandy wrote, 'is an Indian game accidentally discovered by the English.' It inspires at least as much passionate devotion as religion. It should be a conversational gift: I am from Yorkshire, itself a place with a proud cricketing tradition. (Cricket has made Indian geography strange: the common man is more likely to have heard of New Zealand than Argentina, simply because of the Kiwis' love of balls.) When Indian fans learn my birthplace their eyes light up. 'Ah, Geoff Boycott! Do the accent.'

Cricket was a colonial import—the ICC was formerly known as the Imperial Cricket Council—and former British colonies continue to dominate. But the game's centre of gravity has gradually moved towards the subcontinent and its enormous cricket-watching populations. Advertisers now rely on good performances by India and Pakistan to boost World Cup profits. The two are deadly sporting enemies: as relations deteriorated in the 1990s cricket became 'war minus the shooting'. Indian cricket took on a shrill chauvinist new edge, to the extent that recently deceased Hindu extremist Bal Thackeray said, 'It is the duty of Indian Muslims to prove they are not Pakistanis. I want to see them with tears in their eyes every time India loses to Pakistan.' Conversely, 'cricket diplomacy' has often been used to calm bilateral relations at moments of high tension, somewhat hampered by the current prime minister's immovable face.

Since 2008, India has revolutionized the game with the Indian Premier League, a fast-paced combination of sport and entertainment. It is sodden with money. Models and celebrity owners, most famously Bollywood star Shahrukh Khan, watch the world's leading players compete, some defying national call-ups to play. The ten-year television rights were eventually (re)sold for US$1.6 billion, and advertisers hurled money at the franchise; in 2010 IPL players were the second-highest-paid athletes in the world after America's strike-prone National Basketball Association. Victory in the 2011 World Cup, with a thrilling semifinal defeat of Pakistan, boosted India's claim to be the world's new cricketing superpower—and certainly its financial capital.

This commercialization was controversial, however: a Communist Party spokesman called the decision to auction off players the 'death knell' of the gentleman's game. The dedication of some non-Indian players has been questioned—are 'white men in India just for the money'?— and viewer figures have fallen since the heights of the first three tournaments; the opportunistic trading of players each season undermines fan loyalty. The gentleman's game with its puritanical morality risks falling into disrepute with a series of corruption and spot-fixing scandals. In 2000 each one-day international attracted an estimated US$227 million in (illegal) Indian bets: the subcontinent also lies at the heart of cricket's murkier geography.

The fashion-show-cum-afterparty, hosted at a luxury hotel, therefore whispered of illicit thrills. To preserve the social order the tickets turned out to require that we (a) travelled in couples and (b) gave up all our personal details and Facebook access to the sponsor—which, inevitably, was a whiskey offshoot of the United Breweries empire, which also produces India's largest-selling beer, Kingfisher. Even after several months of exposure I couldn't tell if I liked the beer. The taste was OK, especially the dark 'Strong' brew. But it gave me awful hangovers almost instantaneously. Apparently it's the preservatives: I met a bunch of Irishmen who swiftly upended every bottle into a glass of water to counter this. The glycerine floated out, shimmering innocently.

The Kingfisher brand has taken surrogate advertising to a whole new level. Its billionaire chairman, Vijay Mallya, took it upon himself to embody the beer's slogan and proclaimed himself 'the King of Good Times'. He is of course also an independent MP in India's upper house. A swanky new complex in Bangalore, complete with helipad and sky-grazing bars, is named 'UB City' after the brewery, shrugging off the failure of Kingfisher Airlines, perhaps the most dramatic effort to surmount advertising restrictions. Mallya even snapped up an India Premier League cricket team himself and named it after one of UB's whiskey brands. Yet even the might of UB has not been sufficient to break Bangalore's early closing times. The elite might sip in comfort in India's 'pub city', but other more demagogic groups wield power outside the bars.

It was one of the more surreal chunks of my fieldwork. At the hotel door I quickly honey-trapped a nice young man into handing over his details to the brewery. A security scanner or two later and we were inside, facing a huge food table and trying to look as though we did this all the time.

The young man's phone flashed: the whiskey had taken over his identity on Facebook.

Alas, we were distracted from the freebies by the entry of some bored bristly-faced blokes: the Delhi Daredevils. 'That's ⚕☾⚥⚜☼!' exclaimed someone. The small crowd surged, a mixture of eyelash-fluttering girls and distinctly unsporty boys, expensive camera phones flashing at all angles.

At one side I spotted England batsman Kevin Pietersen, just about the only cricket player I could pick out of a lineup. He was looking even more unimpressed than usual, skunk hair scuffed. This seemed a bit rich given he was ending his stint as the IPL's most expensive player, reportedly earning over US$1 million for a month's work.

As I was picking pensively at the buffet, my ever-resourceful Nepali friend grabbed my hand. 'Quick!'

She dragged me towards the ladies' toilets at high speed. I feared a biological emergency, but once inside she nudged me and wiggled her eyebrows. A very tall pale woman was retouching her hair with deliberate slowness.

The Nepali nudged me again, harder. 'That's whatshername!

From *Rock Star*! Quick, click a photo.' She thrust herself forward at the exhausted smile of the Bollywood actress, who teetered at least a foot above us in murderous heels. Feeling a little stalkerish, I pulled out my phone, trying to dodge the toilet bowls.

Outside, the show began with a spurt of violent lighting. A couple of oiled shirtless chaps with pectorals like unripe yellow Alphonsos shuffled sheepishly down the runway. Every now and then a female model stalked through wearing an expensive skirt made of teatowels and glared at the indifferent crowd. All proceeds to charity.

I hiccuped happily.

Next came the walking confirmation that the IPL is the heir of American sporting traditions: a cheerleading troupe. Called 'White Mischief', it appeared to be composed of women from the former Soviet bloc in heavy tangerine makeup, the same group often associated with high-end prostitution. The IPL players perked up.

By this point we had well and truly sampled the delights of India's vineyards. The dancing began—alas, only for us, and with an attempt to dive into the VIP section. We managed precisely 24 glorious seconds of dancing with the beautiful people before the muscular security guards threw us back into the prole pen.

Finally, we danced with a bona fide dwarf. Just how I'd shoehorn this into my PhD I wasn't sure, but boy was I going to try.

Never fear: paddling in the murky pond of nighttime Delhi, every now and then I accidentally swallowed some Culture. The upmarket Delhi bars boasted Indo-Iranian fusion, sweaty house music, Congolese jamming, even a bad Serge Gainsbourg tribute band. But elite Delhi seemed to have another mission besides keeping up with the latest international fads/deceased French sleazebags: to reinvent Indian culture for the international stage.

Delhi may be developing the flashy nightlife of a megacity, but India is ambivalent about it. Alcohol, nightclubs and skimpily clad cheerleaders are immoral, the argument goes; they are not authentically Indian. Pressure from traditionalists and Hindu conservatives explains Bangalore's early closing times and the 2006 ban on Bombay's famous dance bars. The night, and especially the problem of women within it, is a key battleground for the conflict between 'Indian tradition' and Westernized world city. Far better to stay at home, or to embrace instead a pristine classical Culture.

There are many areas of Delhi where the line between rural and urban feels blurred. Pigs roam the roadsides, dairy farms line the Yamuna river, and small farms encircle the city's densely urban core; their vegetables and flowers make it to Old Delhi's Chandni Chowk and North Delhi's Azadpur Sabzi Mandi. Middle-class entrepreneurs have got into the act as organic vegetable retailers, while the coupon website Groupon crashed under heavy traffic after it offered discounted onions.

But South Delhi's 'farmhouses', though legally they are meant to be agricultural, have little of the farm about them. They are like fairytale woods, containing both the most surreally artsy of Delhi life and some of its most wolfish edges. The lanes of Chhattarpur and Ghitorni are quiet and green-lined. Privacy is all: the houses have guards, high walls, metal gates, chauffeured SUVs and CCTV cameras; their grounds and swimming pools are visible only on Google Earth (if you squint). US$50,000 might secure you one to host a wedding. Every now and then one of the capital's shadier success stories will be embroiled in a gunfight on such isolated properties.

Other farmhouses have begun to reinvent themselves as patrons of the arts. Surrounded by all burbling brooks and art-loving insects, I goggled at classical dances from across India. From North India, *Kathak*, a mixture of temple and Mughal court styles, which saw the dancers whirl like sobered-up dervishes. From eastern India, *Odissi*, a 2,000-year-old style that built from a sedate start to a frantic climax of vermillion-coated stomps, associated with *gotipuas*, young dancing boys who dressed as girls. From Kerala, *Mohiniyattam*, Vishnu's 'dance of the enchantress', a frankly deranged mix of swooping arm movements and clownish facial expressions; and *Kathakali*, a tourist-friendly and drum-heavy flourish with a green-painted all-male cast. From its neighbour Tamil Nadu, the famous *Bharatanatyam*, a flouncy genitalia-obsessed Tamil style set to fluttering beats and syncopated religious chants; it was traditionally performed by *devadasis*, girls who were 'married' off to deities and frequently ended up as high-end temple prostitutes.

To say Indian classical culture is enjoying a resurgence might be going too far—but Bollywood hits have not entirely vanquished their ancestors. Instead musical fusion, beat-heavy updates and elite evenings ensure it remains another resource for cultural pride. Washed down with *masala chai* in artfully traditional clay pots, of course, not Kingfisher. Such internationally recognizable cultural symbols—Bharatanatyam, sufi music, yoga—are 'the software of their country's soft power', the *Times of India* argued in 2009.

Later that week I headed off again to gobble up culture— but in the polar opposite setting, a multi-faith mix that has yet to be fully disciplined and packaged up.

Nizamuddin is one of Delhi's more schizophrenic neighbourhoods. It is named after the great Sufi saint Nizamuddin Auliya, and simultaneously manages to host a urine-tinged railway station, a rather covetable residential area, and a series of grubby chattering alleys of staring eyes and pirate DVDs; I winced as I took off my shoes. At the end of these alleys is the saint's shrine, and a host of other tombs—including that of Inayat Khan, bearer of Sufism to London and the father of a glamorous British spy.

Sufism is a mystical, ascetic brand of Islam, which over the centuries fused bits and bobs of magic and other devotional traditions with Quranic meditation—to the extent that 'un-Islamic' Sufi shrines are frequent targets for suicide bombings in Pakistan today. It welcomes all faiths; people of all religions visit to pray for favours.

Nizamuddin's Chishti order preached the power of music to bring believers closer to God. It it is for these hymns of devotion and remembrance, the sacred qawwalis, that clumps of tourists join the barefoot praying crowds. The *dargah* is an oddly welcoming mausoleum, an onion-domed and pillared shelter for the coloured tomb inside.

Two harmonium players struck up a dirge, two tabla players drummed, and another two joined in as they began to sing, a high throaty tremble. It was gritty rather than melodious, but oddly gripping—especially because the musicians were like a boyband inverted in a funhouse mirror, a motley collection of snouty, battered men with gnarled mouths dripping lurid red paan-juice onto the tiles. The music began to build with a clatter of tabla and a collective howl.

This evening, alas, devotees didn't fall into a trance and whirl like the famous Sufi dervishes. Fat drops of rain began to pelt the musicians. A rather impressive stripey roof whirred down—but alas, there was a tear just above the most senior wailer and the wads of devotional rupees were getting wet. God was packed up with the harmonium case for another day.

As a prophylactic measure against all that culture—it's terribly distracting for one's research—I turned from djinn to gin again. The months were getting on, and I was suddenly slightly homesick for the pub. I found myself sitting in another bar, in one of the 'toniest' parts of town (a slang borrowing from nineteenth-century America).

Only two miles from Nizamuddin Dargah, Khan Market is an odd area, a U-shaped crack between dust and globalization. It lies ensconced within a sprawling hush of bungalows, nameplates at the entrance discreetly announcing the presence of 'VVIPs'. The curved alleys are not immune to the syndrome afflicting most Indian streets—cracked pavements, sleeping dogs—and they seem to sweat, full of hot gusts and unsettling drips from AC units. But with typical perversity these alleys make up Delhi's most expensive shopping real estate, twenty-first dearest in the world. The crowd is rich, glossy, heavy on expats and Ladies Who Lunch. The shops cater to their whims: artisanal baguettes, big brands, caustic Anglophone non-fiction, canine treats, organic bruschetta. Every now and then I window-shopped, ogling European cheeses and insanely priced cushions.

I lingered over my not-quite-pint. As usual, the AC ethos was more is more: it was gooseflesh-cold. A fog of torpid American indie music descended.

Wherever there are bars and girls, there are guys talking big. A pause in conversation and *swoosh!* In swooped a white knight.

Lean, with cockroach-coloured hair, he had been all but waving at me from two tables over. I'd tried to dodge his gaze, but it was like trying to avoid a pair of black holes. He was one of those men who doesn't stare out of idle timepass habit, but out of an unshakable conviction that the ladies want to catch his eye.

His opening gambit was strong. 'You're from UK.'

'Well observed, my good man.' Unfortunately, the once wide-eyed newcomer had become a hardened old battle-axe, and this was a line of conversation designed to get my goat. 'How did you know I'm not from Delhi?'

I had baited the trap, and took a sort of grim satisfaction when he toppled into it. The knight smiled and his head swaggered left and right. With a crinkled palm he gestured at my whiteness.

Forget the crush, forget the staring, forget my disturbing new smell. Forget the fact I was starting to feel homesick for what Wolfgang Tillmans calls Britain's 'mix of damp carpet and apricot-scented potpourri, Marmite and repressed but omnipresent sexuality'. I felt depressed that no matter how long I live in Delhi, for all my Indian surname, I'll never belong. People will always look at me with $$$ or lechery or loathing in their eyes as a blank white cipher with blank white breasts. And when I say I'm doing a PhD—an entire blood-sweat-tears umpteen-year festival of geekery—on Indian politics, they'll still say things like, 'There's this thing called the caste system, you probably haven't heard of it...'

I know it's greedy and quite possibly neo-imperialist to want to belong. But dang it, if Delhi really wants to be a world city, it needs to realize that the whole *point* of them is that they're fizzing cross-fertilizing kaleidoscopes of people.

Just to add insult to injury, while I was minding my own business with a bag of onions in the street a burqa-clad woman shouted at me, 'Go back to where you came from!'

I'll check my privilege here of course: I know I have it easy. The Indian obsession with skin colour and good breeding has far worse repercussions for others. Whisper it: India is racist. Gandhi's non-violent civil disobedience inspired Martin Luther King; under Nehru India portrayed itself as an international moral force; the country stood up against South African apartheid when Thatcher's Britain despicably cowered.

But it's assumed that Indian *always* = brown, and the right kind of brown. In May 2013 the *Washington Post*, using World Values Survey data, revealed that India is the second-most racist country in the world (after Jordan) by a long way: 43.5 percent are *happy to declare* that they don't want a neighbour of a different race.

At a conference in Delhi I met a Nigerian who was studying in Pune (near Mumbai—even more famous for its intolerance to migrants). She spoke of insults in the street, of strangers touching her hair uninvited, and how no Indian student would be seen hanging out with her. Nepalis are stereotyped; Tibetan refugees are put in preventive detention; the government scowls at dual nationality.

Nor is racism confined to foreigners. Migrants from Bihar are mocked as crude, alien and endlessly breeding; even Delhi's chief minister got in on the act. Poor Muslims are accused of being 'Bangladeshi infiltrators', Kashmiris suspected of being terrorists, and everyone is judged by how dark they are. All this is complicated by caste. It is no longer a rigid and inescapable system, its influence diminishing in the big cities, but still the fracture lines are real. Even British Hindu organizations have been accused of caste discrimination.

Northeasterners face particular discrimination, the beautiful Nagamese wife of a rugby player told me: constantly asked for ID, called 'chinki'—an insult recently made punishable with imprisonment—and treated as outsiders. In 2007, the Delhi police produced the infamous *Security Tips for Northeast Students/Visitors in Delhi*. 'Dress code: When in rooms do as Roman does,' it instructs, cryptically. It goes on to warn Northeasterners against 'creating ruckus' by cooking their 'smelly dishes'. Boy does New Delhi know how to win over the already disenchanted margins.

Nagaland, close to the border with Myanmar, is India's frontier, and for decades it has been handled with more discreet brutality than Kashmir. In 2010 I visited, a nauseating potholed eleven-hour journey through lush green hills to a village half in India, half Myanmar. A watch-post glinted on the other side of the valley, although the villagers crossed the border with impunity. Old men, faces tattooed from old head-hunting wars, clutched self-made muskets and spent the evenings smoking opium, freshly plucked from individual bushes that the government tactfully ignored. We were shown the re-excavated skulls of old victims, dug from their respectful if bemused Catholic resting place under a tree. The younger people were slender, the men in neat tracksuits, the girls in vest tops that would outrage much of Delhi. The Nagas have become justly famous for their linguistic skills—'the air is full of them!' a middle-aged man told me, glaring at the plane's stewardesses—and all spoke four or five languages. But in the village there was little employment, crap roads, no electricity— although wires stretched to the nearby army camp, home to battalions of the notorious Assam Rifles. The old insurgency bubbled just under the surface.

I said something tactful like all this to the white knight, who gave a neck-shrug. 'Throughout our history India has been invaded. It is not a powerful country. So we cannot be racist.'

Then the white knight made a knight's move, something not unfamiliar but a little leftfield for lady-wooing: 'UK is finished.' He steepled his fingers with an objective air. 'It is a small island only. Nothing to offer to the twenty-first century.'

'Oh,' I said, for it is fairly difficult—and certainly unBritish—to disagree. 'And India?'

'India is now a powerful country.'

'But you just said—'

Another knight's move. This was like talking geopolitics with a goldfish. 'India should take over Pakistan. It is a failed state. They should be happy to be part of us instead…'

Get me a stiff drink.

14

NOSES

My genius is in my nostrils.

—Friedrich Nietzsche

The end of my quest was nigh. I'd laughed, cried, sweated, listened, scribbled and danced, and now only one task remained: to collect mementos. But my mind, addled with sweat and gin, seemed to be playing tricks.

I woke in the middle of the night with a strange unsettled feeling, sitting heavily in the pit of my belly like an unwanted meal. There was something wrong. Very, very wrong.

For days I had been twisting my neck in shops and on the metro. I discreetly cocked my head and flared my nostrils wide, unwary shell-pink interiors exposed to the outside world. And I murmured to myself, 'What *is* that smell?'

The smell lurked everywhere, not entirely pleasant but not unpleasant either. It was like déjà vu, alien but oddly familiar.

It lurked in my clothes, my books, hovered over my bed like a mosquito whine.

My treacherous nose did at least provide a brief distraction. A bad life decision, best discreetly whipped over, managed to knock out my nose piercing. I was embroiled in a race against time to find a new bit of metal to shove into my face before it healed. Surely it would be easy, given many Indians seem to love sticking things in the old *nak*, as is well evidenced on public transport.

'Do you have a thing for my nose?' I asked jeweller after jeweller. Before the fateful knock, virtual strangers would advise me on whether my own stud was in the correct side ('Your nose, it is wrong'). Now the sales assistants, who invariably had their own noses pierced, goggled at me as though I'd just proposed sticking a tiara in my mouth and calling myself Lil Wayne.

I was about to resort to gold wedding nose jewellery, most of which looked to weigh several kilograms and somehow chain your nose to your ear, when I finally found a nose stud—in an American chain store. Watched by a few curious children, I jammed one back into my flesh and breathed a slightly bloody sigh of relief.

Then I realized: the smell was back. It followed me east to the drab sprawl of Ghaziabad, where it mingled with my paan-flavoured icecream. It followed me to the lavish Imperial Hotel, host of many discussions over independence and Partition, where it inspected the art deco flourishes and caressed the red-clad bellhops' noses. The smell followed me north to the Tibetan refugee colony of Majnu-ka-Tilla, where together we failed to enjoy yak-butter tea under posters of runners haloed in violent orange, young men who had burnt themselves in their nation's cause. Self-immolation is a cheap, imitable and media-savvy form of protest. The Arab Spring has made it newly fashionable, but India has long been a world leader: six weeks in 1990 saw a wave of at least 200 self-immolations by high-caste students protesting the increase in reserved places for lower castes.

With rising panic I searched for the smell's source. Perhaps I'd left a morsel of dinner under my pillow. Perhaps I'd sprayed so much mosquito repellent that it'd destroyed the ozone layer. Perhaps Kamala had stubbed out cigarettes in the laundry again.

Of course, the weird smell was *me*.

There is nothing more unsettling, nothing that can make you more suddenly aware of your own newfound foreignness, than being surprised by your own smell. It's even odder than being surprised by your own reflection—at least you can wave and see your mirror image do the same. I'd come to Delhi wanting a transformation, and got one: I felt body-snatched.

I must have missed something. India is meant to be all soul. Yet rather than firing the higher reaches of my spirit, Delhi seemed determined to make me live more in the body. The heat, the sizzle of spice on monoglot tongue, the oft-burbling intestines, the new smells seeping from my pores: my soul was overwhelmed and passive in the face of it all.

At the centre of all this sudden bodily experience was my nose. Formerly a passive (if rather substantial) outcropping, it was suddenly unleashed.

The capital has been called many things, but no unhappy moniker has stuck faster than the cruelly rhyming 'smelly Delhi'.

That India smells is a motif almost as classic as its spirituality. Most Western books are unforthcoming on life's little reeks and whiffs. Indian books, though, not only explode with colours: they stink. *Midnight's Children* bubbles with simmering chutneys, the smell of the narrator's lover, and the famous encounter of his grandfather's proud schnozzle—in which dynasties are contained 'like snot'—with a prayer mat. The protagonist of *Animal's People* crawls at waist height and notes the profusion of smells with a sort of masochistic glee: his is a world of farts and unwashed groins. Kiran Desai's Darjeeling district smells of mice, boiled vegetables, kerosene and the forest's rich dark humus; the scents of Arundhati Roy's beautiful Kerala are toxically evocative: yellow teeth, old urine, sourmetal handcuffs, blood. (The India of *Eat, Pray, Love*, of course, is pleasantly perfumed with incense and jasmine.)

This is alarming for the modern tourist. Blogs burst with horrified ramblings of travellers who have forgotten their nose pegs. They complain about the smell of urine-soaked walls and beaches covered in (human) turds. They complain about garlicky body odour on public transport and rotting garbage in the heat. They complain about the smell of cow dung, rivers of raw sewage, and offal around the Old Delhi butchers.

Young women apparently feel disgust particularly keenly (along with fear of flying, incidentally), so I am hardly immune to bad smells. But I think India's stinkiness is seriously overplayed.

First, we must be careful not to assume that our noses automatically sniff out the Truth. We are simple creatures. The same parts of our brain appear to handle physical and moral disgust, so when we feel repelled by strong or unfamiliar odours it is easy to react emotionally. We sometimes speak as though our nostrils are truth seekers—as though we can actually smell the stink of corruption or the maggoty rottenness of political villains in the air, just as Victorian aristocrats caught the dangerous anarchic whiff of 'the great unwashed'.

But noses can be misled (perfume being the multi-billion-dollar example). Often they mix up Unfamiliar and *Evil*. It's notable that racist demonization of immigrants everywhere, from Singapore to Australia, heavily focuses on their smells. But Unfamiliar can be interesting. To paraphrase T.S. Eliot paraphrasing Rudyard Kipling, the first condition of understanding a foreign place is to smell it. You came wanting difference, and Delhi offers many olfactory experiences you don't get from visiting Edinburgh, say, or Mont Blanc.

Second, it's a thrill to finally smell *something*. The problem is that modernity is anti-smell. It might even be anti-nose entirely, if we consider that Michael Jackson was a modern icon. 'Civilization' means freeing us from streams of shit in the street, oniony dinner-table burps, flatulent beasts and B.O. Instead the world is scrubbed clean and neutered. Our workspaces are chilled, food wrapped, flowers scentless, armpits deodorized, sewage safely sealed on the other side of the U-bend. Noses dormant, retired like old hound-dogs, we fall in thrall into our eyes. We goggle and sightsee (what an odd word), big glassy vein-lined eyeballs rolling unstoppably forth to hoover up the exotic through our gaping black retinas and camera lenses. Meanwhile our noses are ignored, except perhaps at mealtimes, and when they choose to dribble in the winter.

In India the nose is restored to its queenly place.

Third, and most importantly in my end-of-days state, the nose is the organ of nostalgia. Though none of us has read Proust, we know a picture is worth a thousand words and a scent a thousand pictures. As your memories fade, you risk overrelying on a few hasty snapshots. Your nose, however, contains multitudes.

Put down your camera, and this book, so you can close your eyes. Now: flare your nostrils. (Probably best to open your eyes again every now and then. Swiss Chick, international booty call of one of my language school housemates, plunged straight into a drain on her first day, reemerging monstrous and slimy from the neck down à la 1950s B-movie *The Blob*.)

Ah! Like a dreaming dog or a bee to nectar, my nose is twitching wistfully just thinking of it all:

1. Kamala's illicit bathroom cigarette mingling with laundry powder and the kitchen's overripe fruit
2. The faint coconut scent of a woman's hair oil, caught across a table
3. Hot itchy air around the Old Delhi spice market, where traders sneeze morosely beside their chilli piles
4. Wood smoke
5. Sweat and cologne on the metro
6. Sweat and cheap cologne on the bus
7. Corn cobs on small roadside grills, served with chilli oil and a squeeze of lime juice

8. The faded warmth of incense in old houses, beneath solemn photos
9. A mysterious goaty smell
10. An Auntie's unashamedly public fart
11. The lingering wholesome smell of warm old grass (perhaps the cow, a surprisingly rare sight in Delhi, is just around the corner)
12. The mustiness of vegetable-dyed cloth, bought cheap from Lajpat Nagar
13. Freshly baked rotis from a clay tandoor
14. The warm peppered Christmassy smell of chai
15. Generator diesel mixing with car fumes and honeyed spring blossoms
16. Handfuls of curry leaves and spices, fried until the seeds ricochet against iron
17. The chemical burn of DEET
18. The chemical burn of a cheap local whisky, flat and hot
19. The bland chemical scent of old-fashioned Pears soap, still strangely popular in India despite the fact its 1899 slogan was 'The first step towards lightening [*sic*] THE WHITE MAN'S burden is through teaching the virtues of cleanliness'
20. The glorious flat burnt smell of rain on hot dry earth: called *manvasanai* in Tamil, in English its little-known but evocative name is 'petrichor', Greek gods' blood through veins of rock.

And so many more, a whole theatre of memories. Traditionally, Indian odours form a whole series of languages.

On one hand, bad smells play a potent role in upper-caste prejudice: traditional 'untouchable' work often involved 'unclean' substances with unpleasant smells, like blood, corpses, leatherwork or human waste. Once again, smell, disgust and bigotry appear closely linked.

On the other hand, as in the West, virtue is fragrant. Fragrant breezes waft divine messages and draw mythical actors together or carry them to new places, like Mary Poppins. Pleasant or auspicious smells are offered up to the gods: golden ghee lamps, the bright manly scent of sandalwood paste, burning cremation pyres. Statues are garlanded with flowers, from the cool scent of lotus to the headier jasmine, and sometimes bathed with honey and milk. Some of this aromatic language is now familiar in the West, like joss sticks, incense, the old hippie favourite patchouli. Indian perfume production also goes back centuries, both for worship and as an aphrodisiac, and the Mughals were fond of oily attars of rose and jasmine.

Try to relax. The smells won't kill you. At their best they are glorious; even at their worst they can be pretty interesting. Delhi can be a bouillabaisse, a compost heap, a blue cheese, a fine wine, with all the fun of trying to find pretentious adjectives to describe those things like a connoisseur. Let your nose voyage too. Each of these scents is worth twelve postcards and twelve hours on Instagram.

Perhaps it's wise to get in training at home first, though, by sniffing a few wet dogs and men's locker rooms.

Oh, to be able to bottle those scents and instantly whip friends and family to—well, most likely a traffic jam on the Outer Ring Road, or my armpit. Fair enough, I needed tangible trophies. Some would be gifts to apologize for all those long-delayed emails and missed birthdays. Some were just for me.

Finding the perfect trinket is a buzz, albeit a slightly shameful one. I was leaving Delhi behind, maybe forever. Love, hate, relief, regret: were my emotions really reducible to a little plastic snowglobe of the Taj Mahal? Ought I instead admit the souvenirs were for showing off, bribing British snowglobe lovers into reaccepting me, or (the best case scenario) compensating for a memory so bad that I needed stuff to weight it down? Would I rather be smug, trite, forgetful or manipulative?

Still, Delhi looks infinitely promising through the souvenir seeker's hungry lenses. It bulges with cheap and cheerful markets, successful chains, and thickets of boutiques. The pickings are rich: Aladdin pants at Paharganj, cheap knickknacks at Janpath, shady DVDs from Palika Bazaar, fake birdcages at Meharchand Market, achingly fashionable clothes at Shahput Jat, copies of achingly fashionable clothes from Chandni Chowk...

The haul from my end-of-days souvenir binge included, but was not confined to:

- A spidery gold Gandhi statuette (walking stick detachable)
- A cushion screen-printed with a truck's rear, screaming HORN PLEASE
- A set of coasters depicting cartoon *hijras*, the traditional 'third gender' (often employed as sex workers, cursers of weddings, and more recently as highly effective tax collectors)

- A large and photogenically battered cowbell
- An ashtray lined with a garish cartoon Rajput prince, moustache-twirled and beturbanned
- A small plump Ganesh figurine
- A fake Mughal lamp
- A gold filigree bookmark in the shape of India, which I intended to use as a Christmas decoration
- A conference ID lanyard with the inaccurate but flattering designation 'PhD Professor Elizabeth Chatterjee'.

Delhi is a souvenir natural. It (deservedly) has a reputation as a macho, aggressive city—for gang rapes, institutional misogyny, violence and sleaze. But it has another side, too, one readily distilled down into the garish and sentimental. Whisper it (a touch breathily, with a coy pout and a flirtatious twirl): D-Town is *camp*.

Imperial rule of course had more than its fair share of high camp, as the foppish Britishers Carried On Up The Khyber with their cocktails, uniforms and obsession with deviant sexuality. If kitsch is the artistic expression of camp, colonial-era 'tropical gothic' architecture is archetypal: the flamboyance, the clichéd imagery of power, the fakery (wealthy Brits like Thomas Metcalfe even built faux-mediaeval monuments to spice up their Mehrauli views), the sentimental imitation of Home. In Lutyens' extravagantly orchestrated New Delhi, neoclassical lines flirt with odd domes, cupolas, and elephant motifs, in two shades of pink Agra sandstone. Butch, *non*?

Everywhere you turn in Delhi today, you glimpse camp's

potential, sitting prettily atop the muscular highways and throbbing noise. It's there, largely unselfconscious, in the sashaying yellow hips of autorickshaws in traffic, in the painted trucks with their big warbling horns and the sultry-eyed, improbably skinny young Roadside Romeos slinking snake-hipped down the streets in their shiny purple shirts. It's there in the childishly sweet vivid orange whirl of jalebis, the love of song and dance, the pot-bellied jollity of Buddha and Ganesh, the tendency for melodrama in politics and relationships alike. It's *definitely* there in Bollywood, in Salman Khan's pierced navel and the perpetually twinkling Shahrukh Khan's drag-queen pirouettes for Indian film awards. It's even sometimes there in the faint undercurrent of slightly self-conscious menace on some streets or some evenings—like staring at Steve Buscemi's upper lip fur.

Journalist and professional sociopath A.A. Gill wrote, 'If New York is a wise guy, Paris a coquette, Rome a gigolo and Berlin a wicked uncle, then London is an old lady who mutters and has the second sight. She is slightly deaf, and doesn't suffer fools gladly.' Delhi, then, might be an ageing tsarina: ruthless, capricious, avaricious, paranoid—and fond of bright colours, pretty trinkets, and sex scandals. Like all grandes dames, she's showy, cash-splurging, hard to love, easy to photograph. Or perhaps, given her recent reinvention, she's more like a nouveau riche socialite—exactly as above but on Twitter. The whole city jangles with theatricality, bling and the so-bad-it's-good.

All of this is effortlessly gift-wrapped into trinket form. It's easy to pick up something instantly recognizable as 'Indian'. India is an A-grade iconographer.

In fact, in the face of massive internal diversity, India's government has desperately tried to harness icons to stimulate everyday nationalism. The country therefore has an unusually large pantheon of official national symbols, some more famous and T-shirt-friendly than others. They include the Bengal tiger, the peacock, the banyan tree, the Ganges River, the four conjoined lions of Ashoka, and the lotus flower (this latter now more heavily associated with rightwing political party BJP). In 2010 the elephant finally joined the roster as 'national heritage animal'. India even has a National Reptile (the king cobra), a National Fruit (the mango), and a National Aquatic Animal— the blind, toothy and half-poisoned Gangetic dolphin, one local nickname of which, *susu*, unfortunately means 'pee' in Hindi, and which looks like a porpoise whose face has been slammed in a door; it has yet to really take off in the souvenir world.

To this list we might informally add Ganesh, the PR natural in the Hindu stable; Gandhi, face of the rupee; holy cows; the unmistakeable silhouette of the Taj Mahal; and, judging by their ubiquitous green-and-yellow presence in souvenir shops, the autorickshaw. It is also obligatory for tourists both male and female to buy a kurta, destined never to be worn; I have several aggressively dowdy efforts from left-liberal-darling-cum-Louis Vuitton-sell-out Fabindia, all resembling something Julie Andrews would make out of curtains. Optional extras include Bollywood posters, curly-toed Punjabi *jootis*, and saris.

These icons are not *Delhi* icons, though. There is no real Brand Delhi, beyond the odd phallic image of the Qutub Minar. Dilliwallas are by and large too disloyal and the city's reputation too shady for such things.

Instead the capital excels in packaging the entirety of India into manageable morsels. Once confined to dingy state warehouses, this has become much slicker. The state-run souvenir emporium Dilli Haat, site of my mango-based TV humiliation, presents a carefully groomed selection of regional handicrafts and foodstuffs for a small entrance fee. Middle-class girls and genteel tourists rub shoulders on its paths.

Corporate India has got in on the action too. One weekend I ventured to Gurgaon's Kingdom of Dreams, a sticky borrowed three-year-old suctioned to my torso. It featured an indoor beach, star-studded musical shows, and a clown who left the three-year-old weeping hot suncreamy tears. In the midst of all this—*Time Out* describes it as 'the happy lovechild of Dilli Haat and Las Vegas'; its exterior sculptures were oddly reminiscent of Akshardham—on display was the same taxidermied range of Indian souvenirs. Only twice as pricey, of course.

'Somewhere between the exotic and the kitsch is real Delhi,' says Ranjana Sengupta. She's right that Delhi's exotic side—the 'irretrievably lost worlds' of the Mughals and Lutyens—is just that, irretrievably lost. But kitsch is not. Never underestimate the power of kitsch.

All this makes for excellent souvenir shopping—but it comes at a price. Kitsch items are 'instantly and effortlessly identifiable', the Israeli philosopher Tomas Kulka said, and 'highly charged with stock emotions'. They reassure rather than challenge. Our emotional responses to India's icons teeter on the verge of shallowness, so overexposed are they that we borrow sentiment from elsewhere rather than reflecting. India's real problems are only admitted in their most photogenic and sentimental guises, and difficult questions vanish in a puff of Old Spice.

Rich Delhi has repackaged India for its own tastes. Delhi kitsch is both hyper-Indian and totally divorced from Indian realities. A rich Dilliwalla can eat at the Claridges hotel's Dhaba restaurant, which 'recreates the ambience of the archetypical rustic highway eatery', complete with truck mural, Hindu imagery, 'an old radio belting out golden oldies', and even 'walls replicating the uneven mud painted texture of a village hut' (the food is incidentally very good, though calling Punjabi cuisine 'wholesome' is an artery-clogging oversell). Maybe he sips a vodka *nimbu pani* and heads to a swanky boutique, full of unashamedly garish (and pricey) consumer goods covered in Quintessentially Indian Symbols. He feels nostalgic—but for what?

What is the relationship between Dhaba and a roadside *dhaba*, or between a cartoon cycle rickshaw and the impoverished reality? For that matter, what is the relationship between Delhi's visible politics, in which politicians assiduously wear traditional dress and storm out of parliament—the media obsessing over every minute—and the cynical backdoor reality of deals and contempt for public service? Kitsch photoshops reality, places a pair of heart-shaped rose-tinted Lolita spectacles on it, sugarcoats it and spoonfeeds it. This India is a fantasy. It replaces the stereotypes of 'smelly Delhi' with something prettier but equally caricatured.

This is why Akshardham is so successful and so alarming.

It takes something good and noble—religious piety—and processes it. The difference was neatly captured by Milan Kundera. Kitsch, he said, was marked by two tears flowing down the cheek. 'The first tear says: How nice to see children running on the grass!' This is the household shrine, the family temple visit, the humble meditator.

'The second tear says: How nice to be moved, together with all mankind, by children running on the grass!' And, Kundera might have added, how nice to buy the souvenir brochure. This is the self-congratulatory back-pat of Akshardham, soothing nationalism all packaged up ready to be consumed. Consumption *is* nationalism. It's the overblown Bollywood love scenes, the elephant statues outside Noida, and the raising of the national flag in swanky Gurgaon housing complexes, where the idea of a unified public is all but ridiculous.

Don't mistake the prevalence of such symbols for unalloyed confidence, though. India's new middle classes believe in their own hype, in love with their own newness and potential and the promise of the great global marketplace. But this is a fragile ego. It is deeply sensitive to the fraught relationship with 'Westernization', to perceived slights, and to the threat posed by scapegoats. In Indian politics, cultural pride is obsessively sought and must be defended at all costs. Symbols are a key battleground, from political statues to the razing of the Babri Mosque in Ayodhya. In fact the cultural sphere is sublime, versus the corrupting realities of the political world.

The state, collaborating in the reinvention of India as an emergent world power for all that the middle classes dislike it, feels this insecurity too. It takes some of India's icons very seriously. The country's unity has always been problematic and so fetishized. Nobody must interfere with the icon of India itself, that fat-hipped diamond with one scrawny arm slung over Bangladesh. Its borders are vigilantly guarded in the visual media. Somewhere in South Block, deep in the bowels of the Secretariat building, there must be an officer employed full-time to complain about the maps used by Google and British magazines.

Or take the Indian national flag, Ashoka's wheel of law—originally a Gandhian spinning wheel—in the centre of a saffron, white and green tricolour (representing courage/renunciation, truth/peace, and the soil/prosperity, though saffron is also the traditional colour of Hinduism and green of Islam). Only one company may legally manufacture flags, and the symbol is heavily protected under the Prevention of Insults to National Honour Act. In 2007 Sachin Tendulkar, cricket's 'little master', incurred wrath by cutting a celebratory cake decorated with the national flag—thereby irrevocably slashing Mother India. The law got involved, while protestors set fire to Tendulkar posters and beat them with cricket bats.

This last was not unusual. Icons are made for punishment as well as veneration. Britain's *Daily Telegraph* put it with typical sensitivity: burning effigies of powerful people—politicians, Bollywood stars, and especially cricket players—is 'such a common event in India that it more or less doubles the smog levels'.

The very accusation of kitschiness is a snobbish one, of course, and indeed kitsch lies at the centre of a quiet culture war. I say 'war', but this is at best a guerrilla scrap, in which the battle lines are blurred, and the rivals are quite content to stay in their own cushy bastions and take potshots at the others.

'Class,' a woman explained one evening over beers. 'There is no substitute for it.'

The word is everywhere in certain circles, pronounced with the sigh of the British upper crust: *'klahhhss'*. It doesn't refer to the class system so much as some ineffable quality of good taste. This is the social grouping that Jan Morris in 1975 found 'stupendously British still'. They may be more distant from Britain now, but they still preserve a certain distance from the hoi polloi.

She continued: 'We have education, we have, *this thing'*— that little filler phrase beloved of some Dilliwallas, the equivalent of the Americanized 'um, like'—'we have cultural capital. Money cannot buy this.'

Class, good taste, is a key defence of the old-school elites against the arrivistes. Their reference points are an idealized period of noble scarcity, primarily under Nehru, back when men were real men, etc. In contrast, they castigate India's cash-splurging, kitsch-loving new middle classes as materialistic, self-interested, rude and ideologically barren.

The other side retorts with an accusation of elitism—not unfairly, given some of the old-school Anglophone lot are fond of provocation. As one Oxbridge-educated politico quipped: 'I cannot believe he wrote that letter himself. It contains words like "dichotomous" which I cannot believe that a BA Pass from Hansraj College [one of Delhi University's seventy-seven colleges] would know.'

The battle is ongoing. Definitions of 'good taste' will always be contested, and their boundaries will always change with the times, on one hand to exclude upstarts, and on the other to expand in the name of nationalist pride. Bollywood, for example, has changed from 'a medium that was considered infra dig'—*infra dignitatem*, beneath one's dignity, says Amitabh Bachchan; imagine a Hollywood star dropping Latin into his tweets—into a respectable form. Conversely, certain credentials are becoming devalued, as too many business graduates and MBAs enter the workplace. It is through such tastes that social groups define themselves. Given the ferment within the middle classes, permanently aspiring, permanently afraid of falling, these internal conflicts can only intensify.

At least these competing groups take themselves seriously. With my Taj Mahal snowglobe I am in a guilty outside set. The alternative to nationalist kitsch and nostalgic snobbery is a new elitism that embraces kitsch—*ironically*. Transnational elite youngsters make memes, laugh (bitterly), buy up kitschy cushions, make ironic mix tapes of Punjabi farmhouse tunes. For them, as for me, braving the dirt of sprawling Old Delhi is a touristy adventure—dare we gobble a real kebab? (Answer: yes, because Delhi Belly is surely ironic and self-referential.) It cannot be long before the dictatorial moustaches of its power elites are colonised by Hauz Khas wannabe hipsters. This is a generation that knows that countries are brands but are no less important for that.

Rather than offering a solution to the dichotomy, the ironic stance is permanently 'disengaged, depoliticized—or at least apolitical'. Through such mementos my memories are made trivial, sanitary and entirely odourless. What potential can revolution have in such circumstances? The new leftwing May Day Cafe even sells latte mugs with the hammer and sickle emblazoned on them in an (unwitting?) pastiche of coffee-house revolution.

I bought one of those too.

15

BACK

Such, then, was the anthropologist's return—only a shade more dismal than the ceremony which had marked his departure.

—Claude Lévi-Strauss, *Tristes Tropiques*

When I arrived back in Oxford, I submitted the manuscript of this book as my PhD dissertation, and we all lived happily ever after.

Just kidding!

The end was rushed, as ever. Packing up was a dismal affair. A sense of relief and sadness and something like defeat mingled. I said my au revoirs, handed over various possessions to Kamala, and forlornly counted my remaining business cards: 84. There was no room for sleep before the taxi came at 5 am. I made aimless bluebottle polygons around the airport, alighting on a final nostalgic *masala dosa*, and boarded the plane. Just like that: over.

There had been no dramatic rite of passage, no academic *Eureka!* moment, no silver bullet to 'cure' Indian electricity. I hadn't found any easy answers. I hadn't had a spiritual revelation. My Hindi was still ignored by most of the world, though I'd finally reached page 26 of *Harry Potter aur Paras Patthar* and learnt such useful words as 'wand' and 'broom'. I hadn't mastered interviewing, though now I approached books containing the dry phrase 'based on semi-structured interviews' with a healthy new suspicion. I avoided ice bars at all costs. The doctorate still stretched out endlessly. In any case, as an anonymous wag wrote, 'A PhD is like a heavily spicy meal—it doesn't matter how much you enjoy it, once you're finished, half of the pain is still ahead.'

Instead there had been a quiet replacement of certain cells. Hidden in my notebooks were a few modest spools of knowledge, ready to open with a little teasing as bright new ferns unfurl to the light. Within them, like pearls in seaweed, glinted hints of self-understanding. I had my smells and souvenirs and friends. It was enough.

And looming large over my memories was the heavy-set silhouette of Delhi.

Delhi: delirious city, city of the tense present, future imperfect. Yes, it's easy to criticize. It is sprawling, aggressive, authoritarian, water-starved, paranoid, and has had so many facelifts that you can get lost on your own street. Like the ice bar, it's frequently tasteless, materialistic, immensely inegalitarian, environmentally destructive, and full of faintly lecherous men. Its weather is diabolical, it can be ludicrously expensive, and often it smells. Oh, and its monkeys occasionally carry out savage and unprovoked attacks, just to liven things up. (In perhaps a microcosm of Delhi society at large, wealthy Dilliwallas' solution has naturally been to pay even larger, scarier monkeys to piss on their property.)

If my rite of passage came to the humblest of ends, Delhi's is barely beginning. In its current form it is, after all, a gangling adolescent of a city, with all the overconfidence and painful attempts at self-assertion that entails. It combines the hallmarks of the global twenty-first century: an increasingly wealthy elite, a precariously employed majority, an obsession with security, and looming environmental crisis. Inequality, corruption, violence, greed, fear, boredom, lust, smog: these are the snakes and ladders of modernity. It is impossible to be purely optimistic about the city's future.

But Delhi is a sophisticated cougar next to plain-Jane Chennai and glossy Bangalore. Even compared with its nemesis Mumbai, it has history, nightlife, internal diversity, flashes of green, and the sort of insecure desire to please that's hard to refuse. And Delhi boasts power, the electric pulse at the city's heart, reviled and ineffectual as India's rulers often are. If it seems to lack an overarching identity or the great chroniclers of its rivals, it is only a matter of time.

Still, what do I know? Can you ever step into the same city twice?

And then *just like that*—too fast—*too easy*—I was back Home. The coach ride from Heathrow was unsettlingly smooth. Barely a pothole or a leer, not a haggle or a horn blast. The weather and the faces were all lettuce-cool. The only thing I could smell was my own familiar foreignness.

Outside my Oxford window, the blue statue of the boy still winked his buttocks. My map of India grew yellowish in the patient sun. Here I was free to do all sorts of things, to walk and queue and drink straight out of the taps. To be drunk and immodest and nocturnal. To eat Cheddar whenever I felt like it.

I put on my shortest shorts and picked up a block of cheese. Suddenly, everything seemed very quiet.

ACKNOWLEDGEMENTS

As the old chestnut goes, people make the city. I am deeply grateful to all the friends, relatives, acquaintances, colleagues, students, diplomats, barflies, auto drivers, cricket fans, politicos, chatty strangers, and miscellaneous others who helped shape my time in Delhi. Particular thanks must go to my doctoral interviewees for their wit and generosity.

Mrs Rita Roy, my newfound cousin-brothers Indrajit and Prithvijit, Melodika Sadri, Tashiya Mirando and Suranga Rajapakse, Harsh Vardhan Sahni, and Anika Gupta all provided memorable conversation and places to rest my head. My thanks go too to the ever-entertaining Sweta Adhikari, Cecilia Allegra, David Chatterjee, Ujjwal Chattopadhyay, Jean-Nicolas Dangelser, Suparna Dubey, Neha Gupta, Raghu Karnad, Neela Majumdar, Nithiyananthan Muthusamy, Divya Nambiar, Ashleigh O'Mahony, Shreya Sarawgi, Puja Singhal, Aayush Soni, and the Delhi Hurricanes Rugby Club.

Several wonderful women have helped me along the way. Early on Anna Ruddock made invaluable comments. Trisha Bora was an unfailingly patient editor. But my biggest debt by far is to Danielle Yardy, for providing everything: encouragement, curiosity, advice, self-improvement, and snacks. All errors, flaws, idiosyncrasies, and lapses of memory and judgment are, of course, mine alone.

I owe many things to my strange and wonderful family, including my original itch to explore India. This book is dedicated to the memories of

Santosh Hari Chatterjee (1915–1995)
Sveja 'Eija' Gunvor Chatterjee (1924–2009)
Charles Byrne (1918–2004)
Agnes Byrne (1921–2013)
and
Jitendra 'Milan' Hari Chatterjee (1926–2013)

A NOTE ON THE AUTHOR

Born and raised in Yorkshire, Elizabeth Chatterjee is a perpetual student. After a history degree, she moved on to study contemporary Indian politics. She is currently working on her doctorate. In 2008, she was elected a Fellow of All Souls College, Oxford, where she eats alarming amounts of cheese in between visits to Delhi.

A Note on the Type

Sabon is the name of an old style serif typeface designed by the German-born typographer and designer Jan Tschichold (1902–74) in the period 1964–7. A distinguishing feature of the typeface was that the roman, italic, and bold weights all occupy the same width when typeset—an unusual feature, but this meant that the typeface then only required one set of copyfitting data (rather than three) when compositors had to estimate the length of a text prior to actual typesetting (a common practice before computer-assisted typesetting).